THE McGRAW-HILL

QUICK SPELLER

THE McGRAW-HILL

20,000+ Words Spelled and Divided for Quick Reference

ELEVENTH EDITION

Mary Margaret Hosler

 **Glencoe McGraw-Hill**

New York, New York
Columbus, Ohio
Woodland Hills, California
Peoria, Illinois

Glencoe/McGraw-Hill

A Division of The **McGraw·Hill** *Companies*

The McGraw-Hill Quick Speller, Eleventh Edition

Send all inquiries to:
Glencoe/McGraw-Hill
21600 Oxnard St., Suite 500
Woodland Hills, CA 91367

ISBN: 0-07-821983-3

Printed in the United States of America.

1 2 3 4 5 6 7 8 9 0   004   05 04 03 02 01 00

The McGraw-Hill Quick Speller

A Quick Guide to
20,000+WORDS

Foreword

Since the publication in 1934 of the first edition of *The McGraw-Hill Quick Speller,* originally entitled *20,000+ Words* by Dr. Louis A. Leslie, thousands of administrative assistants, document processors, students, teachers, and writers have come to rely on it as one of their most valued reference books.

With each edition, the word list has been updated to keep pace with the changing language of business and society. The eleventh edition provides listings that reflect both the latest technological advances and the global nature of business, thus keeping the book current and useful for anyone who communicates in writing.

The word list in *The McGraw-Hill Quick Speller, Eleventh Edition,* is a dictionary without definitions. Since most references to a standard dictionary are to verify spelling or to determine an acceptable point for word division, the absence of definitions increases the ease with which a given word may be found.

In general, the word list is in agreement with *Merriam Webster's Collegiate Dictionary, Tenth Edition,* 1999. Many other reference works have been consulted in the process of compiling and checking the word list, including *Random House Webster's College Dictionary,* 1999, and *Webster's II New College Dictionary,* 1999, published by Houghton Mifflin.

New Features of the Eleventh Edition

Three new features of *The McGraw-Hill Quick Speller, Eleventh Edition*, will make the book more encompassing and more helpful to the user.

1. Technology terms. The eleventh edition includes terms frequently used when writing about technology. Many of these terms, such as *mouse pad, newbie,* and *trackball,* have only come into use in the 1990s. These terms are conveniently located within the word list.

2. Geographic locations and ethnic terms. Information and news are generated from all parts of the globe, making international locations a part of many writing activities. The entries for names of countries, cities, and ethnic groups from around the world have been broadened and are included within the word list.

3. Updated word list. The word list has been revised, updated, and expanded to over 27,000 words. Words no longer in common use have been deleted, while words now in current use have been added. As a result, the eleventh edition contains an up-to-date listing of words used frequently in today's writing.

Useful Features

Several features of *The McGraw-Hill Quick Speller, Eleventh Edition,* aid the writer in correct spelling and ease of locating a word.

1. **Guide letters and guide words.** The guide letters and guide words at the top of each page assist the user in locating a needed reference.

2. **Bolded words.** Five hundred of the words most commonly misspelled in business writing are set in bold-face print to make them easy to locate in the word list.

3. **Derivatives.** Many derivatives are included along with base words. Derivatives often cause spelling questions: for example, when to double a consonant in forming a past tense or when to drop a final *e* before adding *-ing*. These and many other troublesome spellings that arise when using derivatives can be found in the word list. Many irregularly formed plurals are also included.

4. **Often-confused pairs and groups of words.** Sometimes a writer faces the challenge of choosing from two or more often-confused words—words such as *affect* and *effect* or *cite, sight,* and *site.* Entries for confusing pairs and groups include both simple definitions and cross-references. For example, the entry for the word *main* is followed by a brief definition—*chief,* which is followed by the *cf.* notation (meaning "compare with") and the word or words easily confused with the entry word—*mane.* The writer can easily confirm a correct choice or can reference other possibilities.

5. One Word, Two Words, or Hyphenated? A major problem for the writer is to determine whether a compound word or term is written as one word, as two words, or with a hyphen. For example, the *ice age* was a time of widespread glaciation that left many areas *icebound* and *ice-cold*.

Many expressions go through an evolutionary process of first being written as two separate words, then as a hyphenated word, and finally as one word. The word list shows a number of terms that may be written in all three ways depending on their use in context. A quick check can help a writer use the appropriate compound.

6. Appendix. The Appendix provides additional information that one may need in writing. It covers spelling tips, numbers style, common abbreviations and acronyms, and a list of troublesome place names in the United States, Canada, and Mexico. A helpful reference feature on the inside back cover is the list of abbreviations for states and territories of the United States.

Clear, concise rule statements followed by a variety of appropriate examples make the reference task easy. Users needing more comprehensive rule statements should consult *The Gregg Reference Manual, Ninth Edition,* by William A. Sabin.

The Word List

The alphabetic word listing in *The McGraw-Hill Quick Speller* serves two primary purposes: first, it is a quick reference for checking spelling; and second, it is an indicator of appropriate word division in writing. The eleventh edition of *The McGraw-Hill Quick Speller* follows the syllabication and the rationale as shown in *Merriam Webster's Collegiate Dictionary, Tenth Edition*, 1999.

Checking Spelling

The word list in *The McGraw-Hill Quick Speller, Eleventh Edition*, is a dictionary without definitions. The number of entries on each page and absence of definitions make scanning a column or a page for a certain word very easy. Guide letters and guide words make use of the book even easier. The guide letters—the bold letters at the top outside corner of each page—help locate the right section of the book. The pair of guide words on each page assists in finding the needed page quickly.

Word Division

Correct syllabication and appropriate word division in writing may not be the same. Word divisions shown in the following word list are acceptable points for breaking a word at the end of a line of print or writing. The word list shows these points with a dot (sometimes called a bullet).

For example, the noun *con·nec·tiv·i·ty* may be ended on one line at any of the following points: *con-, connec-,* or *connectivi-*. The hyphen after the word part shows that the word is incomplete; that is, part of the word appears at the beginning of the next line.

Words should not be divided after a single initial letter or before a single terminal letter. Therefore, dots are not shown in those positions even though a single beginning or ending letter may be a separate syllable. For example, the verb *emit* is shown without division marks.

The writer should keep in mind that excessive word division is distracting to the reader. In general, avoid dividing words at the ends of more than two consecutive lines or at the end of a page.

If a writer must divide a word, certain points of division are preferable to others. In a hyphenated word such as *self-employed* the best division point is at the hyphen. In a solid or closed compound such as *timetable* the best division point is between the words that make up the compound (*time·table*). Other preferable points for word division include after prefixes (*super·highway*), before suffixes (*advertise·ment*), and after single-vowel syllables (*consoli·date* rather than *consol·idate*).

In the word list, word division points are indicated by centered dots, sometimes called bullets:

com·put·er·ese   In·ter·net

Hyphenated words appear in the word list just as they should be written or typed, with hyphens between words that make up the compound. The hyphen should be included in these expressions whether the word is used in the middle or at the end of a line.

loose-leaf   co-payment   pay-TV

Certain expressions written as two or more separate words also appear in the word list. These terms are included because the combinations occur often enough to make people think they may be written as solid or hyphenated compounds rather than as separate words. A writer should not use a hyphen to divide these expressions between the words of the open compound.

ad hoc   ex officio   oil slick

Certain words may be spelled, punctuated, or divided differently depending on their part of speech. In such situations, variations appear with part-of-speech designations (*n* for *noun, v* for *verb, adj* for *adjective,* and *adv* for *adverb*). Indications of acceptable word division may vary in such pairs or groups of entries.

car·ry out (v) car·ry·out (n)

Cross-reference

Many pairs or groups of words cause problems for writers because of similarities in spelling or pronunciation. Cross-references between these confusing pairs of words can help the writer not only spell and divide the word correctly but also to make sure of choosing the right word for the intended meaning. A parenthetical notation indicating a brief definition for the entry word and a cross-reference to easily confused words follows the entry.

aid (help; cf. *aide*) aide (assistant; cf. *aid*)

Derivatives

An entry may include both a base word and one or more derivatives. Derivatives appear below and slightly indented from the base word. If a hyphen precedes a derivative, the user must look at both the base word and the derivative to find the spelling. As much of the base word is shown as is necessary to understand the correct spelling of the derivative. When multiple derivatives appear for a single base word, the same part of the base word is shown for each derivative.

> ini·tial·ize
>   -ized, -izing

The abbreviation (*pl*) following an entry indicates the plural form when there may be confusion in identifying the entry.

> daugh·ter-in-law
>   daugh·ters-in-law (pl)

A

aba·cus
ab·a·lo·ne
aban·don
  -don·er, -don·ment
aban·doned
abase
  abased, abas·ing,
  abase·ment
abash
abate
  abat·ed, abat·ing,
  abat·er
abate·ment
ab·bé
ab·bess
ab·bey
  -beys
ab·bot
ab·bre·vi·ate
  -at·ed, -at·ing,
  -a·tor
ab·bre·vi·a·tion
ab·di·cate
  -cat·ed, -cat·ing,
  -ca·tion, -ca·tor
ab·do·men
  -dom·i·nal,
  -dom·i·nal·ly

ab·duct
  -duc·tor
ab·duc·tion
ab·er·rant
ab·er·rat·ed
ab·er·ra·tion
abet
  abet·ted,
  abet·ting,
  abet·ment
abey·ance
ab·hor
  -horred, -hor·ring
ab·hor·rence
ab·hor·rent
abide
  abode or abid·ed,
  abid·ing, abid·er
abil·i·ty
  -ties
ab·ject
  -ject·ly, -ject·ness
ab·jec·tion
ab·jure
  -jured, -jur·ing,
  -jur·er
ablaze
able
able-bod·ied

ab·lu·tion
ably
ab·ne·gate
  -gat·ed, -gat·ing,
  -ga·tor
ab·ne·ga·tion
ab·nor·mal
  -mal·ly
ab·nor·mal·i·ty
  -ties
aboard
abode
abol·ish
  -ish·able, -ish·er,
  -ish·ment
ab·o·li·tion
ab·o·li·tion·ism
  -tion·ist
A-bomb
abom·i·na·ble
  -bly
abom·i·nate
  -nat·ed, -nat·ing,
  -na·tor
abom·i·na·tion
ab·orig·i·nal
  -nal·ly
ab·orig·i·ne
abort

abor·tion
abor·tion·ist
abor·tive
abound
about
about-face
above
above all
above·board
above·ground
abrade
abra·sion
abra·sive
  -sive·ly, -sive·ness
abreast
abridge
  abridged,
  abridg·ing,
  abridg·er
abridg·ment
abroad
ab·ro·gate
  -gat·ed, -gat·ing,
  -ga·tion
abrupt
  abrupt·ly,
  abrupt·ness
ab·scess
  -scess·es, -scessed
ab·scond
  -scond·er
ab·sence
ab·sent

ab·sen·tee
ab·sen·tee·ism
ab·sent·mind·ed
  -ed·ly, -ed·ness
ab·so·lute
ab·so·lute·ly
ab·so·lu·tion
ab·so·lut·ism
ab·solve
  -solved, -solv·ing,
  -solv·er
ab·sorb
  -sorb·abil·i·ty,
  -sorb·able,
  -sorb·er
ab·sor·bance
ab·sor·ben·cy
  -cies
ab·sor·bent
ab·sorb·ing
ab·sorp·tion
ab·stain
  -stain·er
ab·ste·mi·ous
ab·sten·tion
ab·sti·nence
ab·sti·nent
ab·stract
  -stract·ness
ab·stract·ed
ab·strac·tion
ab·strac·tion·ism

ab·surd
  -surd·ness
ab·sur·di·ty
abun·dance
abun·dant
abuse
  abused, abus·ing,
  abus·er
abu·sive
  -sive·ly, -sive·ness
abut
  abut·ted,
  abut·ting
abut·ment
abys·mal
  -mal·ly
abyss
aca·cia
ac·a·deme
ac·a·de·mia
ac·a·dem·ic
  -dem·i·cal·ly
ac·a·de·mi·cian
acad·e·my
  -mies
a cap·pel·la
ac·cede (agree; cf.
  exceed)
  -ced·ed, -ced·ing
ac·cel·er·ate
  -at·ed, -at·ing,
  -at·ing·ly
ac·cel·er·a·tion

6

ac·cel·er·a·tor
ac·cel·er·a·tor card
ac·cent
ac·cen·tu·ate
  -tu·a·tion
ac·cept (take; cf.
  except)
ac·cept·able
  -able·ness, -ably,
  -abil·i·ty
ac·cep·tance
ac·cept·ed
ac·cess (admit-
  tance; cf. *excess*)
ac·ces·si·ble
  -si·ble·ness,
  -si·bly, -si·bil·i·ty
ac·ces·sion
ac·ces·so·rize
  -rized, -riz·ing
ac·ces·so·ry
  -ries
ac·ci·dent
ac·ci·den·tal
  -tal·ly, -tal·ness
ac·claim
ac·cla·ma·tion
ac·cli·mate
  -mat·ed, -mat·ing
ac·cli·ma·tize
ac·co·lade
ac·com·mo·date
  -dat·ed, -dat·ing

ac·com·mo·da·tion
ac·com·pa·ni·ment
ac·com·pa·nist
ac·com·pa·ny
  -nied, -ny·ing
ac·com·plice
ac·com·plish
  -plish·able,
  -plish·er
ac·com·plished
ac·com·plish·ment
ac·cord
ac·cor·dance
ac·cord·ing·ly
ac·cor·di·on
ac·cost
ac·count
ac·count·able
  -able·ness, -ably,
  -abil·i·ty
ac·coun·tan·cy
ac·coun·tant
ac·count·ing
ac·cou·ter·ment
ac·cred·it
  -cred·i·table,
  -cred·i·ta·tion
ac·crete
ac·cre·tion
ac·cru·al
ac·crue
  -crued, -cru·ing,
  -cru·able

ac·cu·mu·late
  -lat·ed, -lat·ing
ac·cu·mu·la·tion
ac·cu·mu·la·tive
ac·cu·mu·la·tor
ac·cu·ra·cy
  -cies
ac·cu·rate
  -rate·ly,
  -rate·ness
ac·cursed
ac·cu·sa·tion
ac·cu·sa·tive
ac·cu·sa·to·ry
ac·cuse
  -cused, -cus·ing,
  -cus·er
ac·cus·tom
ac·cus·tomed
ac·er·bate
  -bat·ed, -bat·ing
ac·e·tate
ace·tic
ac·e·tone
acet·y·lene
ache
  ached, ach·ing
achieve
  achieved,
  achiev·ing,
  achiev·able,
  achiev·er
achieve·ment

ach·ro·mat·ic
ac·id
ac·id re·flux
   dis·ease
acid·ic
acid·i·fy
  -fied, -fying,
  -fi·ca·tion
acid·i·ty
  -ties
acid·u·lous
ac·knowl·edge
  -edged, -edg·ing,
  -edge·able
ac·knowl·edg·ment
ac·me (highest
  point; cf. *acne*)
ac·ne (skin disorder;
  cf. *acme*)
ac·o·lyte
acorn
acous·tic
acous·tics
ac·quaint
ac·quain·tance
ac·qui·esce
  -esced, -esc·ing
ac·qui·es·cence
ac·qui·es·cent
  -cent·ly
ac·quir·able
ac·quire
  -quired, -quir·ing

ac·quire·ment
ac·qui·si·tion
ac·quis·i·tive
  -tive·ly, -tive·ness
ac·quit
  -quit·ted,
  -quit·ting,
  -quit·ter
ac·quit·tal
acre
acre·age
ac·rid
ac·ri·mo·ni·ous
  -ous·ness
ac·ri·mo·ny
ac·ro·bat
  -bat·ic, -bat·i·cal·ly
ac·ro·nym
across
across-the-board
acros·tic
acryl·ic
act·ing
ac·tion
ac·tion·able
ac·tion·less
ac·ti·vate
  -vat·ed, -va·ting,
  -va·tion
ac·tive
  -tive·ly, -tive·ness
ac·tive ma·trix
  LCD

ac·tive wear
ac·tiv·ism
  -tiv·ist
ac·tiv·i·ties
ac·tiv·i·ty
ac·tor
ac·tress
ac·tu·al
ac·tu·al·i·ty
ac·tu·al·ly
ac·tu·ar·i·al
ac·tu·ary
  -ar·ies
ac·tu·ate
  -at·ed, -at·ing
ac·tu·a·tor
acu·ity
acu·men
acu·punc·ture
  -tur·ist
acute
  acute·ly,
  acute·ness
ad (advertisement;
  cf. *add*)
ad·age
ada·gio
ad·a·mant
adapt (adjust; cf.
  adept, adopt)
adapt·ed prod·uct
  strat·e·gy

adapt·able
  -abil·i·ty
ad·ap·ta·tion
adapt·er
add (plus; cf. *ad*)
ad·den·da (pl)
  -den·dum (sing)
ad·dict
ad·dic·tion
ad·dic·tive
ad·di·tion
  (increase; cf.
  edition)
ad·di·tion·al
  -al·ly
ad·di·tive
add-on
ad·dress
ad·dress·able
ad·dress·ee
ad·dress·ees
ad·dress·ing
ad·duce
ad·e·noid
ad·e·noi·dal
ad·ept (skillful; cf.
  adapt, adopt)
ad·e·qua·cy
  -cies
ad·e·quate
  -quate·ly,
  -quate·ness

ad·here
  -hered, -her·ing
ad·her·ence
ad·her·ent
ad·he·sion
ad·he·sive
  -sive·ly, -sive·ness
ad hoc
adieu
  adieus (pl)
adi·os
ad·i·pose
ad·ja·cen·cy
  -cies
ad·ja·cent
ad·jec·tive
ad·join (be next to;
  cf. *adjourn*)
ad·journ (suspend;
  cf. *adjoin*)
ad·journ·ment
ad·ju·di·cate
  -cat·ed, -cat·ing,
  -ca·tor
ad·ju·di·ca·tion
ad·junct
ad·ju·ra·tion
ad·jure
  -jured, -jur·ing
ad·just
  -just·abil·i·ty,
  -just·able
ad·just·ed

ad·just·er
ad·just·ment
ad·ju·tant
ad lib (adv)
ad-lib (v, n, adj)
  ad-libbed,
  ad-lib·bing
ad·min·is·ter
  -tered, -ter·ing
ad·min·is·tra·tion
ad·min·is·tra·tive
ad·min·is·tra·tor
ad·min·is·tra·trix
ad·mi·ra·ble
ad·mi·ral
ad·mi·ral·ty
ad·mi·ra·tion
ad·mire
  -mired, -mir·ing
  -mir·er
ad·mis·si·ble
  -bil·i·ty
ad·mis·sion
ad·mit
  -mit·ted, -mit·ting,
  -mit·ted·ly
ad·mit·tance
ad·mix·ture
ad·mon·ish
  -ish·er, -ish·ing·ly
  -ish·ment
ad·mo·ni·tion
ad·mon·i·to·ry

ad nau·se·am
ado·be
Ado·be Ac·ro·bat
  Read·er
ad·o·les·cence
ad·o·les·cent
adopt (accept; cf.
  adapt, adept)
  adopt·abil·i·ty,
  adopt·able,
  adopt·er
adop·tion
adop·tive
ador·able
ad·o·ra·tion
adore
  adored, ador·ing,
  ador·er
adorn
adorn·ment
ad·re·nal
adren·a·line
adrift
adroit
adsorb
ad·sor·bent
ad·sorp·tion
ad·u·late
  -lat·ed, -lat·ing,
  -la·tion
adult
adul·ter·ate
  -at·ed, -at·ing

adul·ter·a·tion
adul·tery
ad va·lo·rem
ad·vance
  -vanced, -vanc·ing
Ad·vanced Mi·cro
  De·vic·es
Ad·vanced
  Re·search
  Pro·jects
  Agen·cy
  Net·work
  (ARPANET)
ad·vance·ment
ad·van·tage
  -taged, -tag·ing
ad·van·ta·geous
  -geous·ly,
  -geous·ness
ad·vent
ad·ven·ti·tious
ad·ven·ture
  -tured, -tur·ing
ad·ven·tur·er
ad·ven·ture·some
ad·ven·tur·ous
ad·verb
ad·ver·bi·al
ad·ver·sar·i·al
ad·ver·sary
  -sar·ies
ad·verse (unfavor-
  able; cf. *averse*)

ad·ver·si·ty
ad·vert
ad·ver·tise
  -tised, -tis·ing,
  -tis·er
ad·ver·tise·ment
ad·vice (n)(counsel;
  cf. *advise*)
ad·vis·able
  -abil·i·ty
ad·vise (v)(give
  counsel; cf.
  advice)
  -vised, -vis·ing,
  -vis·er
ad·vis·ee
ad·vise·ment
ad·vi·so·ry
  -ries
ad·vo·ca·cy
ad·vo·cate
  -cat·ed, -cat·ing,
  -ca·tion
Ae·ge·an
ae·on
aer·ate
  -at·ed, -at·ing,
  -a·tion
ae·ri·al (adj)
aer·i·al (n)
ae·ri·al·ist
ae·rie
aer·o·bat·ics

aer·o·bic
aero·dy·nam·ics
 -nam·i·cal·ly
aero·nau·tics
 -ti·cal·ly, -ti·cal·ly
aero·sol
aero·space
aes·thet·ic
 -thet·i·cal·ly
aes·thet·ics
afar
af·fa·ble
af·fair
af·fect (influence; cf.
 effect)
af·fec·ta·tion
af·fect·ed
af·fect·ing
af·fec·tion
af·fec·tion·ate
 -ate·ly
af·fec·tive
 -tive·ly, -tiv·i·ty
af·fi·ance
af·fi·da·vit
af·fil·i·ate
 -at·ed, -at·ing,
 -a·tion
af·fin·i·ty
 -ties
af·firm
af·fir·ma·tion
af·fir·ma·tive

af·fix
af·flict
af·flic·tion
af·flu·ence
af·flu·en·cy
 -cies
af·flu·ent (well-to-
 do; cf. *effluent*)
af·ford
af·fright
af·front
af·ghan
Af·ghan·i·stan
afield
afire
afloat
afoot
afore
afore·men·tioned
afore·said
afore·thought
afraid
afresh
Af·ri·ca
Af·ri·can
Af·ri·kaans
Af·ro-Amer·i·can
af·ter
af·ter·care
af·ter·ef·fect
af·ter·glow
af·ter-hours
af·ter·life

af·ter·math
af·ter·noon
af·ter·shock
af·ter·taste
af·ter·tax
af·ter·thought
af·ter·ward
again
against
ag·ate
age
 aged, ag·ing
age-group
age-re·lat·ed
ageless
agen·cy
agen·cies
agen·da
Agent Orange
age-old
ag·glom·er·ate
ag·gran·dize
 -dized, -dizing,
 -dize·ment
ag·gra·vate
 -vat·ed, -vat·ing
ag·gra·va·tion
ag·gre·gate
 -gat·ed, -gat·ing
ag·gre·ga·tion
ag·gres·sion
ag·gres·sive
 -sive·ly, -sive·ness

ag·gres·sor
ag·grieve
  -grieved,
  -griev·ing
aghast
ag·ile
agil·i·ty
  -ties
ag·i·tate
  -tat·ed, -tat·ing,
  -ta·tion
ag·i·ta·tor
ag·let
aglitter
aglow
ag·nos·tic
ago
ag·o·nize
  -nized, -niz·ing
ag·o·ny
  -nies
ag·o·ra·pho·bia
agrar·i·an
agree
  agreed, agree·ing
agree·able
agree·ment
ag·ri·busi·ness
ag·ri·cul·tur·al
ag·ri·cul·ture
agron·o·my
aground
ahead

ahoy
aid (v)(help; cf. *aide*)
aide (n)(assistant; cf.
  aid)
aide-de-camp
AIDS
ail (be ill; cf. *ale*)
ai·le·ron
ail·ment
aim
  aim·less,
  aim·less·ness
air (atmosphere; cf.
  heir)
air bag
air base
air·borne
air brake
air·brush
air coach
air-con·di·tion
  -tion·er, -tion·ing
air·craft
air-drop (v)
air·drop (n)
air-dry (adj)
Aire·dale terrier
air·fare
air·field
air·flow
air·foil
air force
air·freight

air gun
air hole
air·ing
air lane
air letter
air·lift
air·line
air·lin·er
air lock
air·mail
air·man
air mass
air mile
air piracy
air·plane
air pock·et
air·port
air pump
air raid
air·ship
air·sick
air·space
air·speed
air·stream
air·strip
air·tight
air·time
air-to-air
air·wave
air·way
air·wor·thy
  -thi·ness
airy

aisle (passageway;
  cf. *isle*)
aka·maize
akim·bo
al·a·bas·ter
a la carte
alac·ri·ty
a la king
a la mode
alarm
alarm·ism
  -ist
alas
Al·ba·nia
Al·ba·ny
al·ba·tross
  -tross·es (pl)
al·be·it
al·bi·no
  -nos
al·bum
al·bu·men
al·co·hol
al·co·hol·ic
al·co·hol·ism
al·cove
al·der·man
al·der·wom·an
ale (beer; cf. *ail*)
al·fal·fa
al·fres·co
al·ga
  al·gae (pl)

al·ge·bra
al·ge·bra·ic
  -bra·i·cal·ly
Al·ge·ria
Al·giers
al·go·rithm
alias
al·i·bi
  -bied, -bi·ing
alien
alien·able
alien·ate
  -at·ed, -at·ing
alien·ation
alife
align
align·ment
alike
al·i·mo·ny
  -nies
al·ka·li
  -lies
al·ka·line
al·ka·loid
all (wholly; cf. *awl*)
all-Amer·i·can
all-around
al·lay (v)(soothe; cf.
  alley, ally)
al·le·ga·tion
al·lege
  -leged, -leg·ing

al·leged
  -leg·ed·ly
al·le·giance
al·le·gor·i·cal
al·le·go·ry
  -ries
al·le·gret·to
al·le·gro
al·le·lu·ia
al·ler·gic
al·ler·gy
  -gies
al·le·vi·ate
  -at·ed, -at·ing,
  -a·tion
al·ley (n)(passage;
  cf. *allay, ally*)
al·leys
al·ley·way
al·li·ance
al·lied
al·li·ga·tor
all-im·por·tant
all-in·clu·sive
al·lit·er·ate
  -at·ed, -at·ing
al·lit·er·a·tion
al·lit·er·a·tive
all-nighter
al·lo·ca·ble
al·lo·cate
  -cat·ed, -cat·ing,
  -ca·tion

al·lo·cu·tion
al·lot
  -lot·ted, -lot·ting
al·lot·ment
al·low
al·low·able
al·low·ance
al·lowed (permit-
  ted; cf. *aloud*)
al·low·ed·ly
al·loy
all right
all-star
al·lude (refer to; cf.
  elude)
  -lud·ed, -lud·ing
al·lure
  -lured, -lur·ing,
  -lure·ment
al·lu·sion
  -lu·sive·ly,
  -lu·sive·ness
al·lu·vi·al
al·ly (n, v)(associate;
  cf. *allay, alley*)
  -lies, -lied, -ly·ing
al·ma ma·ter
al·ma·nac
al·mighty
al·mond
al·most
alms (charity; cf.
  arms)

al·oe
aloft
alo·ha
alone
along
along·side
aloud (adv)(audibly;
  cf. *allowed*)
al·pha·bet
al·pha·bet·ic
  -bet·i·cal·ly
al·pha·bet·ize
  -ized, -izing
al·pha·nu·mer·ic
  -mer·ics
al·pha·nu·mer·ic
  field
al·pha·nu·mer·ic
  keys
al·pine
al·ready
al·so
al·tar (n)(for wor-
  ship; cf. *alter*)
al·tar·piece
al·ter (v)(change; cf.
  altar)
  -tered, -ter·ing
al·ter·ation
al·ter·cate
  -cat·ed, -cat·ing
al·ter·ca·tion
al·ter ego

al·ter·nate
  -nat·ed, -nat·ing
al·ter·na·tion
al·ter·na·tive
al·ter·na·tor
al·though
al·tim·e·ter
al·ti·tude
al·to
  al·tos
al·to·geth·er
al·tru·ism
  -ist, -is·tic,
  -is·ti·cal·ly
al·um
alu·mi·nize
  -nized, -niz·ing
alu·mi·num
alum·na (fem sing)
  alum·nae (fem pl)
alum·nus (sing)
  alum·ni (pl)
al·ways
alys·sum
Alz·hei·mer's
amal·gam
amal·gam·ate
  -at·ed, -at·ing
amal·gam·ation
am·a·ryl·lis
amass
am·a·teur
  -teur·ism

amaze
  amazed,
  amaz·ing,
  amaz·ing·ly
amaze·ment
am·bas·sa·dor
am·ber
am·bi·dex·trous
am·bi·ence
am·bi·ent
am·bi·gu·i·ty
  -ities
am·big·u·ous
am·bi·tion
am·bi·tious
am·biv·a·lence
am·ble
  -bled, -bling
am·bly·opia
am·bro·sia
am·bu·lance
am·bu·late
  -lat·ed, -lat·ing,
  -la·tion
am·bu·la·to·ry
am·bush
ame·lio·rate
  -lio·rat·ed,
  -lio·ra·tion
amen
ame·na·ble
amend (to change;
  cf. *emend*)

amend·ment
ame·ni·ty
  -ties
Am·er·asian
Amer·i·ca On·line
  (AOL)
Amer·i·can
Amer·i·can
  Stan·dard Code
  for
  In·for·ma·tion
  In·ter·change
  (ASCII)
Amer·i·ca·na
Amer·i·can·ism
Amer·i·can·iza·tion
am·e·thyst
ami·a·ble
  -ble·ness, -bly,
  -bil·i·ty
am·i·ca·ble
  -ble·ness, -bly,
  -bil·i·ty
amid
amid·ships
ami·go
  -gos
ami·no acid
Amish
am·i·ty
  -ties
am·me·ter
am·mo·nia

am·mu·ni·tion
am·ne·sia
am·nes·ty
am·nio·cen·te·sis
amoe·ba
  -bas
among
amor·al
amo·ral·i·ty
am·o·rous
amor·phous
am·or·ti·za·tion
am·or·tize
  -tized, -tiz·ing,
  -tiz·able
amount
am·per·age
am·pere
am·per·sand
am·phib·i·an
am·phib·i·ous
am·phi·the·ater
am·ple
  -ple·ness, -ply
am·pli·fi·ca·tion
am·pli·fi·er
am·pli·fy
  -fied, -fy·ing
am·pli·tude
am·pu·tate
  -tat·ed, -tat·ing,
  -ta·tion
am·pu·tee

Am·ster·dam
am·u·let
amuse
  amused, amus·ing
amuse·ment
amus·ing
  -ing·ness
anach·ro·nism
  -nis·tic,
  -nis·ti·cal·ly
an·aer·o·bic
  -bi·cal·ly
ana·gram
  -grammed,
  -gram·ming
An·a·heim
an·al·ge·sia
an·a·log
an·a·log·i·cal
anal·o·gous
anal·o·gy
  -gies
anal·y·sis
  -y·ses (pl)
an·a·lyst (one who
  analyzes; cf.
  annalist)
an·a·lyt·ic
an·a·lyt·i·cal
  -cal·ly
an·a·lyze
  -lyzed, -lyz·ing,
  -lyz·er

an·ar·chic
an·ar·chism
an·ar·chist
an·ar·chy
anath·e·ma
an·a·tom·ic
  -tom·i·cal,
  -tom·i·cal·ly
anat·o·mist
anat·o·mize
  -mized, -miz·ing
anat·o·my
  -mies
an·ces·tor
an·ces·tral
  -tral·ly
an·ces·try
an·chor
  -chored, -chor·ing
an·chor·age
An·chor·age
an·chor·man
an·chor·peo·ple
an·chor·per·son
an·chor·wom·an
an·cho·vy
  -vies
an·cient
an·cil·lary
an·dan·te
and·iron
and/or
An·dor·ra

an·drog·y·nous
an·droid
an·ec·dot·al
an·ec·dote
ane·mia
  ane·mic
an·e·mom·e·ter
anem·o·ne
an·en·ceph·a·ly
an·er·oid
an·es·the·sia
an·es·the·si·ol·o·gist
an·es·thet·ic
anes·the·tist
anes·the·tize
  -tized, -tiz·ing
an·eu·rysm
anew
an·gel (spiritual
  being; cf. *angle*)
an·gel·fish
an·ger
  -gered, -ger·ing
an·gi·na
an·gle (in geometry;
  cf. *angel*)
  -gled, -gling
an·gle iron
an·gler
an·gle·worm
An·gli·can
an·gli·cism

an·gli·cize
  -cized, -ciz·ing
an·gling
An·glo·phile
An·glo·phobe
An·glo-Sax·on
An·go·la
an·go·ra
an·gry
  -gri·er, -gri·est,
  -gri·ly
An·guil·la
an·guish
an·gu·lar
an·gu·lar·i·ty
an·i·mal
an·i·mate
  -mat·ed, -mat·ing,
  -mate·ly
an·i·ma·tion
an·i·mos·i·ty
  -ties
an·i·mus
an·ise
ani·seed
an·kle
an·kle·bone
an·klet
an·nal·ist (writer of
  annals; cf.
  analyst)
an·nals
An·nap·o·lis

an·neal
an·nex
  -nex·ation,
  -nex·ation·ist
an·ni·hi·late
  -lat·ing, -la·tion,
  -la·tor
an·ni·ver·sa·ry
  -ries
an·no·tate
  -tat·ed, -tat·ing
an·no·ta·tion
an·nounce
  -nounced,
  -nounc·ing
an·nounce·ment
an·nounc·er
an·noy
an·noy·ance
an·noy·ing
an·nu·al
  -al·ly
an·nu·al·ize
  -ized, -iz·ing
an·nu·itant
an·nu·ity
  -ities
an·nul
  -nulled, -nul·ling
an·nu·lar
an·nul·ment
an·nun·ci·a·tion
an·nun·ci·a·tor

an·ode
an·od·ize
  -ized, -iz·ing
an·o·dyne
anoint
anom·a·lous
anom·a·ly
  -lies
an·o·nym·i·ty
anon·y·mous
anon·y·mous FTP
  ar·chive
an·orex·ia
an·orex·ic
an·oth·er
an·swer
  -swered, -swer·ing
an·swer·able
ant (insect; cf. *aunt*)
ant·ac·id
an·tag·o·nism
an·tag·o·nist
an·tag·o·nis·tic
an·tag·o·nize
  -nized, -niz·ing
ant·arc·tic
Ant·arc·ti·ca
ant·eat·er
an·te·bel·lum
an·te·ced·ent
an·te·cham·ber
an·te·date
an·te·di·lu·vi·an

17

an·te·lope
  -lope (pl)
an·te me·ri·di·em
an·te·na·tal
  -tal·ly
an·ten·na
  -nae (pl)
an·te·pe·nult
  -pen·ul·ti·mate
an·te·ri·or
an·te·room
an·them
ant·hill
an·thol·o·gy
  -gies
an·thra·cite
an·thrax
an·thro·poid
an·thro·pol·o·gy
  -gist
an·thro·po·mor·phic
  -phi·cal·ly
an·ti·a·li·as·ing
an·ti·bac·te·ri·al
an·ti·bi·ot·ic
an·ti·body
an·ti·busi·ness
an·tic
an·tic·i·pate
  -pat·ed, -pat·ing
an·tic·i·pa·tion
an·tic·i·pa·to·ry

an·ti·cli·mac·tic
an·ti·cli·max
an·ti·dote
an·ti·freeze
an·ti·gen
An·ti·gua
an·ti-
  in·flam·ma·to·ry
an·ti·knock
an·ti·lock
an·ti·log·a·rithm
an·ti·mag·net·ic
an·ti·mo·ny
an·ti·node
an·ti·nu·cle·ar
an·ti·ox·i·dant
an·ti·pa·thet·ic
  -thet·i·cal·ly
an·tip·a·thy
  -thies
an·ti·per·son·nel
an·ti·per·spi·rant
an·ti·phon
an·ti·quar·i·an
an·ti·quate
  -quat·ed,
  -quat·ing
an·tique
  -tiqued, -tiqu·ing
an·tiq·ui·ty
an·ti-Sem·i·tism
an·ti·sep·tic
  -sep·ti·cal·ly

an·ti·so·cial
an·tith·e·sis
  -e·ses (pl)
an·ti·thet·i·cal
an·ti·tox·in
an·ti·trust
an·ti·vi·rus
an·ti·vi·rus
  soft·ware
an·ti·vi·rus util·i·ty
ant·ler
  -lered
ant·onym
Ant·werp
an·vil
anx·i·ety
  -eties
anx·ious
  -ious·ness
any
any·body
any·how
any·more
any·one
any·place
any·thing
any·time
any·way
any·where
aor·ta
  -tas
aor·tic
apace

apart
apart·heid
apart·ment
ap·a·thet·ic
ap·a·thy
aper·i·tif
ap·er·ture
apex
  apex·es
apha·sia
  -sic
aphid
aph·o·rism
api·ary (for bees; cf. *aviary*)
  -ar·ies
apiece
aplomb
ap·nea
apoc·a·lypse
apoc·a·lyp·tic
apo·gee
apo·lit·i·cal
Apol·lo
apol·o·get·ic
  -get·i·cal·ly
apol·o·gize
  -gized, -giz·ing
apol·o·gy
  -gies
ap·o·plec·tic
ap·o·plexy

apos·ta·sy
  -sies
apos·tate
a pos·te·ri·o·ri
apos·tle
apos·to·late
ap·os·tol·ic
apos·tro·phe
apoth·e·cary
  -car·ies
Ap·pa·la·chia
Ap·pa·la·chian
ap·pall
  -palled, -pall·ing
Ap·pa·loo·sa
ap·pa·ra·tus
  -tus·es (pl)
ap·par·el
  -eled, -el·ing
ap·par·ent
ap·par·ent·ly
ap·pa·ri·tion
ap·peal
  -peal·abil·i·ty,
  -peal·able
ap·peal·ing
ap·pear
ap·pear·ance
ap·pease
  -peas·ing,
  -peas·able,
  -pease·ment
ap·pel·lant

ap·pel·late
ap·pel·lee
ap·pend
ap·pend·age
ap·pen·dec·to·my
  -mies
ap·pen·di·ci·tis
ap·pen·dix
  -dix·es or -di·ces
  (pl)
ap·per·ceive
  -ceived, -ceiv·ing
ap·per·cep·tion
ap·per·tain
ap·pe·tite
ap·pe·tiz·er
ap·pe·tiz·ing
ap·plaud
ap·plause
ap·ple
ap·ple·jack
app·let
ap·pli·ance
ap·pli·ca·ble
  -bil·i·ty
ap·pli·cant
ap·pli·ca·tion
ap·pli·ca·tive
ap·pli·ca·tor
ap·plied
ap·pli·qué
ap·ply
  -ply·ing

ap·point
ap·poin·tee
ap·point·ive
ap·point·ment
ap·por·tion
ap·por·tion·ment
ap·po·site
ap·po·si·tion
ap·prais·al
ap·praise (value; cf.
   apprise)
  -praised,
  -prais·ing
ap·prais·er
ap·pre·cia·ble
ap·pre·ci·ate
  -at·ed, -at·ing
ap·pre·ci·a·tion
ap·pre·cia·tive
ap·pre·hend
ap·pre·hen·si·ble
ap·pre·hen·sion
ap·pre·hen·sive
ap·pren·tice
  -ticed, -tic·ing,
  -tice·ship
ap·prise (inform; cf.
   appraise)
  -prised, -pris·ing
ap·proach
ap·proach·able

ap·pro·bate
  -bat·ed, -bat·ing,
  -ba·to·ry
ap·pro·ba·tion
ap·pro·pri·ate (v)
  -at·ed, -at·ing
ap·pro·pri·ate (adj)
  -ate·ly, -ate·ness
ap·pro·pri·a·tion
ap·prov·al
ap·prove
  -proved, -prov·ing
ap·prox·i·mate
  (v, adj)
  -mat·ed, -mat·ing
ap·prox·i·mate·ly
ap·prox·i·ma·tion
ap·pur·te·nance
ap·pur·te·nant
apri·cot
April
a pri·o·ri
apron
ap·ro·pos
apt
  apt·ly, apt·ness
ap·tent
ap·ti·tude
aqua·cul·ture
aqua·ma·rine
aqua·naut
aquar·i·um
Aquar·i·us

aquat·ic
aq·ue·duct
aque·ous
aqui·fer
aq·ui·line
ar·a·besque
Ara·bia
Ar·a·bic
ar·a·ble
arach·noid
ar·bi·ter
ar·bi·tra·ble
ar·bi·trage
  -traged, -trag·ing
ar·bit·ra·ment
ar·bi·trary
  -trari·ly,
  -trari·ness
ar·bi·trate
  -trat·ed, -trat·ing,
  -tra·tive
ar·bi·tra·tion
ar·bi·tra·tor
ar·bor
ar·bo·re·al
ar·bo·re·tum
ar·bor·vi·tae
ar·bu·tus
arc (curved line; cf.
   ark)
ar·cade

ar·chae·ol·o·gy
  -o·log·i·cal,
  -o·log·i·cal·ly,
  -ol·o·gist
ar·cha·ic
arch·an·gel
arch·bish·op
arch·dea·con
arch·di·o·cese
arch·duch·ess
arch·duchy
arch·duke
arch·en·e·my
  -mies
ar·cher
ar·chery
ar·che·type
arch·fiend
Ar·chie
ar·chi·epis·co·pal
ar·chi·pel·a·go
  -goes
ar·chi·tect
ar·chi·tec·tur·al
ar·chi·tec·ture
ar·chiv·al
ar·chive
  -chived, -chiv·ing
ar·chi·vist
arch·way
arc·tic
ar·dent
ar·dor

ar·du·ous
ar·ea (space; cf.
  aria)
ar·ea·way
are·na
Ar·gen·ti·na
ar·gon
ar·go·sy
  -sies
ar·got
ar·gu·able
ar·gue
  -gued, -gu·ing
ar·gu·ment
ar·gu·men·ta·tion
ar·gu·men·ta·tive
ar·gyle
aria (melody; cf.
  area)
ar·id
  arid·i·ty,
  ar·id·ness
ari·o·so
  -sos
ar·is·toc·ra·cy
  -cies
aris·to·crat
aris·to·crat·ic
Ar·is·to·te·lian
arith·me·tic
  -met·i·cal,
  -met·i·cal·ly,
  -me·ti·cian

arith·me·tic log·ic
  unit (ALU)
ark (refuge; cf. *arc*)
ar·ma·da
ar·ma·dil·lo
  -los
ar·ma·ment
ar·ma·ture
arm·chair
Ar·me·nia
arm·ful
  -fuls
arm·hole
ar·mi·stice
ar·mor
ar·mor·er
ar·mory
  -mor·ies
arm·pit
arm·rest
arms (weapons; cf.
  alms)
ar·my
  -mies
aro·ma
ar·o·mat·ic
around
around-the-clock
arouse
  aroused,
  arous·ing
ar·peg·gio
  -gios

ar·raign
  -raign·ment
ar·range
  -ranged, -rang·ing,
  -rang·er
ar·range·ment
ar·rant
ar·ras
  ar·ras (pl)
ar·ray
ar·rear
ar·rear·age
ar·rest
ar·riv·al
ar·rive
  -rived, -riv·ing
ar·ro·gance
ar·ro·gant
ar·ro·gate
ar·row
ar·row·head
ar·row·root
ar·royo
  -royos
ar·se·nal
ar·se·nic
ar·son
  -son·ist, -son·ous
ar·te·ri·al
ar·te·rio·scle·ro·sis
ar·tery
  -ter·ies
art·ful

ar·thri·tis
  -thrit·i·des (pl)
ar·ti·choke
ar·ti·cle
  -cled, -cling
ar·tic·u·late
  -lat·ed, -lat·ing
ar·tic·u·la·tion
ar·ti·fact
ar·ti·fice
ar·ti·fi·cer
ar·ti·fi·cial
  -ci·al·i·ty, -cial·ly,
  -cial·ness
ar·ti·fi·cial
  in·tel·li·gence
ar·ti·fi·cial life
ar·til·lery
ar·ti·san
art·ist
ar·tiste
ar·tis·tic
art·ist·ry
art·less
art·work
Aru·ba
Ary·an
ASAP
as·bes·tos
as·cend
as·cen·dan·cy
as·cen·dant
as·cend·ing

as·cen·sion
as·cent (motion
  upward; cf.
  assent)
as·cer·tain
  -tain·able,
  -tain·ment
as·cet·ic
  -cet·i·cal·ly,
  -cet·i·cism
ASCII
as·cribe
  -cribed, -crib·ing
asep·sis
asep·tic
  -ti·cal·ly
asex·u·al
ashamed
ash can (n)
ash·can (adj)
ash·en
ashore
ash·tray
ashy
Asian
Asi·at·ic
aside
as·i·nine
ask
  asked, ask·ing
askance
askew
asleep

22

as·par·a·gus
as·pect
as·pen
as·per·i·ty
  -ties
as·perse
  -persed, -pers·ing
as·per·sion
as·phalt
as·phyx·ia
as·phyx·i·ate
  -at·ed, -at·ing,
  -a·tion
as·pic
as·pi·rant
as·pi·rate
  -rat·ed, -rat·ing
as·pi·ra·tion
as·pi·ra·tor
as·pire
  -pired, -pir·ing
as·pi·rin
  as·pi·rin (pl)
as·sail
  -sail·able, -sail·ant
as·sas·sin
as·sas·si·nate
  -nat·ed, -nat·ing,
  -na·tion
as·sault
as·say (analyze; cf.
  essay)
as·sem·blage

as·sem·ble
  -bled, -bling,
  -bler
as·sem·bly
  -blies
as·sem·bly·man
as·sem·bly·wom·an
as·sent (consent; cf.
  ascent)
as·sert
as·ser·tion
as·ser·tive
as·sess
  -sess·able
as·sess·ment
as·ses·sor
as·set
as·si·du·i·ty
  -ities
as·sid·u·ous
as·sign
as·sig·na·tion
as·sign·ee
as·sign·ment
as·sim·i·la·ble
as·sim·i·late
  -lat·ed, -lat·ing,
  -la·tor
as·sim·i·la·tion
as·sim·i·la·tive
as·sim·i·la·to·ry
as·sist

as·sis·tance (help;
  cf. *assistants*)
as·sis·tant
  -tants (helpers; cf.
  assistance)
as·sis·tant·ship
as·so·ci·ate
  -at·ing
as·so·ci·at·ed
as·so·ci·a·tion
as·so·cia·tive
as·so·nance
as·sort
as·sort·ment
as·suage
  -suaged,
  -suag·ing,
  -suage·ment
as·sume
  -sumed, -sum·ing,
  -sum·able
as·sump·tion
as·sur·ance
as·sure
  -sured, -sur·ing
as·sured·ly
as·ter
as·ter·isk
as·ter·oid
asth·ma
as·tig·mat·ic
astig·ma·tism
as·ton·ish

as·ton·ish·ment
as·tound
as·tral
astray
astride
as·trin·gent
-gen·cy, -gent·ly
as·tro·dome
as·trol·o·ger
as·trol·o·gy
as·tro·naut
as·tro·nau·tics
as·tron·o·mer
as·tro·nom·i·cal
as·tron·o·my
-mies
as·tute
-tute·ly,
-tute·ness
asun·der
asy·lum
asym·met·ric
asyn·chro·nous
Asyn·chro·nous
   Trans·fer Mode
   (ATM)
at·a·vism
atax·ia
ate·lier
athe·ism
athe·ist
-is·tic
ath·lete

ath·let·ic
ath·let·ics
athwart
At·lan·ta
At·lan·tic
at·las
at·mo·sphere
at·mo·spher·ic
at·om
atom·ic
at·om·ize
at·om·iz·er
aton·al
atone
   atoned, aton·ing
atone·ment
atri·um
   atria (pl)
atro·cious
atroc·i·ty
-ties
at·ro·phy
-phies
at·tach
at·ta·ché
at·ta·ché case
at·tached
at·tach·ment
at·tack
at·tain
-tain·abil·i·ty,
-tain·able
at·tain·der

at·tain·ment
at·tar
at·tempt
at·tend
at·ten·dance
at·ten·dant
at·tend·ee
at·ten·tion
at·ten·tion def·i·cit
   dis·or·der (ADD)
at·ten·tive
at·ten·u·ate
-at·ed, -at·ing,
-a·tion
at·test
at·tic
at·tire
-tired, -tir·ing
at·ti·tude
at·ti·tu·di·nal
at·tor·ney
-neys
at·tor·ney-at-law
   at·tor·neys-at-law
   (pl)
at·tract
at·trac·tion
at·trac·tive
at·trib·ute (n)
at·trib·ute (v)
-ut·ed, -ut·ing,
-ut·able
at·tri·bu·tion

at·trib·u·tive
at·tri·tion
at·tune
atyp·i·cal
au·burn
au cou·rant
auc·tion
auc·tion·eer
au·da·cious
au·dac·i·ty
  -ties
au·di·ble
  -bly, -bil·i·ty
au·di·ence
au·dio
au·dio book
au·di·ol·o·gy
au·dio·phile
au·dio·vi·su·al
au·dit
au·di·tion
  -tioned, -tion·ing
au·di·tor
au·di·to·ri·um
  -riums (pl)
au·di·to·ry
auf Wie·der·seh·en
au·ger (tool; cf.
  augur)
aught (slightest
  thing; cf. *ought*)
aug·ment
aug·men·ta·tion

aug·men·ta·tive
au gra·tin
au·gur (predict; cf.
  auger)
au·gust (majestic)
Au·gust (month)
Au·gus·ta
au jus
auk
auld lang syne
au na·tu·rel
aunt (relative; cf.
  ant)
au·ra
au·ral (heard; cf.
  oral)
  -ral·ly
au·re·ate
au·re·ole
Au·reo·my·cin
au re·voir
au·ri·cle
au·ric·u·lar
au·rif·er·ous
au·ro·ra bo·re·al·is
Ausch·witz
aus·pice
  -pic·es (pl)
aus·pi·cious
  -cious·ly,
  -cious·ness
aus·tere
  -tere·ly, -tere·ness

aus·ter·i·ty
  -ties
Aus·tin
Aus·tra·lia
Aus·tra·lian
Aus·tria
au·then·tic
  -ti·cal·ly, -tic·i·ty
au·then·ti·cate
  -cat·ed, -cat·ing,
  -ca·tion
au·thor
au·thor·ing
  en·vi·ron·ment
au·thor·i·tar·i·an
au·thor·i·ta·tive
au·thor·i·ty
  -ties
au·tho·ri·za·tion
au·tho·rize
  -riz·ing
au·tho·rized
au·thor·ship
au·tism
  -tis·tic,
  -tis·ti·cal·ly
au·to·bahn
au·to·bio·graph·i·cal
au·to·bi·og·ra·phy
au·to·cor·rect
au·toc·ra·cy
  -cies
au·to·crat

25

au·to·crat·ic
au·to·graph
au·to·graph·ic
au·to·im·mune
au·to·in·fec·tion
au·to·in·tox·i·ca·tion
au·to·mate
  -mat·ed, -mat·ing
au·to·mat·ed tell·er
  ma·chine
au·to·mat·ic
au·to·mat·i·cal·ly
au·to·ma·tion
au·tom·a·tism
au·tom·a·ti·za·tion
au·tom·a·tize
  -tized, -tiz·ing
au·tom·a·ton
  -atons
au·to·mo·bile
au·to·mo·tive
au·ton·o·mous
au·ton·o·my
  -mies
au·top·sy
  -sies
au·to·re·spond·er
au·tumn
  -tum·nal,
  -tum·nal·ly
aux·il·ia·ry
  -ries
avail

avail·abil·i·ty
  -ties
avail·able
av·a·lanche
avant-garde
av·a·rice
av·a·ri·cious
avenge
  avenged,
  aveng·ing,
  aveng·er
av·e·nue
aver
  averred, aver·ring
av·er·age
averse (disinclined;
  cf. *adverse*)
aver·sion
avert
avi·ary (for birds; cf.
  apiary)
  -ar·ies
avi·a·tion
avi·a·tor
avi·a·trix
avi·cul·ture
av·id
avid·ity
avi·on·ics
av·o·ca·do
  -dos (pl)
av·o·ca·tion (hobby;
  cf. *vocation*)

avoid
  avoid·able,
  avoid·ably
avoid·ance
avow
avow·al
avun·cu·lar
await
awake
awak·en
  -ened, -en·ing
award
aware
  aware·ness
awash
away (absent; cf.
  aweigh)
aweigh (of anchor;
  cf. *away*)
awe·some
awe·struck
aw·ful
awhile
awk·ward
awl (tool; cf. *all*)
aw·ning
awoke
awry
ax
ax·i·al
ax·i·om
ax·i·om·at·ic

ax·is
   ax·es (pl)
ax·le
aye
ayes
aza·lea
Azer·bai·jan
az·i·muth
Az·tec
azure

B

baa
bab·ble (chatter; cf.
  bauble, bubble)
  -bled, -bling
ba·boon
ba·bush·ka
ba·by
  -bies, -bied,
  -by·hood
baby boom
  boom·er
ba·by-sit
  -sat, -sit·ting,
  sit·ter
bac·ca·lau·re·ate
bac·ca·rat
bach·e·lor
  -lor·hood, -lor·ette
ba·cil·lus
  -li (pl)
back·ache
back·bite
  -bit, -biting, bit·er
back·board
back·bone
back·break·ing
back door (n)
back·door (adj)

back·drop
back·er
back·field
back·fire
back·gam·mon
back·ground
back·hand
  -hand·ed
back·hoe
back·lash
back·log
back off
back·pack
back·rest
back room
back·scat·ter
back·seat
back·slide
  -slid, -slid·ing,
  -slid·er
back·space
back·stage
back·stairs
back·stitch
back·stop
back·stretch
back·stroke
back·swing

back talk
back-to-back
back·track
back up (v)
back·up (n)
back·ward
  -ward·ly,
  -ward·ness
back·wash
back·wa·ter
back·woods
  -woods·man
back·yard
ba·con
bac·te·ria (pl)
  -ri·um (sing)
bac·te·ri·al
  -al·ly
bac·te·ri·cid·al
  -cid·al·ly
bac·te·ri·cide
bac·te·ri·ol·o·gy
  -o·log·ic,
  -o·log·i·cal·ly,
  -ol·o·gist
bad (not good; cf.
  bade)
bade (commanded;
  cf. *bad*)

badge
bad·ger
 -gered,
 -ger·ing
ba·di·nage
bad·land
bad·min·ton
baf·fle
 -fled, -fling,
 -fle·ment
bag
 bagged, bag·ging,
 bag·ger
ba·gel
bag·gage
bag·gy
 -gi·er, -gi·est,
 -gi·ness
Bagh·dad
bag·pipe
Ba·ha·mas
Bah·rain
bail (release; cf.
 bale)
 bailed (set free; cf.
 baled)
bail·ee
bai·liff
bai·li·wick
bail·ment
bail·or
bail out (v)
bail·out (n)

bait (a lure; cf. *bate*)
bake
 baked, bak·ing,
 bak·er
Ba·ke·lite
bak·er's doz·en
bak·ery
 -er·ies
bal·ance
 -anced,
 -anc·ing
bal·ance sheet
bal·co·ny
 -nies
bald (hairless; cf.
 balled, bawled)
 bald·ish, bald·ly,
 bald·ness
bal·der·dash
bale (package; cf.
 bail)
 baled (packaged;
 cf. *bailed),* bal·ing,
 bal·er
bale·ful
balk
bal·kan·ize
 -ized, -iz·ing,
 -iza·tion
Bal·kans
balky
 balk·i·er,
 balk·i·est,
 balk·i·ness

bal·lad
bal·lad·eer
bal·lad·ry
bal·last
ball bear·ing
balled (made a ball;
 cf. *bald, bawled*)
bal·le·ri·na
bal·let
bal·lis·tic
bal·lis·tics
bal·loon
bal·loon·ist
bal·lot
ball·park
ball·point
ball·room
bal·ly·hoo
 -hoos (pl)
balm
balmy
 balm·i·er,
 balm·i·est,
 balm·i·ness
ba·lo·ney
bal·sa
bal·sam
Bal·tic
bal·us·trade
bam·boo
bam·boo·zle
 -zled, -zling
ba·nal

B   banana/barker

ba·nana
band (narrow strip;
    cf. *banned*)
    bands (pl. of *band*;
    cf. *banns, bans*)
ban·da
ban·dage
    -daged, -dag·ing
Band-Aid
ban·dan·na
band·box
ban·deau
    -deaux (pl)
ban·dit
band·mas·ter
ban·do·lier
band saw
band shell
band·stand
band·wag·on
band·width
band·width
    ca·pac·i·ty
ban·dy
    -died, -dy·ing
bane·ful
Bang·kok
Ban·gla·desh
ban·gle
ban·ish
    -ish·er, -ish·ment
ban·is·ter
ban·jo
    -jos (pl), -jo·ist

bank·book
bank·card
bank dis·count
bank·er
bank mon·ey
banknote
bank rate
bank·roll
bank·rupt
bank·rupt·cy
    -cies
banned (prohibited;
    cf. *band*)
ban·ner
ban·ner page
banns (of marriage;
    cf. *bands, bans*)
ban·quet
ban·quette
bans (forbids; cf.
    bands, banns)
ban·shee
ban·tam
ban·ter
ban·yan
ban·zai
bap·tism
bap·tist
bap·tize
    -tized, -tiz·ing,
    -tiz·er
bar
    barred (kept from;
    cf. *bard*), bar·ring

Bar·ba·dos
bar·bar·i·an
bar·bar·ic
bar·ba·rism
bar·bar·i·ty
    -ties
bar·ba·rize
    -rized, -riz·ing
bar·ba·rous
bar·be·cue
bar·bell
bar·ber
    -bered, -ber·ing
bar·ber·shop
bar·bi·tu·rate
bar chart
bar code
bar code read·er
bard (poet; cf.*barred*)
bare (uncover; cf.
    bear), bar·er,
    bar·est, bare·ness,
    bared, bar·ing
bare·back
bare·faced
bare·foot
bare·hand·ed
bare·head·ed
bare·ly
bar·gain
bari·tone
bar·i·um
bar·keep·er
bark·er

30

bar·ley
bar·ley·corn
bar·na·cle
barn·storm
  -storm·er
barn·yard
baro·graph
ba·rom·e·ter
baro·met·ric
  -ri·cal·ly
bar·on (nobleman;
  cf. *barren*)
bar·on·age
bar·on·ess
bar·on·et
bar·on·et·cy
ba·ro·ni·al
bar·ony
  -on·ies
ba·roque
ba·rouche
bar·rack
bar·ra·cu·da
  -da (pl)
bar·rage
  -raged, -rag·ing
barred (shut out; cf.
  bard)
bar·rel
bar·ren (sterile; cf.
  baron)
bar·rette
bar·ri·cade
  -cad·ed, -cad·ing

bar·ri·er
bar·ring
bar·rio
  -rios (pl)
bar·ris·ter
bar·room
bar·row
bar·tend·er
bar·ter
bas·al
ba·salt
base (foundation; cf.
  bass)
  bas·es (pl)
base·ball
base·board
base·line
base·ment
base pay
bash·ful
ba·sic
  -si·cal·ly, -sic·i·ty
BA·SIC
Ba·sic In·put
  Out·put Sys·tem
  (BIOS)
ba·sil
ba·sil·i·ca
bas·i·lisk
ba·sin
bas·i·net (helmet;
  cf. *bassinet*)

ba·sis (foundation;
  cf. *bases*)
  ba·ses (pl)
bas·ket
  -ket·ful
bas·ket·ball
bas·ket·work
bas-re·lief
bass (deep voice; cf.
  base)
  bass (pl)
bas·si·net (cradle;
  cf. *basinet*)
bas·soon
bass·wood
bas·tion
batch
bate (moderate; cf.
  bait)
  bat·ed, bat·ing
ba·teau
  ba·teaux (pl)
bath (n)
  baths
bathe (v)
  bathed, bath·ing
bath·house
ba·thom·e·ter
bath·robe
bath·room
bath·tub
bathy·scaphe
bathy·sphere

31

ba·tiste
ba·ton
Bat·on Rouge
bat·tal·ion
bat·ten
  -tened, -ten·ing
bat·ter
bat·tery
  -ter·ies
bat·tle
  -tled, -tling, -tler
bat·tle-ax
bat·tle cruis·er
bat·tle cry
bat·tle·field
bat·tle·ground
bat·tle·ment
bat·tle-scarred
bat·tle·ship
bau·ble (trifle; cf.
  babble, bubble)
baud
baud rate
baux·ite
Ba·var·i·an
bawl
  bawled (cried; cf.
  bald, balled)
bay·ber·ry
bay·o·net
bay·ou
ba·zaar (market; cf.
  bizarre)

ba·zoo·ka
beach (shore; cf.
  beech)
beach·comb·er
beach·front
beach·head
beach·wear
bea·con
bea·dle
bead·work
beady
bea·gle
bear (n)(animal; cf.
  bare) bears
bear (v)(hold; cf.
  bare)
  bore, borne,
  bear·ing
bear·able
beard
  beard·ed,
  beard·less
bear·er
bear·skin
beat (flog; cf. *beet*)
be·atif·ic
be·at·i·fi·ca·tion
be·at·i·fy
  -fied, -fy·ing
be·at·i·tude
beat·nik
beau (suitor; cf. *bow*)
  beaux (pl)

beau·te·ous
beau·ti·cian
beau·ti·ful
  -ful·ly, -ful·ness
beau·ti·fy
  -fied, -fying,
  -fi·ca·tion
beau·ty
  -ties
bea·ver
  -vers
be·calm
be·cause
beck·on
  -oned, -on·ing
be·cloud
be·come
  -came, -com·ing,
  -com·ing·ly
be·daz·zle
bed board
bed·bug
bed·clothes
bed·ding
be·deck
be·dev·il
bed·fast
bed·fel·low
bed·lam
bed·ou·in
  bed·ou·in (pl)
bed·post
be·drag·gled

32

bed rest
bed·rid·den
bed·rock
bed·room
bed·side
bed·sore
bed·spread
bed·stead
bed·time
beech (tree; cf.
   beach)
   -beech·es
beech·nut
beef·eat·er
beef·steak
bee·hive
bee·keep·er
bee·line
been
beep·er
beer (liquor; cf. *bier*)
bees·wax
beet (vegetable; cf.
   beat)
bee·tle
be·fall
be·fit
   -fit·ted, -fit·ting
be·fore
be·fore·hand
be·fore·time
be·friend
be·fud·dle

beg·gar
   -gared, -gar·ing
beg·gar·ly
   -gar·li·ness
be·gin
be·gin·ner
Be·gin·ners All-
   pur·pose
   Sym·bol·ic
   In·struc·tion
   Code (BASIC)
be·gin·ning
be·go·nia
be·grudge
be·guile
   -guiled, -guil·ing,
   -guile·ment
be·half
be·have
   -haved, -hav·ing,
   -hav·er
be·hav·ior
   -ior·al, -ior·al·ly
be·hav·ior·ism
   -ior·ist, -ior·is·tic
be·head
be·he·moth
be·hind
be·hind-the-scenes
be·hold
be·hoove
   -hooved, -hoov·ing
beige

Bei·jing
be·ing
Bei·rut
be·la·bor
Be·la·rus
be·lat·ed
   -ed·ly, -ed·ness
be·lay
bel can·to
be·lea·guer
   -guered, -guer·ing
Bel·fast
bel·fry
   -fries
Bel·gian
Bel·gium
Bel·grade
be·lie
   -lied, -ly·ing, -li·er
be·lief
be·liev·able
   -ably, -abil·ity
be·lieve
   -lieved, -liev·ing,
   -liev·er
be·lit·tle
   -tled, -tling,
   -tle·ment
Be·lize
bell (that rings; cf.
   belle)
bel·la·don·na
bell·boy

belle (girl; cf. *bell*)
belles let·tres
bell·hop
bel·li·cose
bel·lig·er·ence
bel·lig·er·ent
bell jar
bel·lows
bell·pull
bell tow·er
bell·weth·er
bel·ly
  -lies
bel·ly·ache
belly button
be·long
be·loved
be·low
belt·ing
belt·way
be·moan
bench mark
bench war·rant
bend
  bent, bend·ing
be·neath
bene·dic·tion
bene·dic·to·ry
bene·fac·tion
bene·fac·tor
be·nef·i·cence
be·nef·i·cent
  -cent·ly

ben·e·fi·cial
ben·e·fi·cia·ry
  -ries
ben·e·fit
  -fit·ed, -fit·ing,
  -fit·er
be·nev·o·lence
be·nev·o·lent
be·night·ed
be·nign
Be·nin
ben·zene
be·queath
be·quest
be·rate
be·reave
  -reaved, -reav·ing
be·reave·ment
beri·beri
Ber·lin
ber·ry (fruit; cf.
  bury)
  -ries
ber·serk
berth (place; cf.
  birth)
ber·yl
be·ryl·li·um
be·seech
be·set·ting
be·side
be·sides

be·siege
  -sieged, -sieg·ing,
  -sieg·er
be·smear
be·smirch
be·speak
  -spoke, -spo·ken,
  -speak·ing
bes·tial
bes·ti·al·i·ty
  -ties
best man
be·stow
best-sell·er
  best-sell·ing
bet
  bet·ted, bet·ting
be·ta-car·o·tene
be·ta test
be·tide
be·to·ken
  -kened, -ken·ing
be·tray
  -tray·al, -tray·er
be·troth
be·troth·al
bet·ter (good; cf.
  bettor)
bet·ter·ment
bet·tor (one who
  wagers; cf. *better*)
be·tween
be·tween·times

bev·el
   -eled, -el·ing
bev·er·age
bevy
   bev·ies
be·wail
be·ware
be·wil·der
   -dered, -der·ing,
   -der·ing·ly
be·wil·der·ment
be·witch
be·yond
be·zel
Bhu·tan
bi·an·nu·al (twice
   yearly; cf.
   biennial)
   -al·ly
bi·as
   -as·ness, -ased,
   -as·ing
bi·ble
bib·li·cal
   -cal·ly
bib·li·og·ra·pher
bib·li·og·ra·phy
   -phies
bib·lio·graph·ic
   -graph·i·cal·ly
bib·lio·phile
bi·cam·er·al
bi·car·bon·ate

bi·cen·te·na·ry
bi·cen·ten·ni·al
bi·ceps
   bi·ceps (pl)
bi·chlo·ride
bi·cus·pid
bi·cy·cle
   -cled, -cling, -cler
bi·cy·clist
bid
   bade, bid·den,
   bid·der
bi·di·rec·tion·al
bi·en·ni·al (once in
   two years; cf.
   biannual)
   -al·ly
bi·en·ni·um
   -ni·ums
bier (for funeral; cf.
   beer)
bi·fo·cal
bi·fur·cate
   -cat·ed, -cat·ing
big
   big·ger, big·gest,
   big·ness
big·a·mous
big·a·my
   -mist
Big Ben
big·head
   -head·ed

big·heart·ed
big·horn
   -horn (pl)
bight
big·ot
   -ot·ed, -ot·ed·ly
big·ot·ry
   -ries
bi·ki·ni
bi·lat·er·al
bile
bi·lev·el
bilge
bi·lin·gual
   -gual·ly
bi·lin·gual·ism
bilk
bill·board
billed (charged; cf.
   build)
bil·let-doux
   bil·lets-doux (pl)
bill·fold
bil·liards
bill·ing
bil·lion
   bil·lionth
bil·lion·aire
bill of fare
bill of lad·ing
bil·low
   -lowy
bil·ly goat

35

bi·me·tal·lic
bi·met·al·lism
bi·met·al·list
  -lis·tic
bi·month·ly
bi·na·ry
  -ries
bi·na·ry large
  ob·ject (BLOB)
bind
  bound, bind·ing
bind·er
bind·ery
  -er·ies
bin·go
bin·oc·u·lar
bi·no·mi·al
bio·chem·i·cal
  -cal·ly
bio·chem·is·try
  -chem·ist
bio·chip
bio·de·grad·able
  -abil·i·ty
bio·de·grade
  -deg·ra·da·tion
bio·di·ver·si·ty
bio·feed·back
bi·og·ra·pher
bio·graph·i·cal
bi·og·ra·phy
  -phies

bi·o·log·i·cal
bi·ol·o·gy
  -gist
bi·on·ics
bi·op·sy
bio·rhythm
bio·sci·ence
bio·sphere
bio·tech·nol·o·gy
bi·par·ti·san
  -san·ism,
  -san·ship
bi·par·tite
bi·ped
bi·plane
bi·po·lar
bi·ra·cial
bird·bath
bird·call
bird-dog (v)
  bird-dog·ging
bird·house
bird·ie
bird·lime
bird·man
bird·seed
bird's-eye
birth (born; cf.
  berth)
birth·day
birth·mark
birth·place

birth·rate
birth·right
birth·stone
bis·cuit
bi·sect
bi·sex·u·al
bish·op
bish·op·ric
Bis·marck
bis·muth
bi·son
  bi·son (pl)
bisque
bite
  bit, bit·ten,
  bit·ing
bit·map
bits per sec·ond
  (bps)
bit·ter
  -ter·ish
bit·tern
bit·ter·ness
bit·ter·root
bit·ter·sweet
bit·ter·weed
bi·tu·men
bi·tu·mi·nous
bi·valve
biv·ouac
  -ouack·ed,
  -ouack·ing

bi·week·ly
bi·zarre (odd; cf. *bazaar*)
  -zarre·ly,
  -zarre·ness
bi·zon·al
black·ball
black·ber·ry
black·board
black·en
  -ened, -en·ing,
  -en·er
black·head
black·jack
black light
black·list
black·mail
black out (v)
black·out (n)
black sheep
black·smith
black·top
blad·der
blade
blam·able
blame
  blamed,
  blam·ing,
  blame·less
blame·ful
blame·wor·thy
  -thi·ness
blanch

blan·dish
  -dish·ment
blan·ket
blar·ney
bla·sé
blas·pheme
  -phemed,
  -phem·ing,
  -phem·er
blas·phe·mous
  -mous·ly
blas·phe·my
  -mies
blast off (v)
blastoff (n)
bla·tan·cy
  -cies
bla·tant
  -tant·ly
blaze
  blazed, blaz·ing
blaz·er
bla·zon
  -zoned, -zon·ing,
  -zon·er
bleach
  bleach·able
bleach·er
  -er·ite
blem·ish
blend
  blend·ed,
  blend·ing

bless
  blessed, bless·ing
blew (air; cf. *blue*)
blight
blind
  blind·ness
blind·er
blind·fold
blink·er
blin·tze
bliss·ful
  -ful·ly, -ful·ness
blis·ter
  -tered, -ter·ing
blithe
  blith·er, blith·est,
  blithe·ly
blitz·krieg
bliz·zard
bloat
bloc (political; cf. *block*)
block (of wood; cf. *bloc*)
block·ade
  -ad·ed, -ad·ing,
  -ad·er
block·bust·er
block·head
blond
blood
blood·cur·dling
blood·ed

blood·less
blood·let·ting
blood·mo·bile
blood·root
blood·shed
blood·shot
blood·stain
blood·suck·er
blood·thirsty
blood ves·sel
bloody
   blood·i·er,
   blood·i·est,
   blood·i·ly
blos·som
blotch
blot·ter
blouse
   blous·es
blow-dry
blow·er
blow·fly
blow·gun
blow out (v)
blow·out (n)
blow over
blow·pipe
blow·torch
blub·ber
   -bered, -ber·ing
blub·bery
blud·geon

blue (color; cf. *blew*)
   blu·er, blu·est,
   blue·ness
blue·bell
blue·ber·ry
blue·bird
blue·bon·net
blue book
blue-col·lar
blue·fish
blue flu
blue·grass
blue·jack·et
blue jay
blue jeans
blue law
blue moon
blue-pen·cil
blue·print
blues
blu·et
bluff
blu·ing
blu·ish
blun·der
   -dered, -der·ing,
   -der·er
blun·der·buss
blunt
   blunt·ness
blur
   blurred, blur·ring
blurb

blurt
blus·ter
   -tered, -ter·ing,
   -ter·er
boa
boar (animal; cf.
   bore)
board (wood; cf.
   bored)
board foot
board·ing·house
board·ing school
board·room
board·walk
boast
boast·ful
   -ful·ly, -ful·ness
boat·house
boat·load
boat people
boat·swain
bob
   bobbed, bob·bing
bob·bin
bob·cat
bob·o·link
bob·sled
bob·tail
bob·white
bod·ice
bodi·less
bodi·ly

body
  bod·ies, bod·ied
body·guard
Boer
bo·gey
  -geys (pl)
bo·gey·man
bog·gle
  -gled, -gling
bo·gus
Bo·he·mi·an
boil·er
boil·er·plate
Boi·se
bois·ter·ous
bold
  bold·er (stronger;
  cf. *boulder*)
bold·face
bold-faced
bole (trunk of tree;
  cf. *boll, bowl*)
bo·le·ro
  -ros (pl)
bo·li·var
Bo·liv·ia
boll (of cotton; cf.
  bole, bowl)
boll wee·vil
bol·ster
  -stered, -ster·ing,
  -ster·er
bolt·er

bolt·rope
bomb
bom·bard
  -bard·ment
bom·bar·dier
bom·bast
bom·bas·tic
bomb·shell
bomb·sight
bo·na fide
bo·nan·za
bon·bon
bond·age
bond·hold·er
bonds·man
bone
  boned, bon·ing
bone·meal
bon·fire
bon mot
  bons mots (pl)
bon·net
bon·ny
  -ni·er, -ni·est,
  -ni·ly
bo·nus
bon vi·vant
  bons vivants (pl)
bon voy·age
bony
  bon·i·er, bon·i·est
boo·dle
book

book·bind·er
  -bind·ery
book·bind·ing
book·case
book club
book·end
book·ie
book·ish
book·keep·er
  -keep·ing
book·let
book·mak·er
  -mak·ing
book·man
book·mark
book·mo·bile
book·plate
book·sell·er
book·shelf
book·store
book val·ue
book·worm
Bool·e·an
boom·box
boo·mer·ang
boon·docks
boon·dog·gle
boor·ish
  -ish·ly, -ish·ness
boost·er
boot·able
boot·ed
boo·tee

booth
  booths
boot·jack
boot·leg
boo·ty
  -ties
booze
  boozed, booz·ing,
  booz·er
bo·rate
bo·rax
Bor·deaux
  Bor·deaux (pl)
bor·der (edge)
  -dered, -der·ing
bor·der·line
bore (weary; cf.
  boar)
  bored (tired; cf.
  board), bor·ing
bo·re·al
bore·dom
born-again
bo·ron
bor·ough (division
  of city; cf. *burro,
  burrow*)
bor·row
Bos·nia
Bos·ni·an
bo·som
bossy
  boss·i·er,
  boss·i·est

Bos·ton
bo·tan·i·cal
bot·a·nist
bot·a·ny
botch
both
both·er
  -ered, -er·ing
both·er·some
Bo·tswa·na
bot·tle
  -tled, -tling, -tler
bot·tle·neck
bot·tom
bot·tom·less
bot·u·lism
bou·doir
bouf·fant
bough (of tree; cf.
  bow)
bought
bouil·la·baisse
bouil·lon (soup; cf.
  bullion)
boul·der (rock; cf.
  bolder)
bou·le·vard
bounce
  bounced,
  bounc·ing
bounc·er
bound

bound·ary
  -aries
bound·er
bound·less
boun·te·ous
boun·ti·ful
boun·ty
  -ties
bou·quet
bour·bon
bour·geois (adj, n)
  bour·geois (pl)
bour·geoi·sie
bou·tique
bou·ton·niere
bo·vine
bow (knot; cf. *beau*)
bow (salutation; cf.
  bough)
bowd·ler·ize
  -ized, -iz·ing,
  -iz·er
bow·el
bow·er
bow·ery
  -er·ies
bow·knot
bowl (dish; cf. *bole,
  boll*)
bowl·er
bow·line
bowl·ing
bow·man

bow·sprit

bow·string

bow tie

box·car

box·er

box·ing

box kite

box lunch

box of·fice

box score

box spring

box·wood

boy (youth; cf. *buoy*)

boy·cott

boy·sen·ber·ry

brace·let

brac·er

brack·et

brack·ish

brag

   bragged,
   brag·ging,
   brag·ger

brag·gart

braille

brain·child

brain·less

brain·pow·er

brain·storm

brain trust

brain·wash·ing

brain wave

brainy

   brain·i·er,
   brain·i·est,
   brain·i·ness

braise (cook slowly;
   cf. *braze*)
   braised, brais·ing

brake (on a car; cf.
   break)
   braked, brak·ing

brake·man

bram·ble

brand

bran·dish

brand-new

bran·dy

   -dies, -died,
   -dy·ing

bras·siere

bra·va·do

brav·ery

   -er·ies

bra·vo

   -vos (pl), -vo·ing,
   -voed

bra·vu·ra

brawl

brawny

   brawn·i·er,
   brawn·i·est,
   brawn·i·ness

braze (solder; cf.
   braise)
   brazed, braz·ing,
   braz·er

bra·zen

   -zened, -zen·ing

bra·zier

Bra·zil

bra·zil·wood

breach (violation; cf.
   breech)

bread (food; cf. *bred*)

bread·fruit

bread·stuff

breadth (size; cf.
   breath)

bread·win·ner

break (shatter; cf.
   brake) break·ing,
   broke, bro·ken

break·able

break·age

break·away

break down (v)

break·down (n)

break·er

break-even

break·fast

break·neck

break out (v)

break·out (n)

break through (v)

break·through (n)
break up (v)
break·up (n)
break·wa·ter
breast
breast·bone
breast-feed
breast·stroke
breath (n)(of air; cf. *breadth*)
Breath·a·ly·zer
breathe (v)
  breathed, breath·ing
breath·er
breath·less
breath·tak·ing
breech (rear; cf. *breach*)
breech·load·er
  breech·load·ing
breed
  bred (produced; cf. *bread*), breed·ing
breeze
breeze·way
breezy
  breez·i·er, breez·i·ly, breez·i·ness
breth·ren

bre·vet
  -vet·ted, -vet·ting
bre·via·ry
  -ries
brev·i·ty
  -ties
brew
  brew·ing
brew·ery
  -er·ies
brews (ferments; cf. *bruise*)
bribe
  bribed, brib·ing, brib·er
brib·ery
  -er·ies
bric-a-brac
  bric-a-brac (pl)
brick
  bricks
brick·lay·er
brick red
brick·work
brick·yard
brid·al (wedding; cf. *bridle*)
bride
bride·groom
brides·maid
bridge
  bridged, bridg·ing
bridge·work

bri·dle (harness; cf. *bridal*)
  -dled, -dling
brief
brief·case
brief·less
bri·er
brig
bri·gade
  -gad·ed, -gad·ing
brig·a·dier
bright
bright·en
  -ened, -en·ing, -en·er
bright·ness
bright·work
bril·liance
bril·lian·cy
  -cies
bril·liant
bril·lian·tine
brim
  brimmed, brim·ming
brim·ful
brim·mer
brim·stone
brin·dle
bring
  brought, bring·ing
brink
brink·man·ship

briny
  brin·i·er,
  brin·i·est,
  brin·i·ness
bri·quette
brisk
bris·ket
bris·tle
  -tled, -tling
bris·tol (cardboard)
Britain (nation; cf.
  Briton)
Bri·tan·nic
Brit·ish
Brit·ish·er
Brit·on (person; cf.
  Britain)
brit·tle
  -tler, -tlest,
  -tle·ness
broach (open; cf.
  brooch)
broad
  broad·ly,
  broad·ness
broad·ax
broad·band
broad·cast
  -cast·ed, -cast·ing,
  -cast·er
broad·cloth
broad·en
  -ened, -en·ing

broad jump
broad-leaved (adj)
broad-mind·ed
  -ed·ness, -ed·ly
broad·side
broad·sword
broad·tail
bro·cade
broc·co·li
bro·chette
bro·chure
bro·chure·ware
brogue
broil
broil·er
broke
bro·ken
bro·ken·heart·ed
bro·ker
bro·ker·age
bro·kered
bro·mate
bro·mide
bro·mine
bron·chi·al
bron·chi·tis
bron·cho·scope
bron·co
  -cos
bronze
  bronzed,
  bronz·ing,
  bronz·er

brooch (pin; cf.
  broach)
brood
brood·er
brook
broom·stick
broth
  broths
broth·er
  broth·ers
broth·er·hood
broth·er-in-law
  broth·ers-in-law(pl)
broth·er·ly
brougham
brought
brow
brow·beat
  -beat·en
brown bread
brown·out
brown·stone
brown sug·ar
browse
  browsed,
  brows·ing, browser
bru·in
bruise (crush; cf.
  brews)
  bruised, bruis·ing
bruis·er
bru·net or
  bru·nette

brunt
brush
brush-off (n)
brush up (v)
brush·up (n)
brush·wood
brush·work
brusque
Brus·sels
bru·tal
bru·tal·i·ty
  -ties
bru·tal·ize
  -ized, -iz·ing,
  -iza·tion
brute
brut·ish
brux
  -ed, -ing
bub·ble (soap; cf.
  babble, bauble)
bub·bly
  -bli·er, -bli·est
buc·ca·neer
Bu·cha·rest
buck·et
buck·eye
buck·le
  -led, -ling
buck·ram
buck·saw
buck·shot
buck·skin

buck·wheat
bu·col·ic
Bu·da·pest
Bud·dha
Bud·dhism
bud·ding
bud·get
  -get·ary
Bue·nos Ai·res
buf·fa·lo (sing)
  buf·fa·lo or
  buf·fa·loes (pl)
buff·er
  -ered, -er·ing
buf·fet
buf·foon
buf·foon·ery
bug·bear
bu·gle
  -gled, -gling
build (construct; cf.
  billed)
  built, build·ing
build·er
build up (v)
build·up (n)
built-in
built-up
bul·bous
Bul·gar·i·an
bulge
  bulged, bulg·ing
bu·lim·ia

bulk·head
bulky
  bulk·i·er,
  bulk·i·est,
  bulk·i·ness
bull·dog
bull·doze
bull·doz·er
bul·let
bul·le·tin
bul·le·tin board
  ser·vice
Bul·le·tin Board
  Sys·tem (BBS)
bul·let-proof
bull·fight
bull·finch
bull·frog
bull·head
bul·lion (gold or sil-
  ver; cf. *bouillon*)
bull·ock
bull pen
bull's-eye
  bull's-eyes (pl)
bull·ter·ri·er
bull·whip
bul·ly
  -lies, -lied, -ly·ing
bul·rush
bul·wark
bum·ble·bee
bump·er

bump·kin
bumpy
  bump·i·er,
  bump·i·ly,
  bump·i·ness
bunch
bun·dle
  -dled, -dling, -dler
bun·ga·low
bun·gee
bun·gle
  -gled, -gling, -gler
bun·ion
bunk
bunk beds
bun·ker
  -kered, -ker·ing
bun·ting
buoy (signal; cf.
  boy)
buoy·an·cy
buoy·ant
bur·den
  -dened, -den·ing
bur·den·some
bur·dock
bu·reau
  -reaus (pl)
bu·reau·cra·cy
  -cies
bur·reau·crat
bu·reau·crat·ic
bur·geon

bur·gher
bur·glar
bur·glar·ize
  -ized, -iz·ing
bur·glar·proof
bur·glary
  -glar·ies
bur·go·mas·ter
bur·gun·dy
  -dies
buri·al
bur·lap
bur·lesque
  -lesqued,
  -lesqu·ing
bur·ly
  -li·er, -li·est,
  -li·ness
Bur·mese
burn
  burned, burn·ing
burn·er
bur·nish
bur·noose
burn out (v)
burn·out (n)
burr
bur·ri·to
bur·ro (donkey; cf.
  borough, burrow)
  bur·ros (pl)
bur·row (dig; cf.
  borough, burro)

bur·sar
bur·sa·ry
  -ries
bur·si·tis
burst
Bu·run·di
bury (conceal; cf.
  berry)
  bur·ied, bury·ing
bus·boy
bush·el
  -eled, -el·ing,
  -el·er
busi·ness (enter-
  prise; cf.
  busyness)
busi·ness·like
busi·ness·man
busi·ness·peo·ple
busi·ness·wom·an
bus·ing
bus·tle
  -tled, -tling
busy
  bus·i·er, bus·i·est,
  bus·ied
busy·body
busy·ness (busy
  state; cf. *business*)
busy·work
but (conjunction; cf.
  butt)
bu·tane

45

butch·er
-ered, -er·ing
butch·ery
-er·ies
but·ler
butt (end; cf. *but*)
butte
but·ter
but·ter·fat
but·ter·fly
-flies
but·ter·milk
but·ter·nut
but·ter·scotch
but·ter·weed
but·tery
-ter·ies
but·tock
but·ton
-toned, -ton·er,
-ton·ing
but·ton·hole
but·tress
bux·om
buy (acquire; cf. *by,
bye*)
buy·ing, buy·er,
bought
buy·back
buzz
buz·zard
buzz·er
buzz saw

buzz·word
by (near, farewell; cf.
buy, bye)
by and large
bye (tournament; cf.
buy, by)
by-elec·tion
by·gone
by·law
by·line
by·pass
by·play
by-prod·uct
by·stand·er
byte
by·way
by·word
Byz·an·tine

ca·bana
cab·a·ret
cab·bage
cab·driv·er
cab·in
cab·i·net
cab·i·net·mak·er
cab·i·net·work
ca·ble
  -bled, -bling
ca·ble·gram
ca·boose
cab·o·tage
cab·ri·ole
cab·stand
ca·cao
cac·cia·to·re
cache
  cached, cach·ing
ca·chet
cack·le
  -led, -ling, -ler
ca·coph·o·ny
  -nies
cac·tus
  cacti (pl)
ca·dav·er
ca·dav·er·ous

cad·die
  -dies
ca·dence
ca·den·za
ca·det
cad·mi·um
cad·re
ca·du·ceus
Cae·sar
cae·su·ra
  -su·ras (pl)
ca·fé
caf·e·te·ria
caf·feine
caf·tan
Cai·ro
cais·son
ca·jole
  -joled, -jol·ing,
  -jol·ery
Ca·jun
cake
  caked, cak·ing
cal·a·bash
cal·a·boose
ca·lam·i·tous
ca·lam·i·ty
  -ties
cal·car·e·ous

cal·cif·er·ous
cal·ci·fy
  -fied, -fy·ing,
  -fi·ca·tion
cal·ci·mine
cal·ci·na·tion
cal·cine
  -cined, -cin·ing
cal·ci·um
cal·cu·la·ble
cal·cu·late
  -lat·ed, -lat·ing
cal·cu·la·tion
cal·cu·la·tor
cal·cu·lus
  -li (pl)
cal·dron
cal·en·dar (for
  dates; cf. *calen-*
  der, colander)
  -dared, -dar·ing
cal·en·der (machine;
  cf. *calendar,*
  colander)
  -dered, -der·ing
calf
  calves (pl)
calf·skin
cal·i·ber

47

cal·i·brate
  -brat·ed, -brat·ing,
  -bra·tor
cal·i·bra·tion
cal·i·co
  -coes (pl)
cal·i·per
  -pered, -per·ing
ca·liph
cal·is·then·ics
calk
call·able
cal·lig·ra·pher
cal·lig·ra·phy
call·ing
cal·li·ope
cal·lous (hardened;
  cf. *callus*)
cal·low
cal·lus (hardened
  surface; cf.
  callous)
calm
  calm·ly, calm·ness
ca·lo·ric
cal·o·rie
  -ries
cal·o·rim·e·ter
ca·lum·ni·ate
  -at·ed, -at·ing,
  -a·tion
ca·lum·ni·ous

cal·um·ny
  -nies
cal·va·ry
  -ries
Cal·vin·ism
ca·lyp·so
  -sos (pl)
ca·lyx
  -lyx·es (pl)
ca·ma·ra·de·rie
cam·ber
  -bered, -ber·ing
cam·bi·um
  -bi·ums
Cam·bo·dia
Cam·bo·di·an
cam·bric
cam·cord·er
cam·el
ca·mel·lia
Cam·e·lot
Cam·em·bert
cam·eo
  -eos
cam·era
Cam·e·roon
cam·i·sole
cam·mie
cam·ou·flage
  -flaged, -flag·ing,
  -flage·able
cam·paign
camp·er

cam·pe·si·no
  -nos
camp·ground
cam·phor
camp·site
cam·pus
cam·shaft
cam wheel
can
  canned, can·ning
Can·a·da
Ca·na·di·an
ca·nal
can·a·li·za·tion
can·a·pé
ca·nard
ca·nary
  -nar·ies
ca·nas·ta
can·cel
  -celed, -cel·ing,
  -cel·able
can·cel·bot
can·cel·la·tion
can·cer
  -ous, -ous·ly
can·de·la·bra
can·des·cent
can·did
  -ly, -ness
can·di·da·cy
  -cies
can·di·date

can·died

can·dle
  -dled, -dling, -dler

can·dle·light

can·dle·mas

can·dle·pow·er

can·dle·snuff·er

can·dle·stick

can·dle·wood

can-do (adj)

can·dor

can·dy
  -dies, -died,
  -dy·ing

ca·nine

can·is·ter

can·ker
  -ker·ous, -kered,
  -ker·ing

can·ker sore

can·ker·worm

can·na

can·na·bis

can·nery
  -ner·ies

can·ni·bal

can·ni·bal·ism
  -is·tic

can·ni·bal·ize
  -ized, -iz·ing,
  -iza·tion

can·no·li

can·non (gun; cf.
  canon, canyon)

can·non·ball

can·non·eer

can·not

can·ny
  -ni·er, -ni·est,
  -ni·ness

ca·noe
  -noed, -noe·ing,
  -noe·ist

can·on (rule; cf.
  cannon, canyon)

ca·non·i·cal

can·on·ize
  -ized, -iz·ing,
  -i·za·tion

can·o·py
  -pies

can·ta·loupe

can·tan·ker·ous

can·ta·ta

can·ta·trice

can·teen

can·ter

can·ti·cle

can·ti·le·ver

can·ti·na

can·to
  -tos

can·ton
  -ton·al

Can·ton·ese
  Can·ton·ese (pl)

can·ton·ment

can·tor

can·vas (n)(cloth; cf.
  canvass)

can·vass (v)(solicit;
  cf. *canvas*)
  -vased, -vas·ing,
  -vass·er

can·yon (ravine; cf.
  cannon, canon)

ca·pa·bil·i·ty

ca·pa·bil·i·ties

ca·pa·ble
  -bly

ca·pa·cious

ca·pac·i·tate
  -tat·ed, -tat·ing

ca·pac·i·tor

ca·pac·i·ty
  -ties

ca·par·i·son

ca·per
  -pered, -per·ing

cap·il·lar·i·ty
  -ties

cap·il·lary
  -lar·ies

cap·i·tal (city, property; cf. *capitol*)

cap·i·tal·ism

cap·i·tal·ist
  -is·tic, -is·ti·cal·ly
cap·i·tal·iza·tion
cap·i·tal·ize
  -ized, -iz·ing
cap·i·tate
cap·i·tol (building;
  cf. *capital*)
ca·pit·u·late
  -lat·ed, -lat·ing
ca·pit·u·la·tion
cap·puc·ci·no
ca·price
ca·pri·cious
cap·size
  -sized, -siz·ing
cap·stone
cap·sule
  -suled, -sul·ing
cap·tain
cap·tion
  -tioned, -tion·ing,
  -tion·less
cap·tious
  -tious·ly,
  -tious·ness
cap·ti·vate
  -va·tion, -vat·ed,
  -vat·ing
cap·tive
cap·tiv·i·ty
cap·tor

cap·ture
  -tured, -tur·ing
ca·rafe
car·a·mel
car·a·mel·ize
  -ized, -iz·ing
car·at or kar·at
  (weight; cf. *caret,*
  carrot)
car·a·van
  -vanned,
  -van·ning
car·a·way
car·bide
car·bine
car·bo·hy·drate
car·bol·ic
car·bon
  -bon·less
car·bo·na·ceous
car·bon·ate
  -at·ed, -at·ing,
  -ation
car·bon copy
car·bon dating (n)
  car·bon-date (v)
car·bon·ic
car·bon·if·er·ous
car·bon·ize
  -ized, -iz·ing
Car·bo·run·dum
car·box·yl
  -yl·ic

car·bun·cle
  -cled, -cu·lar
car·bu·re·tor
car·cass
car·cin·o·gen
  -gen·ic, -ge·nic·i·ty
car·ci·no·ma
  -mas, -ma·tous
card·board
card cat·a·log
card·file
card·hold·er
car·di·ac
car·di·gan
car·di·nal
  -nal·ly
car·dio·gram
car·dio·graph
  -dio·graph·ic,
  -di·og·ra·phy
car·di·ol·o·gy
  -ol·o·gist,
  -o·log·i·cal
car·dio·pul·mo·nary
car·dio·vas·cu·lar
ca·reen
ca·reer
care·free
care·ful
  -ful·ler, -ful·lest,
  -ful·ly
care·giv·er

care·less
-less·ly, -less·ness
ca·ress
-res·sive,
-res·sive·ly,
-ress·er
car·et (a symbol; cf.
carat, carrot)
care·tak·er
care·worn
car·fare
car·go (sing)
-goes (pl)
car·hop
Ca·rib·be·an
car·i·bou
car·i·bou (pl)
car·i·ca·ture
-tur·al, -tur·ist,
-tured
car·ies
car·ies (pl)
ca·ri·o·ca
car·jack·ing
car·load
car·mine
car·nage
car·nal
-nal·ity, -nal·ly
car·na·tion
car·nets
car·ni·val

car·niv·o·rous
-rous·ness
car·ol
-oled, -o·ling,
-ol·er
car·om
ca·rot·id
ca·rous·al
ca·rouse
-roused, -rous·ing,
-rous·er
car·ou·sel
car·pal tun·nel
syn·drome
car·pen·ter
-tered, -ter·ing
car·pen·try
car·pet
car·pet·ing
car pool
car·port
car·riage
car·ri·er
car·ri·on
car·rot (vegetable;
cf. *carat, caret*)
car·rou·sel (var. of
carousel)
car·ries
-ried
car·ry
-ry·ing
car·ry·all

car·ry out (v)
car·ry·out (n)
car·ry·over (n)
Car·son City
cart·age
carte blanche
car·tel
car·ti·lage
car·tog·ra·pher
car·tog·ra·phy
car·ton (box; cf.
cartoon)
car·toon (picture; cf.
carton)
-toon·ing,
-toon·ish, -toon·ist
car·tridge
carve
carved, carv·ing,
carv·er
ca·sa·ba
cas·cade
-cad·ed, -cad·ing
case hard·en
case-hard·ened
case·load
case·ment
case·work
cash-and-car·ry
cash·book
ca·shew
cash·ier (n)
ca·shier (v)

cash·mere
ca·si·no
  -nos
cas·ket
casque
cas·sa·va
cas·se·role
cas·sette
cas·sia
cas·sock
cast (throw; cf. *caste*)
  cast·ing
cas·ta·net
cast·away
caste (social class;
  cf. *cast*)
cas·tel·lat·ed
cas·ti·gate
  -gat·ed, -gat·ing,
  -ga·tor
Cas·til·ian
cast iron (n)
cast-iron (adj)
cas·tle
  -tled, -tling
cast-off (adj)
cast·off (n)
cas·tor
ca·su·al
  -al·ly, -al·ness
ca·su·al·ty
ca·su·ist
  -is·tic, -is·ti·cal

ca·su·ist·ry
  -ries
cat·a·clysm
  -clys·mal,
  -clys·mic,
  -clys·mi·cal·ly
cat·a·comb
cat·a·falque
Cat·a·lan
cat·a·lep·sy
  -lep·sies, -lep·tic,
  -lep·ti·cally
cat·a·log
  -loged, -log·ing
ca·tal·pa
ca·tal·y·sis
  -y·ses (pl)
cat·a·lyst
cat·a·lyt·ic
cat·a·ma·ran
cat·a·mount
cat·a·pult
cat·a·ract
ca·tas·tro·phe
  cat·a·stroph·ic
cat·a·ton·ic
Ca·taw·ba
  -ba or -bas (pl)
cat·bird
cat·boat
cat·call
catch·all
catch·er

catch-22
  catch-22's or
  catch-22s (pl)
catch·word
cat·e·che·sis
  -che·ses (pl),
  -chet·i·cal
cat·e·chism
  -chis·mal, -chis·tic
cat·e·chist
cat·e·chu·men
cat·e·gor·i·cal
  -cal·ly
cat·e·go·rize
  -rized, -riz·ing,
  -ri·za·tion
cat·e·go·ry
  -ries
ca·ter
  -ter·er
cat·er·pil·lar
cat·fish
cat·gut
ca·thar·sis
  -thar·ses (pl)
ca·thar·tic
ca·the·dral
cath·e·ter
cath·ode
  cath·od·al,
  ca·thod·ic,
  ca·thod·i·cal·ly
cath·ode-ray tube

cath·o·lic
  ca·thol·i·cal·ly,
  ca·thol·i·cize
Ca·thol·i·cism
cat·like
cat·nip
cat-o'-nine-tails
  cat-o'-nine-tails (pl)
CAT scan
cat·sup
cat·tail
cat·tle
cat·walk
Cau·ca·sian
cau·cus
cau·li·flow·er
caulk
  caulk·er,
  caulk·ing
caus·al
  -al·ly
cau·sal·i·ty
cau·sa·tion
caus·ative
cause
  caused, caus·ing,
  caus·er
cause·way
caus·tic
  -ti·cal·ly, -tic·i·ty
cau·ter·ize
  -ized, -iz·ing,
  -iza·tion

cau·tery (effect of
  burning tissue; cf.
  coterie)
  -ter·ies
cau·tion
  -tioned, -tion·ing
cau·tion·ary
cau·tious
  -tious·ness
cav·al·cade
cav·a·lier
  -lier·ism
cav·al·ry
  -ries
ca·ve·at emp·tor
cav·ern
cav·ern·ous
cav·i·ar
cav·il
  -iled, -il·ing, -il·er
cav·i·ty
  -ties
ca·vort
Cay·man Islands
CD-ROM
cease
  ceased, ceas·ing
cease-fire
cease·less
ce·dar
cede (yield; cf. *seed*)
  ced·ed, ced·ing,
  ced·er

ce·dil·la
ceil
ceil·ing (limit,
  overhead wall; cf.
  sealing)
  -inged
cel·e·brant
cel·e·brate
  -brat·ed, -brat·ing,
  -bra·tion
ce·leb·ri·ty
  -ties
ce·ler·i·ty
Cel·er·on
cel·ery
  -er·ies
ce·les·tial
cel·i·ba·cy
cel·i·bate
cel·lar (under-
  ground store-
  room; cf. *seller*)
cel·lo
  -los, -list
cel·lo·phane
cel·lu·lar
  -lar·i·ty
cel·lu·lite
cel·lu·loid
cel·lu·lose
Cel·sius
Celt·ic
ce·ment

ce·men·ta·tion
cem·e·tery
 -ter·ies
ceno·taph
Ce·no·zo·ic
cen·ser (for incense;
  cf. *censor, sensor*)
cen·sor (supervisor
  of morals; cf.
  censer, sensor)
 -sored, -sor·ing
cen·so·ri·ous
cen·sor·ship
cen·sur·able
cen·sure
 -sured, -sur·ing
cen·sus (count; cf.
  senses)
cent (penny; cf.
  scent, sent)
cen·taur
cen·ta·vo
 -vos
cen·te·na·ry
cen·ten·ni·al
cen·ter·board
cen·ter·piece
cen·ti·grade
cen·ti·gram
cen·ti·li·ter
cen·time
cen·ti·me·ter
cen·ti·pede
cen·tral

Cen·tral Af·ri·can
  Re·pub·lic
cen·tral·ize
 -ized, -iz·ing,
 -iza·tion
cen·tral
  pro·cess·ing unit
cen·trif·u·gal
 -gal·ly
cen·tri·fuge
 -fuged, -fug·ing
cen·trip·e·tal
cen·trist
Cen·tron·ics
  in·ter·face
cen·tu·ry
 -ries
ce·phal·ic
ce·ram·ic
ce·re·al (grain; cf.
  serial)
cer·e·bel·lum
 -bel·lums
ce·re·bral
ce·re·bral pal·sy
ce·re·bro·spi·nal
ce·re·brum
 -brums
cer·e·mo·ni·al
cer·e·mo·ni·ous
cer·e·mo·ny
 -nies
ce·ri·um
cer·tain

cer·tain·ly
cer·tain·ty
 -ties
cer·ti·fi·ably
cer·tif·i·cate
 -cat·ed, -cat·ing,
 -ca·to·ry
cer·ti·fi·ca·tions
cer·ti·fy
 -fied, -fy·ing,
 -fi·able
cer·ti·tude
ce·ru·le·an
cer·vi·cal
cer·vix
 -vi·ces (pl)
ce·sar·e·an
ce·si·um
ces·sa·tion
ces·sion (yielding;
  cf. *session*)
cess·pool
Chab·lis
Chae·bol
chafe (irritate; cf.
  chaff)
 chafed, chaf·ing
chaff (banter; cf.
  chafe)
cha·grin
 -grined, -grin·ing
chain gang
chain mail
chain saw

chain-smoke
  chain-smok·er
chain stitch
chair·man
  -maned, -man·ing
chair·per·son
chair·wom·an
chaise longue
  chaise longues
chal·ce·do·ny
  -nies
cha·let
chal·ice
chalk
  chalky
chal·lenge
  -lenged, -leng·ing
chal·lis
  -lises (pl)
cham·ber
  -bered, -ber·ing
cham·ber·lain
cham·ber·maid
cha·me·leon
cham·ois
cham·pagne (wine;
  cf. *champaign*)
cham·paign (plain;
  cf. *champagne*)
cham·per·ty
  -per·tous
cham·pi·on
cham·pi·on·ship

chan·cel
chan·cel·lery
  -ler·ies
chan·cel·lor
chan·cery
  -cer·ies
chan·de·lier
chan·dler
change
  changed,
  chang·ing
change·able
  -able·ness, -ably,
  -abil·i·ty
change·less
change·over
chan·nel
  -neled, -nel·ing
chan·teuse
cha·os
  cha·ot·ic
chap·ar·ral
chap·book
cha·peau
  -peaus (pl)
cha·pel
chap·er·on
  -oned, -on·ing,
  -on·age
chap·lain
  -lain·cy
chap·let
  -let·ed

chap·ter
char·ac·ter
char·ac·ter
  an·i·ma·tion
char·ac·ter field
char·ac·ters per
  inch (cpi)
char·ac·ters per
  sec·ond (cps)
char·ac·ter·is·tic
char·ac·ter·iza·tion
char·ac·ter·ize
  -ized, -iz·ing
char·ac·ter print·er
cha·rade
char·broil
char·coal
charge
  charged,
  charg·ing
charge·able
charge ac·count
char·gé d'af·faires
  chargés d'affaires
  (pl)
char·i·ot
cha·ris·ma
char·i·ta·ble
  -ta·bly
char·i·ty
  -ties
char·la·tan
  -tan·ism, -tan·ry

Charles·ton
char·ley horse
char·nel
char·ter
char·treuse
char·wom·an
chase (pursue)
   chased (past tense
   of *chase*; cf.
   chaste), chas·ing
chasm
chas·sis
   chas·sis (pl)
chaste (virtuous; cf.
   chased)
   chast·er, chast·est,
   chaste·ness
chas·ten
   -tened, -ten·ing
chas·tise
   -tised, -tis·ing,
   -tise·ment
chas·ti·ty
cha·su·ble
châ·teau
   -teaus (pl)
chat line
chat room
chat·tel
chat·ter
chat·ter·box
chauf·feur
   -feured, -feur·ing

chau·vin·ism
cheap·en
   -ened, -en·ing
cheap·skate
Chech·nya
check·book
check·er
check·er·board
check in (v)
check-in (n)
check·list
check mark
check·mate
check off (v)
check·off (n)
check out (v)
check·out (n)
check·point
check·rein
check·room
check up (v)
check·up (n)
cheek·bone
cheer·ful
   -ful·ly, -ful·ness
cheer·less
cheery
   cheer·i·er,
   cheer·i·est,
   cheer·i·ly
cheese·burg·er
cheese·cake
cheese·cloth

chef
chef d'oeu·vre
   chefs d'oeu·vre (pl)
chem·i·cal
   -cal·ly
che·mise
chem·ist
chem·is·try
   -tries
che·mo·ther·a·py
che·nille
cher·ish
Cher·no·byl
Cher·o·kee
   Cher·o·kee (pl)
cher·ry
   -ries
cher·ub
   cher·u·bim or
   cher·ubs (pl)
Ches·a·peake
chess
   chess·board,
   chess·man
chest·nut
che·va·lier
chev·ron
Chey·enne
   Chey·enne (pl)
Chi·an·ti
chiar·oscu·ro
chi·ca·nery
   -ner·ies

Chi·ca·no
   -nos (pl)
chick·a·dee
chick·en
   -ened, -en·ing
chick·en·heart·ed
chick·en pox
chick-pea
chic·o·ry
   -ries
chide
chief·ly
chief·tain
chif·fon
chig·ger
chi·gnon
Chi·hua·hua
chil·blain
child
   chil·dren (pl),
   child·less,
   child·less·ness
child·bear·ing
child·birth
child·hood
child·ish
   -ish·ly, -ish·ness
child·like
child·proof
Chil·e
chili or chile (pep-
   per sauce; cf.
   chilly)

chill
   chill·ing·ly,
   chill·ness
chilly (cold; cf. *chili*
   or *chile*)
   chill·i·er,
   chill·i·est,
   chill·i·ness
chi·me·ra
chim·ney
   -neys
chim·pan·zee
Chi·na
chi·na·ber·ry
Chi·na·town
chi·na·ware
chin·chil·la
Chi·nese
   Chi·nese (pl)
Chi·no (of China; cf.
   chino)
chi·no (cloth; cf.
   Chino)
Chi·nook
   Chi·nook (pl)
chintz
chip
   chipped,
   chip·ping
chip jewelry
chip·munk
chi·rop·o·dy
   -dist

chi·ro·prac·tic
   -prac·tor
chis·el
   -eled, -eling, -el·er
chit-chat
chiv·al·rous
   -rous·ness
chiv·al·ry
   -ries
chlo·ral
chlo·rate
chlor·dane or
   chlor·dan
chlo·ride
chlo·ri·nate
   -nat·ed, -nat·ing,
   -na·tion
chlo·rine
chlo·rite
   -rit·ic
chlo·ro·fluo·ro·car·bon
chlo·ro·form
chlo·ro·phyll
chock-full
choc·o·late
Choc·taw
   Choc·taw (pl)
choice
   choic·er, choic·est,
   choice·ness
choir (singers; cf.
   quire)
choke·cher·ry

57

chok·er
cho·ler
chol·era
cho·ler·ic
cho·les·ter·ol
choose (select; cf.
   chose)
   chose, cho·sen,
   choos·ing
chop·per
chop·py
chop·stick
chop su·ey
   chop su·eys (pl)
cho·ral (of a chorus;
   cf. *chorale, coral,*
   corral)
cho·rale (sacred
   song; cf. *choral,*
   coral, corral)
chord (music; cf.
   cord)
chore
cho·rea
cho·re·og·ra·phy
   -phies
cho·ris·ter
chor·tle
   -tled, -tling
cho·rus
chose (selected; cf.
   choose)
chow·der

chow mein
chrism
chris·ten
   -tened, -ten·ing
Chris·ten·dom
Chris·tian
Chris·tian·i·ty
Chris·tian·ize
   -ized, -iz·ing
Christ·mas
Christ·mas·tide
chro·mate
chro·mat·ic
chro·ma·tog·ra·phy
chrome
chro·mite
chro·mi·um
chro·mo·some
chron·ic
chron·ic fa·tigue
   syn·drome
chron·i·cle
   -cled, -cling, -cler
chro·no·graph
chro·no·log·i·cal
   -cal·ly
chro·nol·o·gy
   -gies
chro·nom·e·ter
chro·no·met·ric
chry·san·the·mum
chuck·le
   -led, -ling,
   -le·some

chum
   chummed,
   chum·ming
chum·my
   -mi·er, -mi·est,
   -mi·ness
chunk
church·go·er
church·yard
churl
churl·ish
   -ish·ly, -ish·ness
churn
chute (slide; cf.
   shoot)
chut·ney
   -neys (pl)
chutz·pah
ci·bo·ri·um
   -ria (pl)
ci·ca·da
   -das (pl)
ci·ca·trix
   -tri·ces (pl)
ci·der
ci·gar
cig·a·rette
cinc·ture
cin·der
Cin·der·el·la
cin·e·ma
cin·e·ma·tog·ra·pher
cin·na·bar

cin·na·mon
cinque·foil
ci·pher
-phered, -pher·ing
cir·cle
-cled, -cling
cir·clet
cir·cuit
cir·cuit board
cir·cuit-switched
line
cir·cu·itous
-itous·ness
cir·cuit·ry
-ries
cir·cu·lar
-lar·ity, -lar·ly
cir·cu·lar·ize
-ized, -iz·ing,
-iza·tion
cir·cu·late
-lated, -lat·ing
cir·cu·la·tion
cir·cu·la·to·ry
cir·cum·cise
-cised, -cis·ing
cir·cum·ci·sion
cir·cum·fer·ence
-fer·en·tial
cir·cum·flex
cir·cum·lo·cu·tion
cir·cum·nav·i·gate
cir·cum·scribe

cir·cum·spect
-spec·tion,
-spect·ly
cir·cum·stance
cir·cum·stan·tial
-ti·al·i·ty, -tial·ly
cir·cum·stan·ti·ate
-at·ed, -at·ing
cir·cum·vent
-ven·tion
cir·cus
cir·rho·sis
-rho·ses (pl)
cir·ro·cu·mu·lus
cir·ro·stra·tus
cir·rus (cloud; cf.
serous)
cis·tern
cit·a·del
ci·ta·tion
cite (quote; cf. *sight,
site*)
cit·ed, cit·ing,
cit·able
cit·i·zen
cit·i·zen·ry
-ries
cit·i·zen·ship
cit·rate
cit·ron
cit·ro·nel·la
cit·rus
cit·rus (pl)

city
cit·ies
civ·ic
civ·i·cal·ly
civ·il
ci·vil·ian
ci·vil·i·ty
-ties
civ·i·li·za·tion
civ·i·lize
-lized, -liz·ing
civ·il·ly
claim
claim·er,
claim·able
claim·ant
clair·voy·ance
clair·voy·ant
cla·mant
clam·bake
clam·ber (climb; cf.
clamor)
-bered, -ber·ing
clam·my
-mi·er, -mi·est,
-mi·ness
clam·or (outcry; cf.
clamber)
-ored, -or·ing
clam·or·ous
clam·shell
clam up (v)

clan·des·tine
  -tine·ly, -tine·ness
clang
clan·nish
  -nish·ness
clans·man
clap·board
clap·per
clar·et
clar·i·fy
  -fied, -fy·ing,
  -fi·ca·tion
clar·i·net
  -net·ist
clar·i·on
clar·i·ty
clas·sic
clas·si·cal
clas·si·cism
clas·si·cist
clas·si·fi·ca·tion
clas·si·fy
  -fied, -fy·ing,
  -fi·able
class·ism
class·mate
class·room
clat·ter
  -ter·er, -ter·ing·ly
clause (grammati-
  cal; cf. *claws*)
claus·tro·pho·bia
  -phobe

clav·i·cle
claw
  claws (sharp toes;
  cf. *clause*)
clean
  clean·ness
clean-cut
clean·er
clean·ly
  -li·er, -li·est,
  -li·ness
cleanse
  cleansed,
  cleans·ing
cleans·er
clear·ance
clear-cut
clear-eyed
clear-head·ed
  -head·ed·ly,
  -head·ed·ness
clear·ing·house
clear-sight·ed
cleav·age
cleav·er
cleft pal·ate
cle·ma·tis
clem·en·cy
  -cies
clem·ent
cler·gy
  -gies
cler·gy·man

cler·gy·wom·an
cler·ic
cler·i·cal
cler·i·cal·ism
clev·er
  -er·ish, -er·ly,
  -er·ness
clew or clue
  clewed or clued,
  clew·ing or
  clue·ing
cli·ché
click (noise; cf.
  clique)
cli·ent
cli·en·tele
cli·ent serv·er
  com·put·ing
cliff-hang·er
cli·mac·tic (of a cli-
  max; cf. *climatic*)
cli·mate
cli·ma·tic (of
  climate; cf.
  climactic)
cli·ma·tol·o·gy
  -tol·o·gist,
  -to·log·i·cal,
  -to·log·i·cal·ly
cli·max
clin·ic
clin·i·cal
cli·ni·cian

clin·ker

clip
  clipped, clip·ping

clip art

clip·board

clip·book

clip-on (adj, n)

clique (narrow
  group of people;
  cf. *click*),
  cliqu·ish,
  clique·ish·ness

cloak-and-dag·ger

clob·ber
  -bered, -ber·ing

clock-watch·er

clock·wise

clock·work

clod·hop·per

clog
  clogged, clog·ging

clois·ter
  -tered, -ter·ing

clone
  cloned, clon·ing

closed

closed-cap·tioned

closed-end

close·fist·ed

close-hauled

close-knit

close·ness

close-out

clos·et
  -et·ful

close-up (n, adv, adj)

clos·ing

clo·sure

cloth (n)
  cloths

clothe (v)
  clothed, cloth·ing

clothes·pin

cloth·ier

cloud·burst

cloudy
  cloud·i·er,
  cloud·i·est,
  cloud·i·ness

clout

cloven foot

clo·ver

clo·ver·leaf

club
  clubbed,
  club·bing

club chair

club·foot
  -foot·ed

club·house

club steak

clue·less

clum·sy
  -si·er, -si·ly,
  -si·ness

clus·ter
  -tered, -ter·ing

clutch

clut·ter

coach·man

co·ad·ju·tor

co·ag·u·late
  -lated, -lat·ing,
  -la·tion

co·alesce
  co·alesced,
  co·alesc·ing,
  co·ales·cent

coal gas

co·ali·tion

coal tar

co·an·chor

coarse (rough; cf.
  corse, course)
  coars·er, coars·est,
  coarse·ly

coars·en
  coars·ened,
  coars·en·ing

coast
  coast·al

coast·er

coast guard

coast·line

coast-to-coast

coat·tail

co·au·thor

coax

co·ax·i·al
co·balt
cob·bler
cob·ble·stone
CO·BOL
co·bra
cob·web
  -webbed
co·caine
coc·cyx
  coc·cy·ges or
  coc·cyx·es (pl)
co·chair
co·chair·man
cock·a·too
  -toos
cock·boat
cock·crow
cock·eyed
cock·le
cock·le·bur
cock·le·shell
cock·ney
  cock·neys (pl)
cock·pit
cock·roach
cock·sure
cock·tail
co·coa
co·co·nut
co·coon
code
  cod·ed, cod·ing

co·de·fen·dant
co·deine
co·dex
  co·di·ces (pl)
cod·fish
cod·i·cil
cod·i·fy
  -fied, -fy·ing,
  -fi·ca·tion
co·ed
co·ed·i·tor
  co·ed·it
co·ed·u·ca·tion
co·ef·fi·cient
coel·acanth
co·erce
  -erced, -erc·ing,
  -erc·ible
co·er·cion
co·er·cive
co·eval
co·ex·ist
  -is·tence, -is·tent
cof·fee
cof·fee·house
cof·fee·mak·er
cof·fee·pot
cof·fee shop
cof·fee ta·ble
cof·fer
cof·fin
co·gen·cy
co·gent

cog·i·tate
  -tat·ed, -tat·ing
cog·i·ta·tion
cog·i·ta·tive
co·gnac
cog·nate
  -nate·ly
cog·ni·zance
cog·ni·zant
cog·wheel
co·hab·it
co·heir
co·here
  -hered, -her·ing
co·her·ence
co·her·en·cy
  -cies
co·her·ent
  -ent·ly
co·he·sion
co·he·sive
  -sive·ly
co·hort
co·host
coif·feur (person; cf.
  coiffure)
coif·fure (style; cf.
  coiffeur)
coin
coin·age
co·in·cide
  -cid·ed, -cid·ing
co·in·ci·dence

co·in·ci·dent
co·in·ci·den·tal
co·in·sur·ance
co·in·sure
co·ition
coke
 coked, cok·ing
col·an·der (perfo-
 rated utensil; cf.
 calendar, calender)
cold-blood·ed
cold cream
cold cuts
cold frame
cold front
cold sore
cold sweat
cold war
cold wave
co·le·op·tera
 -tera (pl), -ter·ous
cole·slaw
col·ic
col·ic·root
col·i·se·um
co·li·tis
col·lab·o·rate
 -rat·ed, -rat·ing,
 -ra·tion
col·lage
col·lapse
 -lapsed, -laps·ing,
 -laps·ible

col·lar
col·lar·bone
col·late
 -lat·ed, -lat·ing,
 -la·tor
col·lat·er·al
col·la·tion
col·league
col·lect
 -lect·ible
col·lect·ed
 -lect·ed·ness
col·lec·tion
col·lec·tive
 -tive·ly
col·lec·tiv·ism
col·lec·tor
col·lege
col·le·gial
col·le·gi·al·i·ty
col·le·gian
col·le·giate
col·le·gi·um
 -gia or -gi·ums (pl)
col·lide
 -lid·ed, -lid·ing
col·lie (dog; cf.
 coolie, coolly)
col·lier
col·liery
 -lier·ies
col·li·sion (crash; cf.
 collusion)

col·loid
col·lo·qui·al
 -qui·al·ly
col·lo·qui·al·ism
col·lo·qui·um
 -qui·ums or -quia
 (pl)
col·lo·quy
 -quies (pl)
col·lu·sion (secret
 agreement; cf.
 collision)
 -sive
co·lo·ca·tion
co·logne
 -logned
Co·lom·bia
Co·lom·bi·an
co·lon
 colons or co·la (pl)
col·o·nel (officer; cf.
 kernel)
 -nel·cy
co·lo·nial
co·lo·nial·ism
col·o·nist
col·o·ni·za·tion
col·o·nize
 -nized, -niz·ing
col·on·nade
col·o·ny
 -nies
col·o·phon

col·or
col·or·ation
col·or·a·tu·ra
col·or-blind
col·ored
col·or·fast
col·or·ful
col·or guard
col·or·less
co·los·sal
  -sal·ly
col·os·se·um
co·los·sus
  -si (pl)
Co·lum·bia
Co·lum·bus
col·umn
  -umned
co·lum·nar
col·um·nist
co·ma (insensibility;
  cf. *comma*)
co·ma·tose
com·bat
  -bat·ed, -bat·ing
com·bat·ant
com·bat·ive
com·bi·na·tion
com·bine
  -bined, -bin·ing
com·bo
  -bos
com·bus·ti·ble

com·bus·tion
come back (v)
come·back (n)
co·me·di·an
co·me·di·enne (fem)
com·e·dy
  -dies
come·ly
  -li·ness
come on (v)
come-on (n)
co·mes·ti·ble
com·et
com·fit
com·fort
com·fort·able
com·fort·er
com·ic
com·i·cal
com·ing
co·mi·ty
  -ties
com·ma (punctua-
  tion; cf. *coma*)
com·mand (order;
  cf. *commend*)
com·man·dant
com·man·deer
com·mand·er
com·mand·ment
com·mand mod·ule
com·man·do
  -dos

com·mem·o·rate
  -rat·ed, -rat·ing
com·mem·o·ra·tion
com·mem·o·ra·tive
com·mence
  -menced,
  -menc·ing
com·mence·ment
com·mend (praise;
  cf. *command*)
  -mend·able,
  -mend·ably
com·men·da·tion
com·men·da·to·ry
com·men·su·ra·ble
  -bly, -bil·i·ty
com·men·su·rate
  -rate·ly
com·ment
com·men·tary
  -tar·ies
com·men·tate
  -tat·ed, -tat·ing
com·men·ta·tor
com·merce
com·mer·cial
com·mer·cial·ism
com·mer·cial·ize
  -iza·tion
com·min·gle
com·mis·er·ate
  -at·ed, -at·ing
com·mis·er·a·tion

com·mis·sar
com·mis·sary
  -sar·ies
com·mis·sion
  -sioned, -sion·ing
com·mis·sion·aire
com·mis·sion·er
com·mit
  -mit·ting
com·mit·ment
com·mit·ted
com·mit·tee
com·mit·tee·man
com·mit·tee·wom·an
com·mode
com·mo·di·ous
com·mod·i·ty
  -ties
com·mo·dore
com·mon
Com·mon Busi·ness
  Ori·en·ted
  Lan·guage
  (COBOL)
com·mon us·er
  ac·cess (CUA)
com·mon·al·ty
  -ties
com·mon·er
com·mon·place
com·mon sense
  -sen·si·ble
com·mon·wealth

com·mo·tion
com·mu·nal
com·mune
  -muned, -mun·ing
com·mu·ni·ca·ble
com·mu·ni·cant
com·mu·ni·cate
  -cat·ed, -cat·ing
com·mu·ni·ca·tion
com·mu·ni·ca·tive
com·mu·nion
com·mu·ni·qué
com·mu·nism
com·mu·nist
  -nis·tic
com·mu·ni·ty
  -ties
com·mu·ta·tion
com·mute
  -mut·ed,
  -mut·ing,
  -mut·able
com·mu·ter
com·pact
  -pact·ible, -pac·tor
com·pact disc
Com·pact Disc
  Read-Only
  Mem·o·ry (CD-
  ROM)
com·pa·nies
com·pan·ion
com·pan·ion·able

com·pan·ion·ship
com·pan·ion·way
com·pa·ny
  -nied, -ny·ing
com·pa·ra·ble
com·par·a·tive
com·pare
  -pared, -par·ing
com·par·i·son
com·part·ment
com·pass
com·pas·sion
com·pas·sion·ate
com·pat·i·ble
  -bly, -bil·i·ty
com·pa·tri·ot
com·pel
  -pelled, -pel·ling,
  -pel·la·ble
com·pen·di·ous
com·pen·di·um
  -di·ums or -dia (pl)
com·pen·sate
  -sat·ed, -sat·ing
com·pen·sa·tion
  -tive, -to·ry
com·pete
  -pet·ed, -pet·ing
com·pe·tence
com·pe·ten·cy
  -cies
com·pe·tent
com·pe·ti·tion

com·pet·i·tive
-tive·ness
com·pet·i·tor
com·pi·la·tion
com·pile
-piled, -pil·ing
com·pil·er
com·pla·cence
com·pla·cen·cy
-cies
com·pla·cent (self-
satisfied; cf.
complaisant)
com·plain
com·plain·ant
com·plaint
com·plai·sance
com·plai·sant
(obliging; cf.
complacent)
com·ple·ment (full
quantity; cf.
compliment)
com·ple·men·tal
com·ple·men·ta·ry
-ri·ly
com·plete
-plet·ed, -plet·ing
com·ple·tion
com·plex
com·plex·ion
-ion·al, -ioned
com·plex·i·ty

com·pli·ance
com·pli·ant
com·pli·cate
-cat·ed, -cat·ing
com·pli·ca·tion
com·plic·it
com·plic·i·ty
-ties
com·pli·ment
(flattery; cf.
complement)
com·pli·men·ta·ry
com·ply
-plied, -ply·ing
com·po·nent
com·port
com·port·ment
com·pose
-posed, -pos·ing
composed
-pos·ed·ly
com·pos·er
com·pos·ite
-it·ed, -it·ing
com·po·si·tion
com·pos·i·tor
com·post
com·po·sure
com·pound
-pound·able
com·pre·hend
-hend·ible
com·pre·hen·si·ble

com·pre·hen·sion
com·pre·hen·sive
com·press
com·pressed
com·press·ible
-ibil·i·ty
com·pres·sion
com·pres·sor
com·prise
-prised, -pris·ing
com·pro·mise
-mised, -mis·ing
comp·trol·ler
com·pul·sion
com·pul·so·ry
-ri·ly
com·punc·tion
-tious
com·put·able
-abil·i·ty
com·pu·ta·tion
com·pute
-put·ed, -put·ing
com·put·er
-er·like
com·put·er-aid·ed
de·sign (CAD)
com·put·er-aid·ed
draft·ing (CAD)
com·put·er-aid·ed
en·gin·eer·ing
(CAE)

com·put·er-aid·ed
   man·u·fac·tur·ing
com·put·er
   gen·er·ated
   im·ag·ery (CGI)
com·put·er·ese
com·put·er·ist
com·put·er·ize
   -ized, -iz·ing,
   -iz·able, -i·za·tion
com·put·er·nik
com·put·er·phobe
   -pho·bia, -pho·bic
com·rade
con·cave
con·cav·i·ty
   -ties
con·ceal
   -ceal·able
con·cede
   -ced·ed, -ced·ing,
   -ced·ed·ly
con·ceit
con·ceit·ed
con·ceiv·able
   -ably, -abil·i·ty
con·ceive
   -ceived, -ceiv·ing
con·cen·trate
   -trat·ed, -trat·ing,
   -tra·tor
con·cen·tra·tion
con·cen·tric
   -tri·cal·ly

con·cept
con·cep·tion
   -tion·al
con·cep·tu·al
   -al·i·ty, -al·ly
con·cern
con·cerned
con·cern·ing
con·cert
con·cer·ti·na
con·cert·mas·ter
con·cer·to
con·ces·sion
   -sion·al, -sion·ary
con·ces·sion·aire
conch
con·cierge
con·cil·i·ate
   -at·ed, -at·ing,
   -a·tion
con·cise
con·clave
con·clude
   -clud·ed, -clud·ing
con·clu·sion
con·clu·sive
con·coct
   -coc·tion
con·com·i·tant
con·cord
Con·cord
con·cor·dance
con·cor·dat

con·course
con·crete
   -cret·ed,
   -cret·ing,
   -crete·ly
con·cur
   -curred, -cur·ring
con·cur·rence
con·cur·rent
con·cus·sion
   -sive
con·demn
   -dem·nable,
   -dem·na·to·ry
con·dem·na·tion
con·den·sa·tion
   -tion·al
con·dense
   -densed,
   -dens·ing,
   -dens·able
con·dens·er
con·de·scend
con·de·scend·ing
   -scend·ing·ly
con·de·scen·sion
con·di·ment
con·di·tion
   -tioned,
   -tion·ing,
   -tion·able
con·di·tion·al

con·dole
-doled, -dol·ing
con·do·lence
con·do·min·i·um
con·do·na·tion
con·done
con·dor
con·duce
con·du·cive
con·duct
con·duc·tion
con·duc·tor
-to·ri·al
con·duit
con·fab·u·la·tion
con·fec·tion
con·fec·tion·er
con·fec·tion·ery
-er·ies
con·fed·er·a·cy
-er·a·cies, -er·al
con·fed·er·ate
-at·ed, -at·ing,
-a·tive
con·fed·er·a·tion
con·fer
-ferred, -fer·ring,
-fer·ra·ble
con·fer·ee
con·fer·ence
con·fess
-fess·able
con·fessed·ly

con·fes·sion
-sion·al·ly
con·fes·sion·al
con·fes·sor
con·fet·ti
con·fi·dant (friend;
cf. *confident*)
con·fide
-fid·ed, -fid·ing
con·fi·dence
con·fi·dent (sure; cf.
confidant)
con·fi·den·tial
-ti·al·i·ty
con·fig·u·ra·tion
con·fig·ure
-ured, -ur·ing
con·fine
-fined, -fin·ing
con·fine·ment
con·firm
-firm·abil·i·ty,
-firm·able
con·fir·ma·tion
con·firmed
con·fis·cate
-cat·ed, -cat·ing,
-ca·tion
con·fla·gra·tion
con·flict
con·flu·ence
con·form
-form·ist

con·form·able
con·for·ma·tion
con·for·mi·ty
-ties
con·found
con·found·ed
con·fra·ter·ni·ty
con·front
con·fron·ta·tion
Con·fu·cian
con·fuse
-fused, -fus·ing,
-fus·ing·ly
con·fu·sion
con·geal
con·ge·nial
-nial·i·ty
con·gen·i·tal
con·gest
-ges·tion,
-ges·tive
con·glom·er·ate
-at·ed, -at·ing,
-a·tive
con·glom·er·a·tion
Con·go
con·grat·u·late
-lat·ed, -lat·ing,
-la·to·ry
con·grat·u·la·tion
con·gre·gate
-gat·ed, -gat·ing
con·gre·ga·tion

con·gre·ga·tion·al
con·gress
  -gres·sio·nal
con·gress·man
con·gress·wom·an
con·gru·ence
con·gru·ent
con·gru·i·ty
  -ities
con·gru·ous
con·ic
con·i·cal
co·ni·fer
  -nif·er·ous
con·jec·tur·al
con·jec·ture
  -tured, -tur·ing,
  -tur·er
con·ju·gal
con·ju·gate
  -gat·ed, -gat·ing
con·ju·ga·tion
con·junc·tion
con·junc·ti·va
con·junc·ture
con·jure
  -jured, -jur·ing
con·jur·er
con·line·bill
con·nect
  -nect·able,
  -nec·tor
con·nec·tion

con·nec·tive
con·nec·tiv·i·ty
con·niv·ance
con·nive
  -nived, -niv·ing
con·nois·seur
con·no·ta·tion
con·no·ta·tive
con·note
  -not·ed, -not·ing
con·nu·bi·al
con·quer
  -quered, -quer·ing,
  -quer·or
con·quest
con·san·guin·e·ous
con·san·guin·i·ty
  -ties
con·science
con·sci·en·tious
con·scious
con·scious·ness
con·script
con·scrip·tion
con·se·crate
  -crat·ed, -crat·ing,
  -cra·tor
con·se·cra·tion
con·sec·u·tive
  -tive·ly
con·sen·su·al
con·sen·sus
con·sent

con·se·quence
con·se·quent
con·se·quen·tial
con·se·quent·ly
con·ser·va·tion
con·ser·va·tion·ist
con·ser·va·tism
con·ser·va·tive
con·ser·va·to·ry
con·serve
  -served,
  -serv·ing,
  -serv·er
con·sid·er
  -ered, -er·ing
con·sid·er·able
  -ably
con·sid·er·ate
con·sid·er·a·tion
con·sign
  -sign·able,
  -sig·na·tion,
  -sign·or
con·sign·ee
con·sign·ment
con·sist
con·sis·ten·cy
  -cies
con·sis·tent
con·so·la·tion
con·sole
  -soled, -sol·ing,
  -sol·ing·ly

con·sol·i·date
  -dat·ed, -dat·ing
con·sol·i·da·tion
con·som·mé
con·so·nance
con·so·nant
con·sort
con·sor·tium
  -sor·tia (pl)
con·spec·tus
con·spic·u·ous
con·spir·a·cy
  -cies
con·spir·a·tor
con·spire
  -spired, -spir·ing
con·sta·ble
con·stab·u·lary
  -lar·ies
con·stan·cy
  -cies
con·stant
con·stel·la·tion
con·ster·na·tion
con·sti·pate
  -pat·ed, -pat·ing
con·stit·u·en·cy
  -cies
con·stit·u·ent
con·sti·tute
  -tut·ed, -tut·ing
con·sti·tu·tion
con·sti·tu·tion·al

con·sti·tu·tion·al·i·ty
con·sti·tu·tion·al·ly
con·strain
con·straint
con·strict
con·stric·tion
con·struct
  -struct·ible,
  -struc·tor
con·struc·tion
con·struc·tion·ist
con·struc·tive
con·strue
  -strued, -stru·ing,
  -stru·able
con·sul (govern-
  ment official; cf.
  council, counsel)
con·sul·ar
con·sul·ate
con·sult
con·sul·tant
con·sul·ta·tion
con·sul·ta·tive
con·sume
  -sumed, -sum·ing
con·sum·ed·ly
con·sum·er
con·sum·er·ism
con·sum·mate
  -mat·ed, -mat·ing
con·sum·ma·tion
con·sump·tion

con·sump·tive
con·tact
con·ta·gion
con·ta·gious
con·tain·er
con·tain·ment
con·tam·i·nant
con·tam·i·nate
  -nat·ed, -nat·ing
con·tam·i·na·tion
con·tem·plate
  -plat·ed, -plat·ing
con·tem·pla·tion
con·tem·pla·tive
con·tem·po·ra·ne·ous
con·tem·po·rary
  -rar·ies, -rar·i·ly
con·tempt
con·tempt·ible
con·temp·tu·ous
con·tend
con·tent
con·ten·tion
con·ten·tious
con·tent·ment
con·test
con·tes·tant
con·tes·ta·tion
con·text
  -tex·tu·al
con·tex·ture
con·ti·gu·ity
  -ities

con·tig·u·ous
con·ti·nence
con·ti·nent
con·ti·nen·tal
con·tin·gen·cy
  -cies
con·tin·gent
con·tin·u·al
con·tin·u·ance
con·tin·u·a·tion
con·tin·ue
  -tinu·ing, -tin·ued
con·ti·nu·ity
  -ities
con·tin·u·ous
con·tin·u·um
  -ua (pl)
con·tort
  -tor·tion
con·tor·tion·ist
con·tour
con·tra
con·tra·band
con·tra·bass
con·tra·cep·tion
con·tract
  -tract·ibil·i·ty,
  -tract·ible
con·trac·tion
con·trac·tor
con·trac·tu·al
con·tra·dict
  -dict·able

con·tra·dic·tion
con·tra·dic·to·ry
  -ries, -ri·ly
con·tra·dis·tinc·tion
con·tra·in·di·cate
con·tral·to
  -tos
con·trap·tion
con·trari·wise
con·trary
  -trar·ies, -trari·ly,
  -trari·ness
con·trast
  -trast·able
con·tra·vene
  -vened, -ven·ing,
  -ven·er
con·tra·ven·tion
con·tre·temps
con·trib·ute
  -ut·ed, -ut·ing,
  -u·tor
con·tri·bu·tion
con·trib·u·to·ry
con·trite
con·tri·tion
con·triv·ance
con·trive
  -trived, -triv·ing
con·trol
  -trolled, -trol·ling,
  -trol·la·bil·i·ty
con·trol·ler

con·tro·ver·sial
  -sial·ly
con·tro·ver·sy
  -sies
con·tro·vert
con·tu·ma·cy
con·tu·sion
  -tuse
co·nun·drum
con·va·lesce
  -lesced, -lesc·ing,
  -les·cence
con·vec·tion
con·vene
  -vened, -ven·ing
con·ve·nience
con·ve·nient
con·vent
con·ven·tion
con·ven·tion·al
con·ven·tion·al·i·ty
  -ties
con·verge
  -verged, -verg·ing
con·ver·gence
con·ver·sant
con·ver·sa·tion
  -tion·al
con·ver·sa·tion·al·ist
con·verse
  -versed, -ver·sing,
  -verse·ly
con·ver·sion

con·vert
con·vert·er
con·vert·ible
  -ibil·i·ty
con·vex
con·vex·i·ty
  -ties
con·vey
  -veyed, -vey·ing
con·vey·ance
con·vey·er
con·vict
con·vic·tion
con·vince
  -vinced, -vinc·ing,
  -vinc·ing·ly
con·viv·ial
  -i·al·i·ty, -ial·ly
con·vo·ca·tion
con·voke
  -voked, -vok·ing
con·vo·lute
  -lut·ed, -lut·ing
con·voy
con·vulse
  -vulsed, -vuls·ing
con·vul·sion
con·vul·sive
cook·ery
  -er·ies
cook·ie
  -ies
cook·out (n)

cool
  cool·ly (coldly; cf.
  collie, coolie)
cool·ant
cool·er
cool·head·ed
coo·lie (laborer; cf.
  collie, coolly)
co·op·er·ate
co·op·er·a·tion
co·op·er·a·tive
co-opt
co·or·di·nate
co·or·di·na·tor
co·pay
co·pay·ment
cope
  coped, cop·ing
Co·pen·ha·gen
Co·per·ni·can
copi·er
co·pi·lot
co·pi·ous
cop·per
cop·per·head
cop·per·plate
cop·per·smith
cop·u·late
  -lat·ed, -lat·ing
copy
  cop·ies, cop·ied,
  copy·ing
copy·cat

copy·hold·er
copy·ist
copy·read·er
copy·right
copy·writ·er
co·que·try
  -tries
co·quette
cor·al (pink; cf.
  *choral, chorale,
  corral*)
cord (string; cf.
  chord)
cord·age
cor·dial
cor·dial·i·ty
cord·ite
cord·less
cor·don
cor·do·van
cor·du·roy
  -roys
core (center; cf.
  corps, corpse)
  cored, cor·ing,
  cor·er
co·re·spon·dent
  (legal term; cf.
  correspondent)
co·ri·an·der
Co·rin·thi·an
cork·age
cork·screw

cor·mo·rant
corn bor·er
corn bread
corn·cob
corn·crib
cor·nea
cor·ner
 -nered, -ner·ing
cor·ner·stone
cor·ner·wise
cor·net
 -net·ist
corn-fed
corn·field
corn·flakes
corn·flow·er
cor·nice
 -niced, -nic·ing
corn·meal
corn pone
corn·stalk
corn·starch
cor·nu·co·pia
co·rol·la
 -late
cor·ol·lary
 -lar·ies
co·ro·na
cor·o·nary
 -nar·ies
cor·o·na·tion
cor·o·ner
cor·o·net
cor·po·ral

cor·po·rate
cor·po·ra·tion
cor·po·ra·tive
cor·po·re·al
corps (group of
 people; cf. *core,*
 corpse)
 corps (pl)
corpse (body; cf.
 core, corps)
cor·pu·lent
cor·pus
 -po·ra (pl)
Cor·pus Chris·ti
cor·pus·cle
 -cu·lar
cor·ral (animal pen;
 cf. *choral, chorale,*
 coral)
 -ralled, -ral·ling
cor·rect
 -rect·able
cor·rec·tion
cor·rec·tive
cor·re·late
 -lat·ed, -lat·ing,
 -lat·able
cor·re·la·tion
cor·rel·a·tive
cor·re·spond
cor·re·spon·dence
 (letters; cf.
 correspondents)

cor·re·spon·dent
 (writer of letters;
 cf. *corespondent*)
cor·re·spon·dents
 (writers of letters;
 cf. *correspondence*)
cor·ri·dor
cor·rob·o·rate
 -rat·ed, -rat·ing,
 -ra·tion
cor·rode
 -rod·ed, -rod·ing,
 -rod·ible
cor·ro·sion
cor·ro·sive
cor·ru·gate
 -gat·ed, -gat·ing
cor·ru·ga·tion
cor·rupt
 -rupt·er,
 -rupt·ibil·i·ty,
 -rupt·ible
cor·rup·tion
cor·rup·tive
cor·sage
corse (corpse; cf.
 coarse, course)
cor·set
Cor·si·ca
Cor·si·can
cor·tege
cor·tex
 -ti·ces or -tex·es (pl)
cor·ti·sone

co·run·dum
cor·us·cate
cor·vette
cos·met·ic
cos·me·tol·o·gist
cos·me·tol·o·gy
cos·mic
    -mic·al
cos·mog·o·ny
    -mog·o·nies,
    -mo·gon·ic
cos·mol·o·gy
    -gies
cos·mo·naut
cos·mo·pol·i·tan
cos·mos
cost
Cos·ta Ri·ca
cost-ef·fec·tive
cost·ly
    -li·er, -li·est
cost-plus
cos·tume
    -tum·ey, -tumed,
    -tum·ing
cos·tum·er
co·te·rie (close
    group; cf. *cautery*)
co·ter·mi·nous
co·til·lion
cot·tage
cot·ton
    -toned, -ton·ing

cot·ton·tail
cot·ton·wood
cou·gar
could
cou·lomb
coun·cil (assembly;
    cf. *consul, counsel*)
coun·cil·lor
coun·cil·man
coun·cil·wom·an
coun·sel (advice; cf.
    consul, council)
    -sel·ing, -seled
coun·sel·or
count down (v)
count·down (n)
coun·te·nance
    -nanced,
    -nanc·ing
count·er
coun·ter·act
coun·ter·bal·ance
coun·ter·claim
coun·ter·clock·wise
coun·ter·feit
    -feit·er
coun·ter·ir·ri·tant
coun·ter·mand
coun·ter·march
coun·ter·mine
coun·ter·pane
coun·ter·part
coun·ter·point

coun·ter·pro·duc·tive
coun·ter·rev·o·lu·tion
    -tion·ary
coun·ter·sign
coun·ter·spy
coun·ter·top
coun·ter·trade
coun·ter·weight
count·ess
count·ing·house
count·less
coun·try
    -tries
coun·try·man
coun·try·side
coun·try·wom·an
coun·ty
    -ties
coup d'état
    coups d'état (pl)
cou·pé or coupe
cou·ple
    -pled, -pling
cou·pler
cou·plet
cou·pling
cou·pon
cour·age
cou·ra·geous
cou·ri·er
course (way; cf.
    coarse, corse)
    coursed

course·ware
cour·te·ous
cour·te·san
cour·te·sy
  -sies
court·house
court·ier
court·ly
  -li·er, -li·est,
  -li·ness
court-mar·tial
  courts-martial or
  court-martials (pl),
  court-mar·tialed
court·room
court·ship
court·yard
cous·in
cou·ture
cou·tu·ri·er
cov·e·nant
  -nan·tal
cov·er
  -ered, -er·ing,
  -er·able
cov·er·age
cov·er·all (adj)
cov·er·all (n)
  -alled
cov·er charge
cov·er·let
co·vert
cov·er·ture

cov·er up (v)
cov·er-up (n)
cov·et
  -et·able, -et·er
cov·et·ous
cov·ey
  cov·eys
cow·ard (frightened;
  cf. *cowered*)
cow·ard·ice
cow·ard·ly
  -li·ness
cow·bell
cow·boy
cow·ered (crouched;
  cf. *coward*)
cow·girl
cow·hand
cow·hide
cow·lick
cowl·ing
co·work·er
cow·pox
cow·punch·er
cow·slip
cox·comb
cox·swain
coy
coy·ote
  coy·otes
co·zy
  -zi·er, -zi·ly,
  -zi·ness

crab ap·ple
crabbed
crab·grass
crack·brain
  -brained
crack down (v)
crack·down (n)
crack·er
crack·er·jack
crack·le
  -led, -ling
crack·pot
cra·dle
  -dled, -dling
crafts·man
crafts·wom·an
crafty
  craft·i·er, craft·i·ly,
  craft·i·ness
cram
  crammed,
  cram·ming
cran·ber·ry
cra·ni·al
cra·ni·um
  -ni·ums or
  -nia (pl)
crank·case
crank·shaft
cranky
  crank·i·er,
  crank·i·est,
  crank·i·ness

cran·ny
  -nies
crash
cra·ter
cra·vat
cra·ven
craw·fish
cray·on
cra·zy
  -zi·er, -zi·est, -zi·ly
creak (sound; cf.
  creek, crick)
cream·ery
  -er·ies
cream·i·ness
cream puff
cre·ate
  -at·ed, -at·ing
cre·ation
cre·ative
cre·ator
crea·ture
cre·dence
cre·den·tial
  -tialed, -tial·ing
cre·den·za
cred·i·bil·i·ty
cred·i·ble (believ-
  able; cf. *creditable,
  credulous*)
  -bly
cred·it

cred·it·able
  (estimable; cf.
  *credible,
  credulous*)
  -ably, -abil·i·ty
cred·it card
cred·i·tor
cre·do
  cre·dos
cred·u·lous
  (gullible; cf.
  *credible,
  creditable*)
creek (water; cf.
  creak, crick)
creepy
  creep·i·er,
  creep·i·est,
  creep·i·ness
cre·mate
  -mat·ed, -mat·ing,
  -ma·tion
cre·ma·to·ry
  -ries
cre·ole
cre·o·sote
  -sot·ed, -sot·ing
crepe
cre·pus·cu·lar
cre·scen·do
  -dos or -does (pl)
cres·cent

crest·fall·en
Crete
cre·tin
  -tin·ous
cre·tonne
cre·vasse
crev·ice
crew
  crews (group; cf.
  cruise, cruse)
crib
  cribbed, crib·bing
crib·bage
crick (cramp; cf.
  creak, creek)
crick·et
  -et·er
cri·er
crim·i·nal
  -nal·ly
crim·i·nal·i·ty
crim·i·nol·o·gy
crim·son
cringe
  cringed, cring·ing
crin·kle
  -kled, -kling, -kly
crin·o·line
crip·ple
  -pled, -pling
cri·sis
  cri·ses (pl)
criss·cross

cri·te·ri·a (pl)
  -ri·on (sing)
crit·ic
crit·i·cal
  -cal·i·ty
crit·i·cism
crit·i·cize
  -cized, -ciz·ing,
  -ciz·able
cri·tique
  -tiqued, -tiqu·ing
Cro·a·tia
cro·chet
crock·ery
croc·o·dile
cro·cus
  -cus·es (pl)
crois·sant
crop
-cropped, crop·ping
crop·land
crop ro·ta·tion
cro·quet (game; cf.
  croquette)
cro·quette (food; cf.
  croquet)
cro·sier
cross·bar
cross·bow
cross·breed
cross-coun·try
cross-cul·tur·al
cross·cut

cross-ex·am·ine
cross-eyed
cross-grained
cross hair
cross·hatch
cross·ing
cross·over
cross-ques·tion
cross-ref·er·ence
cross·road
cross sec·tion
cross-stitch
cross·walk
cross·wise
crotch·et
crotch·ety
crou·pi·er
crou·ton
crow·bar
cru·cial
cru·ci·ble
cru·ci·fix
cru·ci·fix·ion
cru·ci·form
cru·ci·fy
  -fied, -fy·ing
cru·di·ty
  -ties
cru·el
  -el·er, -el·est, -el·ly
cru·el·ty
cru·et
cruise (sail; cf.
  crews, cruse)

cruised, cruis·ing
cruis·er
crul·ler
crum·ble (break; cf.
  crumple)
  -bled, -bling
crum·pet
crum·ple (wrinkle;
  cf. *crumble*)
  -pled, -pling
crup·per
cru·sade
  -sad·ed, -sad·ing,
  -sad·er
cruse (small cup; cf.
  crews, cruise)
crus·ta·ceous
crux
  crux·es or cru·ces
  (pl)
cry
  cried, cry·ing,
  cries
cryo·bi·ol·o·gy
cryo·gen
cryo·gen·ics
crypt
crypt·anal·y·sis
cryp·tic
cryp·to·gram
cryp·tog·ra·phy
crys·tal
crys·tal·line
crys·tal·li·za·tion

crys·tal·lize
  -lized, -liz·ing,
  -liz·able
Cu·ba
Cu·ban
cu·bic
cu·bi·cal (adj)
cu·bi·cle (n)
cu·bit
cuck·old
cuck·oo
  cuck·oos
cu·cum·ber
cud·dle
  -dled, -dling
cue (signal; cf.
  queue)
  cued, cu·ing
cui·sine
cul-de-sac
  culs-de-sac (pl)
cu·li·nary
cul·mi·nate
  -nat·ed, -nat·ing
cul·mi·na·tion
cu·lotte
cul·pa·ble
  -bly, -bil·i·ty
cul·prit
cul·ti·vate
  -vat·ed, -vat·ing,
  -vat·able
cul·ti·va·tion

cul·ti·va·tor
cul·tur·al
cul·ture
  -tured, -tur·ing
cul·vert
cum·ber·some
cum lau·de
cum·mer·bund
cu·mu·la·tive
cu·mu·lus
cu·ne·i·form
cun·ning
cup·board
cu·pel
cup·ful
  -fuls
cu·pid·i·ty
  -ties
cu·po·la
cur·able
cu·ra·çao
cu·ra·re
cu·rate
cu·ra·tive
cu·ra·tor
  -to·ri·al
curb·stone
cur·dle
  -dled, -dling
cu·rette
  -rett·ed, -rett·ing
cur·few
cu·rio

-ri·os (pl)
cu·ri·os·i·ty
  -ties
cu·ri·ous
cu·ri·ous·ly
curli·cue
  -cued, -cu·ing
cur·rant (berry; cf.
  current)
cur·ren·cy
cur·rent (prevalent;
  cf. *currant*)
  -rent·ly
cur·ric·u·lum
  -la (pl)
cur·ry
  -ried, -ry·ing
cur·ry·comb
cur·sive
cur·sor
cur·so·ry
  -ri·ly
cur·tail
  -tail·er
cur·tain
  -tained, -tain·ing
cur·tain call
cur·va·ture
curve
  curved, curv·ing
cur·vi·lin·ear
cush·ion
  -iony, -ioned,
  -ion·ing

cus·tard
cus·to·di·al
cus·to·di·an
cus·to·dy
  -dies
cus·tom
cus·tom·ary
cus·tom·er
cus·tom·house
cus·tom·ize
  -ized, -iz·ing, -iz·er
cus·tom-made
cut-and-dry
cut-and-paste
cut·away
cut·back
cu·ti·cle
cut·lass
cut·lery
cut·let
cut off (v)
cut·off (n)
cut·out (n, adj)
cut-rate
cut·throat
cut·ting
cut up (v)
cut·up (n)
cut·wa·ter
cut·worm
cy·an·a·mide
cy·an·ic
cy·a·nide

cy·ano·gen
cy·a·no·sis
cy·ber·auc·tions
cy·ber·com·mu·ni·ty
cy·ber·en·tre·
  pre·neurs
cy·ber·junk·ie
cy·ber·na·tion
cy·ber·net·ics
cy·ber·space
cy·ber·trans·mis·sions
cy·brar·i·an
cy·cla·mate
cy·cle
  -cled, -cling, -cler
cy·clic
cy·cli·cal
cy·cloid
cy·clone
cy·clo·pe·dia
cy·clops
  -clo·pes (pl)
cy·clo·ra·ma
cy·clo·tron
cyg·net
cyl·in·der
cy·lin·dri·cal
cym·bal (musical;
  cf. *symbol*)
cyn·ic
cyn·i·cal
cyn·i·cism
cy·no·sure
cy·press

Cy·prus
Cy·rix
cyst
cys·tic
czar
cza·ri·na
Czech
Czech Re·pub·lic
Czech·o·slo·va·kia

dab·ble
  -bled, -bling
dachs·hund
Da·cron
daf·fo·dil
dag·ger
dahl·ia
dai·ly
  -lies
dain·ty
  -ties, -ti·est, -ti·ly
dairy (for milk; cf.
  diary)
  dair·ies
da·is
dai·sy
  -sies
dai·sy wheel
dal·li·ance
dal·ma·tian
dam
  dammed (con-
  fined; cf. *damned*),
  dam·ming
dam·age
  -aged, -ag·ing,
  -ag·er
Da·mas·cus
dam·ask

dam·na·ble
dam·na·tion
damned (cursed; cf.
  dammed)
  damned·er,
  damned·est
damn·ing
damp·en
  -ened, -en·ing
damp·er
damp·ing off
dam·sel
dance
  danced, danc·ing,
  danc·er
dan·de·li·on
dan·druff
dan·ger
dan·ger·ous
dan·gle
  -gled, -gling, -gler
Dan·ish
  Dan·ish (pl)
dan·seuse
dap·ple
dare·dev·il
dark·en
  -ened, -en·ing,
  -en·er

dark horse
dar·kle
  -kled, -kling
dark·ness
dark·room
dar·ling
Dar·win·ian
dash·board
das·tard·ly
da·ta (pl)
  da·tum (sing)
da·ta bank
da·ta·base
da·ta-en·try
da·ta gram
da·ta·high·way
da·ta·ma·tion
da·ta pro·cess·ing
date
  dat·ed, dat·ing,
  dat·er
date·line
daugh·ter
daugh·ter-in-law
  daugh·ters-in-law
  (pl)
dav·en·port
da·vit

daw·dle
  -dled, -dling, -dler
day·bed
day·book
day·break
day care (n)
day·dream
day·flow·er
day·light
day·room
days
day school
day·star
day·time
day-to-day
daz·zle
  -zled, -zling, -zler
dea·con
dead·beat
dead·en
  -ened, -en·ing
dead·eye
dead·fall
dead·head
dead heat
dead·line
dead·lock
dead·ly
  -li·er, -li·est,
  -li·ness
dead·weight
dead·wood
deaf-mute

deal
  dealt, deal·ing,
  deal·er
dear (beloved; cf.
  deer)
dearth
death·bed
death ben·e·fit
death·blow
death·less
death·ly
death's-head
death war·rant
death·watch
de·ba·cle
de·bark
  -bar·ka·tion
de·base
de·bat·able
de·bate
  -bat·ed, -bat·ing,
  -bat·er
de·bauch
de·bauch·ery
  -er·ies
de·ben·ture
de·bil·i·tate
  -tat·ed, -tat·ing,
  -ta·tion
de·bil·i·ty
  -ties
deb·it (bookkeeping
  entry; cf. *debt*)

deb·o·nair
de·brief
de·bris
  de·bris (pl)
debt (obligation; cf.
  debit)
debt·or
de·bug
de·bug·ger
de·bug·ging
de·but
deb·u·tante
de·cade
dec·a·dence
dec·a·dent
de·caf·fein·at·ed
deca·gon
deca·logue
de·camp
de·cant
de·cant·er
de·cap·i·tate
  -tat·ed, -tat·ing,
  -ta·tion
de·cath·lon
de·cay
de·cease
de·ceased (dead; cf.
  diseased)
  de·ceased (pl)
de·ce·dent
de·ceit
de·ceit·ful

81

de·ceive
 -ceived, -ceiv·ing,
 -ceiv·ing·ly
De·cem·ber
de·cen·cy
 -cies
de·cent (proper; cf.
 descent, dissent)
de·cen·tral·ize
de·cep·tion
de·cep·tive
deci·bel
de·cide
 -cid·ed, -cid·ing
de·cid·u·ous
dec·i·mal
dec·i·mate
 -mat·ed, -mat·ing,
 -ma·tion
deci·me·ter
de·ci·pher
de·ci·sion
de·ci·sive
deck chair
de·claim
 -claim·er,
 -cla·ma·tion
dec·la·ra·tion
de·clar·a·tive
de·clare
 -clared, -clar·ing
de·clen·sion

de·cline
 -clined, -clin·ing,
 -clin·able
de·cliv·i·ty
 -ties
de·code
dé·col·le·té
de·com·pose
 -pos·able,
 -po·si·tion
de·com·press
de·con·ges·tant
de·con·tam·i·nate
de·cor
dec·o·rate
 -rat·ed, -rat·ing
dec·o·ra·tion
dec·o·ra·tive
dec·o·ra·tor
de·co·rous
de·co·rum
de·coy
de·crease
 -creased,
 -creas·ing
de·cree (law; cf.
 degree)
 -creed, -cree·ing,
 -cre·er
de·crep·it
de·cre·scen·do
 -dos
de·cry

ded·i·cate
 -cat·ed, -cat·ing,
 -ca·tor
ded·i·ca·tion
de·duce
 -duced, -duc·ing,
 -duc·ible
de·duct·ible
de·duc·tion
de·duc·tive
de·em·pha·size
deep·en
 -ened, -en·ing
deep-root·ed
deep-seat·ed
deer (animal; cf.
 dear)
 deer (pl)
deer·hound
deer·skin
de·es·ca·late
 -la·tion
de·face
de fac·to
de·fal·ca·tion
def·a·ma·tion
de·fam·a·to·ry
de·fame
 -famed, -fam·ing,
 -fam·er
de·fault
 -fault·er
de·feat

de·fect
de·fec·tion
de·fec·tive
de·fend
de·fen·dant
de·fense
  -fensed, -fens·ing
de·fen·si·ble
de·fen·sive
de·fer
  -ferred, -fer·ring
def·er·ence
  (respect; cf.
  difference)
def·er·en·tial
  (respectful; cf.
  differential)
de·fer·ment
de·fer·ra·ble
de·fi·ance
de·fi·ant
de·fi·cien·cy
  -cies
de·fi·cient
def·i·cit
de·file
  -filed, -fil·ing,
  -fil·er
de·fine
  -fined, -fin·ing,
  -fin·able
def·i·nite (clear; cf.
  definitive)
  -nite·ly

def·i·ni·tion
def·in·i·tive (final;
  cf. *definite*)
de·flate
  -flat·ed, -flat·ing,
  -fla·tor
de·fla·tion
de·flect
de·flec·tion
de·fo·li·ant
de·fo·li·ate
de·fo·li·a·tion
de·for·es·ta·tion
de·form
de·for·ma·tion
de·for·mi·ty
  -ties
de·fraud
de·fray
de·funct
de·fy
  -fies, -fied, -fy·ing
de·gen·er·a·cy
  -cies
de·gen·er·ate
de·gen·er·a·tion
deg·ra·da·tion
de·grade
de·gree (from col-
  lege; cf. *decree*)
de·hu·mid·i·fy
de·hy·drate
deign

de·i·ty
  -ties
de·ject·ed
de·jec·tion
de ju·re
deka·gram
Del·a·ware
  Del·a·ware (pl)
de·lay
de·lec·ta·ble
del·e·gate
  -gat·ed, -gat·ing,
  -ga·tor
del·e·ga·tion
de·lete
  -let·ed, -let·ing
del·e·te·ri·ous
de·le·tion
delft·ware
de·lib·er·ate
  -at·ed, -at·ing
de·lib·er·a·tion
  -tive, -tive·ness,
  -tive·ly
del·i·ca·cy
  -cies
del·i·cate
del·i·ca·tes·sen
de·li·cious
de·light
de·light·ful
de·lim·it
de·lim·it·er

de·lin·eate
-eat·ed, -eat·ing,
-ea·tor
de·lin·ea·tion
de·lin·quen·cy
-cies
de·lin·quent
de·lir·i·ous
de·lir·i·um
de·liv·er
-ered, -er·ing,
-er·able
de·liv·er·ance
de·liv·ery
-er·ies
del·phin·i·um
de·lude
-lud·ed, -lud·ing,
-lud·er
del·uge
-uged, -ug·ing
de·lu·sion
de·luxe
delve
delved, delv·ing,
delv·er
de·mag·ne·tize
dem·a·gogue
de·mand
de·mar·cate
-cat·ed, -cat·ing,
-ca·tion

de·mean
-meaned,
-mean·ing
de·mean·or
de·ment·ed
de·men·tia
de·mer·it
demi·god
de·mil·i·ta·rize
de·mise
demi·tasse
de·mo·bi·lize
de·moc·ra·cy
-cies
dem·o·crat
dem·o·crat·ic
de·moc·ra·tize
-tized,
-tiz·ing,
-ti·za·tion
de·mod·u·late
-la·tion,
-la·tor
de·mo·graph·ic
de·mog·ra·phy
de·mol·ish
de·mo·li·tion
de·mon
de·mon·e·tize
-ti·za·tion
de·mon·stra·ble
dem·on·strate
-strat·ed,
-strat·ing

dem·on·stra·tion
de·mon·stra·tive
de·mon·stra·tor
de·mor·al·ize
de·mount
-mount·able
de·mur (delay; cf.
demure)
-murred,
-mur·ring
de·mure (modest;
cf. *demur*)
de·mur·rage
de·mur·rer
de·na·ture
-tured, -tur·ing
de·ni·al
den·im
den·i·zen
Den·mark
de·nom·i·na·tion
de·nom·i·na·tor
de·note
de·noue·ment
de·nounce
-nounced,
-nounc·ing,
-nounce·ment
den·si·ty
-ties
den·tal
den·ti·frice
den·tist

den·tist·ry
den·ture
de·nude
  -nud·ed, -nud·ing
de·nun·ci·a·tion
  -tive, -to·ry
de·ny
  -nied, -ny·ing
de·odor·ant
de·odor·ize
de·part
de·part·ment
  -men·tal,
  -men·tal·ly
de·par·ture
de·pend·able
de·pen·dence
de·pen·den·cy
  -cies
de·pen·dent
de·pict
  -pic·ter, -pic·tion
de·pil·a·to·ry
  -ries
de·plane
de·plete
  -plet·ed, -plet·ing,
  -ple·tion
de·plor·able
de·plore
  -plored, -plor·ing,
  -plor·ing·ly
de·ploy
de·po·lit·i·cize

de·pop·u·late
de·port·able
de·por·ta·tion
de·port·ment
de·pose
  -posed, -pos·ing
de·pos·it
  -it·ed, -it·ing, -i·tor
de·pos·i·tary
  -tar·ies
de·po·si·tion
de·pos·i·to·ry
  -ries
de·pot
de·prave
  -praved, -prav·ing,
  -pra·va·tion
  (corruption; cf.
  deprivation)
de·prav·i·ty
dep·re·cate
  -cat·ed, -cat·ing,
  -ca·tion
dep·re·ca·to·ry
de·pre·ci·ate
  -at·ed, -at·ing,
  -a·tion
dep·re·date
  -dat·ed, -dat·ing,
  -da·tion
de·press
de·pressed
de·pres·sion
de·pres·sur·ize

de·pri·va·tion (loss;
  cf. *depravation*)
de·prive
  -prived, -priv·ing
dep·u·ta·tion
de·pute
dep·u·tize
  -tized, -tiz·ing,
  -ti·za·tion
dep·u·ty
  -ties
de·rail
de·range
  -ranged,
  -rang·ing,
  -range·ment
de·reg·u·la·tion
der·e·lict
der·e·lic·tion
de·ride
  -rid·ed, -rid·ing,
  -rid·ing·ly
de·ri·sion
de·ri·sive
de·ri·so·ry
der·i·va·tion
de·riv·a·tive
de·rive
  -rived, -riv·ing
der·ma·tol·o·gy
  -tol·o·gist,
  -to·log·ic,
  -to·log·i·cal
de·rog·a·to·ry

der·rick
der·vish
de·scend
de·scen·dant
de·scent (going
    down; cf. *decent,*
    dissent)
de·scribe
  -scribed,
  -scrib·ing,
  -scrib·able
de·scrip·tion
de·scrip·tive
des·e·crate
  -crat·ed, -crat·ing,
  -crat·or
des·e·cra·tion
de·seg·re·gate
de·seg·re·ga·tion
de·se·lect
de·sen·si·tize
des·ert (n)(dry coun-
    try; cf. *dessert*)
de·sert (v)(leave; cf.
    dessert)
de·ser·tion
de·serve
  -served, -serv·ing,
  -serv·er
de·served·ly
des·ic·cate
  -cated, -cat·ing,
  -ca·tion

de·sid·er·a·ta (pl)
  -tum (sing)
de·sign
des·ig·nate
  -nat·ed, -nat·ing,
  -na·tor
des·ig·na·tion
des·ig·nee
de·sign·er
de·sir·abil·i·ty
  -ties
de·sir·able
de·sire
  -sired, -sir·ing
de·sir·ous
de·sist
desk·top
  pub·lish·ing
des·o·late
  -lat·ed, -lat·ing
des·o·la·tion
de·spair
des·per·a·do
  -does (pl)
des·per·ate (hope-
    less; cf. *disparate*)
des·per·a·tion
de·spi·ca·ble
de·spise
  -spised, -spis·ing,
  -spis·er
de·spite
  -spit·ed, -spit·ing

de·spoil
de·spond
de·spon·den·cy
de·spon·dent
des·pot
des·pot·ic
des·po·tism
des·sert (food; cf.
    desert)
des·sert·spoon
des·ti·na·tion
des·tine
  -tined, -tin·ing
des·ti·ny
  -nies
des·ti·tute
des·ti·tu·tion
de·stroy
de·struc·ti·ble
de·struc·tion
de·struc·tive
des·ul·to·ry
de·tach
de·tach·ment
de·tail
de·tain
de·tect
  -tect·abil·i·ty,
  -tect·able
de·tec·tion
de·tec·tive
de·tec·tor
de·ten·tion

de·ter
  -terred, -ter·ring,
  -ter·ment
de·ter·gent
de·te·ri·o·rate
  -rat·ed, -rat·ing,
  -ra·tive
de·te·ri·o·ra·tion
de·ter·min·able
de·ter·mi·nant
de·ter·mi·nate
de·ter·mi·na·tion
de·ter·mine
  -mined, -min·ing
de·ter·min·ism
de·ter·rent
de·test
de·test·able
de·tes·ta·tion
de·throne
det·i·nue
det·o·nate
  -nat·ed, -nat·ing,
  -na·tive
det·o·na·tion
det·o·na·tor
de·tract
de·trac·tion
det·ri·ment
det·ri·men·tal
deutsche mark
dev·as·tate
  -tat·ed, -tat·ing,
  -ta·tion

de·vel·op
de·vel·op·er
de·vel·op·ing
de·vel·op·ment
de·vel·op·men·tal
de·vi·ate
  -at·ed, -at·ing,
  -a·tor
de·vi·a·tion
de·vice (n)(inven-
  tion; cf. *devise*)
dev·il·fish
dev·il·ish
dev·il·ment
de·vi·ous
de·vise (v)(invent;
  cf. *device*)
  -vised, -vis·ing,
  -vis·er
de·void
de·volve
  -volved, -volv·ing,
  -volv·ment
de·vote
  -vot·ed, -vot·ing
dev·o·tee
de·vo·tion
de·vo·tion·al
de·vour
de·vout
dew·ber·ry
dew·drop
dew point

dewy
  dew·i·er, dew·i·est,
  dew·i·ness
dex·ter·i·ty
  -ties
dex·ter·ous
dex·trose
di·a·be·tes
di·a·bet·ic
di·a·bol·ic
di·a·bol·i·cal
di·a·crit·i·cal
di·aer·e·sis
  -aer·e·ses (pl),
  -ae·ret·ic
di·ag·nose
  -nosed, -nos·ing,
  -nos·able
di·ag·no·sis
  -ses (pl)
di·ag·nos·tic
di·ag·o·nal
di·a·gram
  -gramed,
  -gram·ing
di·a·gram·mat·ic
di·al
  -aled, -al·ing,
  -al·er
di·a·lect
di·a·lec·tic
di·a·lec·ti·cal
di·a·logue
  -logued, -logu·ing

di·a·log box
dial-up
di·al·y·sis
  -al·y·ses (pl),
  -a·lyt·ic
di·am·e·ter
di·a·met·ric
di·a·mond
di·a·per
  -pered, -per·ing
di·aph·a·nous
di·a·phragm
di·ar·rhea
di·a·ry (journal; cf.
  dairy)
  -ries
di·a·tribe
di·chot·o·my
  -mies
Dic·ta·phone
dic·tate
  -tat·ed, -tat·ing
dic·ta·tion
dic·ta·tor
dic·ta·to·ri·al
dic·ta·tor·ship
dic·tion
dic·tio·nary
  -nar·ies
dic·tum
  dic·ta (pl)
di·dac·tic

die (expire; cf. *dye*)
  died (perished; cf.
  dyed), dy·ing
  (expiring; cf.
  dyeing)
die-hard (adj)
die-hard (n)
di·elec·tric
di·er·e·sis
die·sel
di·et
di·etary
  -etar·ies
di·etet·ic
di·etet·ics
di·eti·tian
dif·fer
  -fered, -fer·ing
dif·fer·ence (unlike-
  ness; cf.
  deference)
  -enced, -enc·ing
dif·fer·ent
dif·fer·en·tial
  (change; cf.
  deferential)
dif·fer·en·ti·ate
  -ti·at·ed, -ti·at·ing,
  -tia·ble
dif·fer·en·ti·a·tion
dif·fi·cult
dif·fi·cul·ty
  -ties

dif·fi·dent
dif·frac·tion
dif·fuse
  -fused, -fus·ing
dif·fu·sion
dig·er·a·ti
di·gest
di·gest·ible
di·ges·tion
di·ges·tive
dig·it
dig·i·tal
  -tal·ly
dig·i·tal au·dio·tape
dig·i·tal cam·era
dig·i·tal com·pu·ter
dig·i·tal
  con·ver·gence
dig·i·tal·is
dig·i·tal vid·eo disc
  (DVD)
dig·i·tize
dig·ni·fy
  -fied, -fy·ing
dig·ni·tary
  -tar·ies
dig·ni·ty
  -ties
di·gress
di·gres·sion
di·lap·i·date
  -dat·ed, -dat·ing,
  -da·tion

di·la·ta·tion
di·late
  -lat·ed, -lat·ing,
  -lat·able
di·la·tion
di·lem·ma
dil·i·gence
dil·i·gent
di·lute
  -lut·ed, -lut·ing,
  -lut·er
di·lu·tion
di·men·sion
  -sioned, -sion·ing
di·min·ish
dim·i·nu·tion
di·min·u·tive
dim·mer
dim·ple
  -pled, -pling
dim·wit (n)
dim·wit·ted (adj)
di·nar (coin; cf.
  diner)
din·er (eater; cf.
  dinar)
di·nette
ding·bat
din·ghy (boat; cf.
  dingy)
  din·ghies (pl)

din·gy (dull; cf.
  dinghy)
  -gi·er, -gi·est
dink
din·ner
din·ner jack·et
din·ner·ware
di·no·saur
di·oc·e·san
di·o·cese
  -ces·es (pl)
di·ode
di·ox·ide
di·ox·in
diph·the·ria
diph·thong
di·plo·ma
  -mas
di·plo·ma·cy
dip·lo·mat
dip·lo·mat·ic
dip·per
dip·so·ma·nia
di·rect
di·rec·tion
di·rec·tive
di·rect·ly
di·rec·tor
di·rec·tor·ate
di·rec·to·ry
  -ries
dirge

di·ri·gi·ble
dirndl
dirty
  dirt·i·er, dirt·i·est,
  dirt·i·ness
dis·abil·i·ty
dis·able
  -abled, -abling,
  -able·ment
dis·abuse
dis·ad·van·tage
dis·ad·van·ta·geous
dis·af·fect·ed
dis·agree
dis·agree·able
dis·agree·ment
dis·al·low
  -low·ance
dis·ap·pear
dis·ap·pear·ance
dis·ap·point
dis·ap·point·ment
dis·ap·pro·ba·tion
dis·ap·prov·al
dis·ap·prove
dis·arm
  -ar·ma·ment,
  -arm·er
dis·arm·ing·ly
dis·ar·range
dis·ar·ray
dis·ar·tic·u·late

dis·as·sem·ble (take
  apart; cf.
  dissemble)
dis·as·so·ci·ate
di·sas·ter
di·sas·trous
dis·avow
  -avow·able,
  -avow·al
dis·band
dis·bar
dis·be·lief
dis·be·lieve
  -liev·er
dis·burse (pay out;
  cf. *disperse*)
  -bursed, -burs·ing,
  -burs·er
dis·burse·ment
disc
dis·card
dis·cern
  -cern·er,
  -cern·ible,
  -cern·ibly
dis·cern·ment
dis·charge
dis·ci·ple
dis·ci·pli·nar·i·an
dis·ci·plin·ary
dis·ci·pline
  -plined, -plin·ing,
  -plin·er

dis·claim
dis·claim·er
dis·close
dis·clo·sure
dis·co
  dis·cos
dis·cog·ra·phy
  -cog·ra·phies
dis·col·or
dis·col·or·ation
dis·com·fit (balk; cf.
  discomfort)
dis·com·fi·ture
dis·com·fort
  (uneasiness; cf.
  discomfit)
dis·com·pose
  -po·sure
dis·con·cert
dis·con·nect
dis·con·so·late
dis·con·tent
  -tent·ment
dis·con·tin·u·ance
dis·con·tin·ue
dis·con·tin·u·ous
dis·cord
dis·cor·dance
dis·cor·dant
dis·co·theque
dis·count
dis·cour·age
  -aged, -ag·ing,
  -ag·ing·ly

dis·cour·age·ment
dis·course
  -coursed,
  -cours·ing,
  -cours·er
dis·cour·te·ous
dis·cour·te·sy
dis·cov·er
  -ered, -er·ing,
  -er·able
dis·cov·ery
  -er·ies
dis·cred·it
dis·cred·it·able
dis·creet (prudent;
  cf. *discrete*)
dis·crep·an·cy
  -cies
dis·crete (separate;
  cf. *discreet*)
dis·cre·tion
dis·cre·tion·ary
dis·crim·i·nate
  -nat·ed, -nat·ing
dis·crim·i·na·tion
dis·crim·i·na·to·ry
dis·cur·sive
dis·cus (athletic
  term; cf. *discuss*)
  -cus·es (pl)
dis·cuss (talk about;
  cf. *discus*)
dis·cus·sion

dis·dain
dis·dain·ful
dis·ease
  dis·eased (ill; cf.
  deceased)
dis·em·bar·rass
dis·em·bow·el
dis·en·chant
  -chant·ing,
  -chant·ing·ly,
  -chant·ment
dis·en·gage
dis·en·tan·gle
dis·fa·vor
dis·fig·ure
  -ure·ment
dis·gorge
dis·grace
dis·grace·ful
dis·grun·tle
  -grun·tled,
  -grun·ting,
  -grun·tle·ment
dis·guise
  -guised, -guis·ing,
  -guis·er
dis·gust
dis·ha·bille
dis·har·mon·ic
dish·cloth
dis·heart·en
di·shev·el
  -eled, -el·ing

dis·hon·est
dis·hon·or
dis·hon·or·able
dish·pan
dish·rag
dish·wash·er
dish·wa·ter
dis·il·lu·sion
  -sioned, -sion·ing,
  -sion·ment
dis·in·cen·tive
dis·in·cli·na·tion
dis·in·fect
  -fec·tion
dis·in·fec·tant
dis·in·gen·u·ous
dis·in·her·it
dis·in·te·grate
dis·in·ter·est·ed
dis·join
dis·junc·tion
dis·junc·tive
disk
disk drive
dis·kette
dis·like
dis·lo·cate
dis·lo·ca·tion
dis·lodge
dis·loy·al
dis·loy·al·ty
dis·mal

dis·man·tle
  -tled, -tling,
  -tle·ment
dis·may
  -mayed, -may·ing,
  -may·ing·ly
dis·mem·ber
  -bered, -ber·ing,
  -ber·ment
dis·miss
dis·miss·al
dis·mount
dis·obe·di·ence
dis·obe·di·ent
dis·obey
dis·oblige
dis·or·der
dis·or·dered
dis·or·der·ly
dis·or·ga·nize
  -ni·za·tion
dis·own
dis·par·age
  -aged, -ag·ing,
  -age·ment
dis·pa·rate (differ-
  ent; cf. *desperate*)
  -pa·rate·ly,
  -pa·rate·ness,
  -par·i·ty
dis·pas·sion·ate
dis·patch

dis·pel
  -pelled, -pel·ling
dis·pen·sa·ry
  -ries
dis·pen·sa·tion
dis·pense
  -pensed, -pens·ing
dis·pers·al
dis·perse (scatter;
  cf. *disburse*)
  -persed, -pers·ing,
  -pers·er
dis·per·sion
dispir·it
dis·place
dis·place·ment
dis·play
dis·please
dis·plea·sure
dis·pos·able
dis·pos·al
dis·pose
  -posed, -pos·ing,
  -pos·er
dis·po·si·tion
dis·pos·sess
dis·proof
dis·pro·por·tion
dis·pro·por·tion·ate
dis·prove
dis·pu·tant
dis·pu·ta·tion
dis·pu·ta·tious

dis·pute
  -put·ed, -put·ing,
  -put·er
dis·qual·i·fi·ca·tion
dis·qual·i·fy
dis·qui·et
dis·re·gard
dis·re·pair
dis·rep·u·ta·ble
dis·re·pute
dis·re·spect
  -spect·ful,
  -spect·ful·ly,
  -spect·ful·ness
dis·robe
dis·rupt
  -rupt·er, -rup·tive,
  -rup·tion
dis·sat·is·fac·tion
dis·sat·is·fied
dis·sect
dis·sec·tion
dis·sem·ble
  (disguise; cf.
  disassemble)
  -sem·bled,
  -sem·bling,
  -sem·bler
dis·sem·i·nate
  -nat·ed, -nat·ing,
  -na·tion
dis·sen·sion

dis·sent (disagree-
  ment; cf. *decent,
  descent*)
dis·sent·er
dis·ser·ta·tion
dis·ser·vice
dis·si·dence
dis·si·dent
dis·sim·i·lar
  -lar·i·ty, -lar·ly
dis·sim·u·late
  -lat·ed, -lat·ing,
  -la·tion
dis·si·pate
  -pat·ed, -pat·ing
dis·si·pa·tion
dis·so·ci·ate
  -at·ed, -at·ing
dis·so·ci·a·tion
dis·sol·u·ble
dis·so·lute
dis·so·lu·tion
dis·solve
dis·so·nance
dis·suade
  -suad·ed,
  -suad·ing,
  -suad·er
dis·sua·sion
dis·taff
  dis·taffs (pl)
dis·tance
  -tanced, -tanc·ing

dis·tant
dis·taste
dis·taste·ful
dis·tem·per
dis·tend
dis·ten·sion
dis·till
  -tilled, -till·ing
dis·til·late
dis·til·la·tion
dis·till·er
dis·till·ery
  -er·ies
dis·tinct
dis·tinc·tion
dis·tinc·tive
  -tive·ly, -tive·ness
dis·tin·guish
dis·tort
dis·tor·tion
dis·tract
dis·trac·tion
dis·traught
dis·tress
dis·trib·ute
  -ut·ed, -ut·ing,
  -u·tee
dis·tri·bu·tion
dis·trib·u·tor
dis·trict
dis·trust
dis·trust·ful
dis·turb
dis·tur·bance

dis·union
dis·use
dit·to
  dit·tos
di·ur·nal
di·va
  di·vas
di·van
div·er
di·verge
  -verged, -verg·ing
di·ver·gence
di·ver·gent
di·vers (various; cf.
  diverse)
di·verse (different;
  cf. *divers*)
di·ver·si·fy
  -fied, -fy·ing,
  -fi·ca·tion
di·ver·sion
di·ver·si·ty
  -ties
di·vert
di·vest
di·vide
  -vid·ed, -vid·ing,
  -vid·able
div·i·dend
div·i·na·tion
di·vine
  -vin·er, -vin·est,
  -vine·ly
di·vin·i·ty

  -ties
di·vi·sion
di·vi·sive
di·vorce
  -vorced, -vorc·ing,
  -vorce·ment
div·ot
di·vulge
  -vulged, -vulg·ing,
  -vul·gence
diz·zy
  -zi·er, -zi·est, -zi·ly
DMZ
DNA
Do·ber·man
  pin·scher
doc·ile
  doc·ile·ly,
  do·cil·i·ty
dock·et
dock·hand
dock·o·min·i·um
dock·side
dock·yard
doc·tor
  -tor·al, -tored
doc·tor·ate
doc·trin·al
doc·trine
doc·u·ment
doc·u·men·ta·ry
doc·u·men·ta·tion

dodge
  dodged, dodg·ing
doe (deer; cf. *dough*)
  does (pl)
do·er
doe·skin
dog·catch·er
dog-eared
dog·fight
dog·ged
  -ged·ly, -ged·ness
dog·ger·el
dog·house
dog·ma
  dog·mas
dog·mat·ic
  -i·cal, -i·cal·ly
dog·ma·tism
do-good·er
dog pad·dle (n)
dog-pad·dle (v)
dog tag
dog·watch
dog·wood
doi·ly
  -lies
dol·drums
dole
  doled, dol·ing
dol·lar
dol·lar day
dol·lar di·plo·ma·cy
dol·lar·i·za·tion

dol·lars-and-cents
dol·man (cloak; cf.
  dolmen)
  dol·mans
dol·men (monu-
  ment; cf. *dolman*)
do·lor
do·lor·ous
  -ous·ly, -ous·ness
dol·phin
do·main
do·mes·tic
  -ti·cal·ly
do·mes·ti·cate
  -cat·ed, -cat·ing,
  -ca·tion
do·mes·tic·i·ty
do·mi·cile
  -ciled, -cil·ing
dom·i·nance
dom·i·nant
dom·i·nate
  -nat·ed, -nat·ing
dom·i·na·tion
dom·i·neer
dom·i·neer·ing
  -ing·ly
Do·min·i·can
Do·min·i·can
  Re·pub·lic
do·min·ion
domino
  -noes

donate
  -nat·ed, -nat·ing
do·na·tion
done (finished; cf.
  dun)
do·nee
don·gle
don·key
do·nor
dooms·day
door·bell
door·keep·er
door·knob
door·mat
door·sill
door·stop
door·way
dor·mant
dor·mer
dor·mi·to·ry
  -ries
dor·mouse
dor·sal
dos·age
dos·sier
dot
  dot·ted,
  dot·ting
dot·age
dot·ard
dot-com
dote
  dot·ed, dot·ing

dot ma·trix

dou·ble
-bled, -bling

dou·ble check (n)

dou·ble-check (v)

dou·ble-click

dou·ble-deal·ing

dou·ble-deck·er

dou·ble-dig·it

dou·ble-faced

dou·ble-park

dou·ble-quick

dou·ble-space

dou·ble-speak

dou·blet

dou·ble take

dou·ble-talk (n)

dou·ble·think

dou·ble time (n)

dou·ble-time (v)

doubt·ful

doubt·less

dough (bread; cf.
doe)

dough·nut

dour

doused
doused, dous·ing

dove·tail

dow·a·ger

dowdy
dowd·i·er,
dowd·i·est,
dowd·i·ness

dow·el
-eled, -el·ing

dow·er

down-and-out

down·beat

down·cast

down·fall

down·grade

down·heart·ed

down·hill

down·home

down·link

down·load
-load·able

down·pour

down·range

down·right

down·size
-siz·ing

down·spout

Down's syndrome

down·stage

down·stairs

down·state

down·stream

down·stroke

down·swing

down·time

down-to-earth

down·town

down·trend

down·trod·den

down·turn

down·ward

down·wind

downy
down·i·er,
down·i·est

dow·ry
-ries

dox·ol·o·gy
-gies

doz·en

drab
drab·ber,
drab·best

drach·ma
drach·mas

dra·co·ni·an

draft (draw; cf.
draught, drought)
draft·able, draft·er

drafts·man

drag
dragged,
drag·ging

drag·line

drag·net

drag·on

drag·on·fly

dra·goon

drain·age

drain·pipe

dra·mat·ic

dra·ma·tist

dra·ma·tize
-tized, -tiz·ing

dra·me·dy
-dies
drap·ery
-er·ies
dras·tic
-ti·cal·ly
draught (drink; cf.
draft, drought)
draw back (v)
draw·back (n)
draw·bar
draw·ee
draw·er
dray·age
dread·ful
dream·land
dream team
dreamy
dream·i·er,
dream·i·est,
dream·i·ly
drea·ry
-ri·er, -ri·est
dredge
Dres·den
dress·er
dress·mak·er
drib·ble
-bled, -bling
drift·wood
drill
drill·mas·ter
drill press
drink·able

drip
dripped, drip·ping
drip-dry
drive
driv·ing, driv·able
drive-by
drive-in
driv·er
drive·way
driz·zle
-zled, -zling
drom·e·dary
drop
dropped,
drop·ping
drop in (v)
drop-in (n)
drop-kick (v)
drop-kick (n)
drop leaf
drop·light
drop out (v)
drop·out (n)
drop·per
drop·sy
drought (dryness;
cf. *draft, draught*)
drowsy
drows·i·er,
drows·i·est,
drows·i·ly
drudg·ery
drug
drugged,

drug·ging
drug·gist
drug·store
drum
drummed,
drum·ming
drum·beat
drum·mer
drum·roll
drum·stick
drunk·ard
drunk·en
dry
dries, dried, dri·er,
dri·est
dry cell
dry-clean (v)
dry clean·ing
dry dock (n)
dry-dock (v)
dry rot (n)
dry-rot (v)
dry run
dry·wall
du·al (twofold; cf.
duel)
du·bi·ous
du·cal
-cal·ly
duch·ess
duchy
duch·ies
duck·ling

dud·geon

due

du·el (combat; cf. *dual*)

du·et

dug·out

duke

  duke·dom

dul·cet

dul·ci·mer

dumb·bell

dumb·wait·er

dum·my

  -mies, -mied,

  -my·ing

dump

dump·site

dump·ing-ground

dump·ling

dun (demand for payment; cf. *done*)

  dunned, dun·ning

dun·ga·ree

dun·geon

duo·dec·i·mal

du·o·de·num

du·plex

du·pli·cate

  -cat·ed, -cat·ing

du·pli·ca·tion

du·pli·ca·tor

du·plic·i·ty

du·ra·ble

  -bil·i·ty

dur·ing

dusky

  dusk·i·er,

  dusk·i·est

dust·bin

dust bowl

dust·cov·er

dust mop

dust·pan

dust storm

dusty

  dust·i·er,

  dust·i·est,

  dust·i·ly

Dutch ov·en

Dutch treat

du·te·ous

du·ti·able

du·ti·ful

du·ty

  -ties

Dvo·rak

dwell·ing

dwin·dle

  -dled, -dling

dye (color; cf. *die*)

  dyed (colored; cf. *died*), dye·ing (coloring; cf. *dying*)

dy·na·base

dy·nam·ic

dy·na·mite

  -mit·ed, -mit·ing

dy·na·mo

  -mos

dy·na·mom·e·ter

dy·nast

dy·nas·ty

dys·en·tery

  -ter·ies (pl)

dys·flu·en·cy

dys·func·tion

  -func·tion·al

dys·gra·phia

dys·lex·ia

  -lex·ic

dys·pep·sia

dys·pep·tic

dys·pha·gia

dys·pha·sia

dys·pho·ria

dys·tro·phy

  -phies

ea·ger
ea·gle
ear·ache
ear·drop
ear·drum
ear·ly
  -li·er, -li·est
ear·mark
earn (gain; cf. *urn*)
ear·nest
earn·ings
ear·phone
ear·ring
ear·shot
ear·split·ting
earth·born
earth·bound
earth·en·ware
earth·ly
  -li·ness
earth·quake
earth·ward
earth·wards
earth·work
earth·worm
ear·wax
ear·wig
ea·sel
ease·ment

eas·i·ly
east·bound
East Ber·lin
Eas·ter
east·ern
East·ern·er
east·ward
easy·go·ing
eat·able
eaves
eaves·drop
ebb
eb·o·ny
  -nies
eBook
ebul·lient
eb·ul·li·tion
ec·cen·tric
ec·cen·tric·i·ty
  -ties
ec·cle·si·as·ti·cal
ech·e·lon
echo
  ech·oes
echo·la·lia
éclair
eclec·tic
eclipse
  eclipsed,

eclips·ing
E coli
ecol·o·gy
  -gies, -gist
e-com·merce
eco·nom·ic
eco·nom·i·cal
  -i·cal·ly
econ·o·mist
econ·o·mize
econ·o·my
  -mies
eco·sys·tem
eco·tour·ism
ec·sta·sy
ec·stat·ic
ec·to·derm
Ec·ua·dor
ec·u·men·i·cal
ec·ze·ma
ed·dy
  -dies, -died,
  -dy·ing
edel·weiss
ede·ma
edge·ways
edg·ing
ed·i·ble
  -bil·i·ty
edict

ed·i·fi·ca·tion
ed·i·fice
ed·i·fy
-fied, -fy·ing
Ed·in·burgh
ed·it
edi·tion (printing;
cf. *addition*)
ed·i·tor
ed·i·to·ri·al
ed·i·to·ri·al·ize
-ized, -iz·ing
ed·u·ca·ble
ed·u·cate
-cat·ed, -cat·ing
ed·u·ca·tion
ed·u·ca·tive
ed·u·ca·tor
ef·face
-faced, -fac·ing,
-face·ment
ef·fect (result; cf.
affect)
ef·fec·tive
-tive·ly,
-tive·ness
ef·fec·tu·al
ef·fec·tu·ate
-at·ed, -at·ing
ef·fem·i·nate
ef·fer·vesce
-vesced, -vesc·ing
ef·fete

ef·fi·ca·cious
ef·fi·ca·cy
-cies
ef·fi·cien·cy
-cies
ef·fi·cient
ef·fi·gy
-gies
ef·flo·res·cence
-cent
ef·flu·ent (flowing
out; cf. *affluent*)
ef·flu·vi·um
-via (pl)
ef·fort
ef·front·ery
ef·fu·sion
ef·fus·sive
egg·head
egg·nog
egg·plant
ego
egos
ego·cen·tric
ego·ism
ego·ist
ego·tism
egre·gious
egress
Egypt
Egyp·tian
ei·der
eight
eigh·teen

-teenth
eighth
eighths
eighty
eight·ies,
eight·i·eth
ei·ther
ejac·u·late
-lat·ed, -lat·ing
ejac·u·la·tion
eject
elab·o·rate
-rat·ed, -rat·ing
élan
elapse (pass; cf.
lapse)
elapsed, elaps·ing
elas·tic
elas·tic·i·ty
ela·tion
el·bow·room
el·der
el·der·ber·ry
el·dest
elect
elec·tion
elec·tive
elec·tor
elec·tor·al
elec·tor·ate
elec·tric
elec·tri·cal
elec·tri·cian
elec·tric·i·ty

99

elec·tri·fi·ca·tion
elec·tri·fy
  -fied, -fy·ing
elec·tro·cute
  -cut·ed, -cut·ing,
  -cu·tion
elec·trode
elec·tro·en·ceph·
  a·lo·gram
elec·trol·y·sis
elec·tro·lyte
elec·tro·mag·net
elec·tro·me·chan·i·cal
elec·tron
elec·tron·ic
elec·tron·ic mail
elec·tro·plate
elec·tro·scope
elec·tro·ther·mal
  -mal·ly
elec·tro·type
el·e·gance
el·e·gant
ele·gi·ac
el·e·gy
  -gies
el·e·ment
el·e·men·tal
el·e·men·ta·ry
el·e·phant
el·e·phan·tine
el·e·vate
  -vat·ed, -vat·ing

el·e·va·tor
elev·en
  -enth
elf
  elves (pl)
elic·it (draw out; cf.
  illicit)
el·i·gi·bil·i·ty
el·i·gi·ble (quali-
  fied; cf. *illegible,
  ineligible*)
elim·i·nate
  -nat·ed, -nat·ing
eli·sion
elite
elix·ir
Eliz·a·be·than
el·lipse
el·lip·sis
  -ses (pl)
el·lip·tic
el·o·cu·tion
elon·gate
  -gat·ed, -gat·ing
elon·ga·tion
elope
  eloped, elop·ing
el·o·quence
el·o·quent
El Sal·va·dor
else·where
elu·ci·date
  -dat·ed, -dat·ing,
  -da·tion

elude (escape; cf.
  allude)
  elud·ed, elud·ing
elu·sive (evasive; cf.
  illusive)
ema·ci·ate
  -at·ed, -at·ing
E-mail
em·a·nate
  -nat·ed, -nat·ing
em·a·na·tion
eman·ci·pate
  -pat·ed, -pat·ing
eman·ci·pa·tion
emas·cu·late
  -lat·ed, -lat·ing
em·balm
em·bank·ment
em·bar·go
  -goes
em·bar·rass
em·bar·rass·ment
em·bas·sy
  -sies
em·bed
  -bed·ded,
  -bed·ding
em·bel·lish
em·bez·zle
  -zled, -zling,
  -zle·ment
em·bit·ter
em·bla·zon
  -zoned, -zon·ing

em·blem
em·blem·at·ic
em·bodi·ment
em·body
  -bod·ied,
  -body·ing
em·bold·en
em·bo·lism
em·boss
em·brace
  -braced, -brac·ing
em·bra·sure
em·broi·dery
  -der·ies
em·broil
em·bryo
  -bry·os
em·bry·on·ic
em·cee
emend (correct; cf.
  amend)
emen·da·tion
em·er·ald
emerge
  emerged,
  emerg·ing
emer·gence
emer·gen·cy
  -cies
emer·gent
emer·i·tus
  -i·ti (pl)

em·i·grant
  (outgoing; cf.
  immigrant)
em·i·grate
  -grat·ed, -grat·ing
émi·gré
em·i·nence
em·i·nent (promi-
  nent; cf. *imma-
  nent, imminent*)
emir
em·is·sary
  -sar·ies
emis·sion
emit
  emit·ted,
  emit·ting
emol·lient
emol·u·ment
emo·ti·con
emo·tion
emo·tion·al
Emo·tion·al quo-
  tient (EQ)
em·pa·thy
em·per·or
em·pha·sis
  -pha·ses (pl)
em·pha·size
  -sized, -siz·ing
em·phat·ic
em·phy·se·ma
em·pire

em·pir·ic
em·pir·i·cal
em·ploy
  -ploy·er
em·ploy·able
em·ploy·a·bil·it·y
em·ploy·ee
em·ploy·ment
em·po·ri·um
  -ri·ums
em·pow·er
em·press (n)(female
  ruler; cf. *impress*)
emp·ty
  -ties, -tied, -ti·ness
emp·ty-head·ed
emu
em·u·late
  -lat·ed, -lat·ing
em·u·la·tion
emul·si·fy
  -fied, -fy·ing,
  -fi·able
emul·sion
en·able
  -abled, -abling
en·act
en·act·ment
enam·el
  -eled, -eling
enam·el·ware
en·am·or
  -ored, -or·ing

en·camp·ment
en·cap·su·late
  -lat·ed, -lat·ing
en·cap·sule
  -suled, -sul·ing
en·ceph·a·li·tis
en·ceph·a·lo·gram
en·chant·ing
en·chant·ment
en·chant·ress
en·chi·la·da
en·cir·cle
en·clave
en·close
en·clo·sure
en·code
en·co·mi·um
  -mi·ums
en·com·pass
en·core
  -cored, -cor·ing
en·coun·ter
  -tered, -ter·ing
en·cour·age
  -aged, -ag·ing
en·cour·age·ment
en·croach
  -croach·ment
en·crypt
  -cryp·tion
en·cum·ber
  -bered, -ber·ing
en·cum·brance
en·cyc·li·cal

en·cy·clo·pe·dia
en·dan·ger
  -gered, -ger·ing
en·dear
en·dear·ment
en·deav·or
  -ored, -or·ing
en·dem·ic
end·ing
en·dive
end·less
end·line
end·long
end·most
end·note
en·do·crine gland
en·do·cri·nol·o·gy
en·dor·phin
en·dorse
  -dorsed, -dors·ing
en·dorse·ment
en·dow
en·dow·ment
end prod·uct
end ta·ble
en·dur·able
en·dur·ance
en·dure
  -dured, -dur·ing
end·ways
en·e·ma
en·e·my
  -mies
en·er·get·ic

en·er·gize
  -gized, -giz·ing
en·er·giz·er
en·er·gy
  -gies
en·er·vate
  -vat·ed, -vat·ing
en·fee·ble
  -bled, -bling
en·fold
en·force
  -force·able,
  -force·ment
en·fran·chise
  -chised, -chis·ing,
  -chise·ment
en·gage
  -gaged, -gag·ing
en·gage·ment
en·gen·der
  -dered, -der·ing
en·gine
en·gi·neer
en·gi·neer·ing
En·glish
En·glish·man
En·glish·wom·an
en·graft
en·grave
  -graved,
  -grav·ing,
  -grav·er
en·gross
en·gross·ing

en·gross·ment
en·gulf
en·hance
  -hanced,
  -hanc·ing,
  -hance·ment
enig·ma
enig·mat·ic
en·join
en·joy
  -joy·able,
  -joy·ably
en·joy·ment
en·large
  -larged, -larg·ing
en·large·ment
en·light·en
  -ened, -en·ing
en·light·en·ment
en·list
  -list·ee, -list·ment
en·liv·en
en·mi·ty
  -ties
en·nui
enor·mi·ty
  -ties
enor·mous
enough
en·rage
en·rap·ture
  -tured, -tur·ing

en·rich
  -rich·ment
en·robe
en·roll
  -rolled, -roll·ee
en·roll·ment
en route
en·sconce
  -sconced,
  -sconc·ing
en·sem·ble
en·shrine
en·shroud
en·sign
en·slave
  -slave·ment
en·snare
en·sue
  -sued, -su·ing
en·sure
  -sured, -sur·ing
en·tail
  -tail·ment
en·tan·gle
en·tan·gle·ment
en·ter
  -ter·ing
en·tered
en·ter·prise
en·ter·pris·ing
en·ter·tain
  -tain·er
en·ter·tain·ment

en·thrall
  -thralled,
  -thrall·ing
en·throne
en·thuse
  -thused, -thus·ing
en·thu·si·asm
en·thu·si·ast
en·thu·si·as·tic
  -ti·cal·ly
en·tice
  -ticed, -tic·ing,
  -tice·ment
en·tire
en·tire·ty
  -ties
en·ti·tle
  -tling
en·ti·tled
en·ti·ty
  -ties
en·tomb
en·tomb·ment
en·to·mol·o·gy
  (insects; cf.
  etymology)
en·tou·rage
en·trails
en·trance
  -tranced,
  -tranc·ing
en·trant

en·trap
  -trap·ment
en·treat
en·treaty
  -treat·ies
en·tree
en·tre·pre·neur
  -neur·ial,
  -neur·ship
en·try
  -tries
en·try·way
en·twine
enu·mer·a·ble
enu·mer·ate
  -at·ed, -at·ing,
  -a·tion
enu·mer·a·tor
enun·ci·ate
  -at·ed, -at·ing,
  -a·tion
en·vel·op (v)
  -op·ment
en·ve·lope (n)
en·ven·om
en·vi·able
  -ably
en·vi·ous
en·vi·ron
en·vi·ron·ment
en·vi·ron·men·tal
en·vis·age
  -aged, -ag·ing

en·vi·sion
en·voy
en·vy
  -vies
en·zyme
ep·au·let
ephem·er·al
ep·ic (poem; cf.
  epoch)
  ep·i·cal
ep·i·cure
ep·i·cu·re·an
ep·i·dem·ic
ep·i·der·mal
epi·der·mis
ep·i·gram (witty
  saying; cf.
  *epigraph, epitaph,
  epithet*)
ep·i·graph (motto;
  cf. *epigram,
  epitaph, epithet*)
ep·i·graph·ic
ep·i·lep·sy
  -sies
ep·i·lep·tic
ep·i·logue
epiph·a·ny
  -nies
epis·co·pal
Epis·co·pa·lian
ep·i·sode
ep·i·sod·ic

ep·i·sod·i·cal
epis·tle
epis·to·lary
  -lar·ies
p·i·taph (inscrip-
  tion; cf. *epigram,
  epigraph, epithet*)
ep·i·thet (curse; cf.
  *epigram, epi-
  graph, epitaph*)
epit·o·me
epit·o·mize
  -mized, -miz·ing
ep·och (era; cf. *epic*)
ep·och·al
ep·oxy
  -ox·ied, -oxy·ing
equa·ble
  equa·bil·i·ty
equal
  equaled,
  equal·ing
equal·i·ty
equal·ize
  -ized, -iz·ing
equal·iz·er
equal·ly
equa·nim·i·ty
equa·tion
equa·tor
equa·to·ri·al
E·qua·to·ri·al
  Guin·ea

eques·tri·an
equi·an·gu·lar
equi·dis·tant
equi·lat·er·al
equi·lib·ri·um
  -ri·ums
equine
equi·nox
equip
  equipped,
  equip·ping
equip·ment
eq·ui·ta·ble
eq·ui·ty
  -ties
equiv·a·lent
equiv·o·cal
equiv·o·cate
  -cat·ed, -cat·ing
era
erad·i·cate
  -cated, -cat·ing,
  -ca·tion
erase
  erased, eras·ing,
  eras·able (can be
  erased; cf.
  irascible)
eras·er
era·sure
erect
erec·tion

er·go·nom·ics
  -nom·i·cal·ly
Er·i·trea
er·mine
  -mines
erode
ero·sion
ero·sive
erot·ic
err
er·rand
er·rant
er·ra·ta (pl)
  -tum (sing)
er·rat·ic
er·ro·ne·ous
er·ror
erst·while
er·u·dite
er·u·di·tion
erupt (break out; cf.
  irrupt)
  erupt·ible
erup·tion
es·ca·late
  -lat·ed, -lat·ing,
  -la·tion
es·ca·la·tor
es·ca·pade
es·cape
  -caped, -cap·ing,
  -cap·er
es·cape·ment

es·cap·ism
es·ca·role
es·cheat
es·chew
es·cort
es·cri·toire
es·crow
Es·ki·mo
  -mo (pl)
esoph·a·gus
  -gi (pl)
es·o·ter·ic
es·pe·cial
es·pe·cial·ly
Es·pe·ran·to
es·pi·o·nage
es·pla·nade
es·pous·al
es·pouse
  -poused,
  -pous·ing,
  -pous·er
espres·so
  -sos
es·prit
es·py
  -pied, -py·ing
es·quire
es·say (try; cf.
  assay)
es·say·ist
es·sence
es·sen·tial

105

es·sen·ti·al·i·ty
  -ties
es·tab·lish
  -lished
es·tab·lish·ment
es·tate
es·teem
es·ti·ma·ble
es·ti·mate
  -mated, -mat·ing,
  -ma·tive
es·ti·ma·tion
Es·to·nia
es·top
  -topped, -top·ping
es·top·pel
es·trange
  -tranged,
  -trang·ing,
  -trange·ment
es·tro·gen
es·tu·ary
  -ar·ies
et cet·era
etch·ing
eter·nal
eter·ni·ty
  -ties
eth·a·nol
ether
ethe·re·al
  -al·i·ty, -al·ize
Ether·net

eth·i·cal
eth·ics
Ethi·o·pia
Ethi·o·pi·an
eth·nic
eth·nic cleans·ing
eth·no·cen·trism
eth·yl
eth·yl·ene
eti·ol·o·gy
et·i·quette
et·y·mol·o·gy
  (words; cf.
  entomology)
  -mol·o·gies,
  -mo·log·i·cal,
  -mo·log·i·cal·ly
Eu·cha·rist
eu·chre
  -chred, -chring
eu·clid·e·an
eu·lo·gize
  -gized, -giz·ing,
  -giz·er
eu·lo·gy
  -gies, -gis·tic
eu·phe·mism
  -mis·tic,
  -mis·ti·cal·ly
eu·pho·ni·ous
eu·pho·ny
  -pho·nies,
  -phon·ic

eu·pho·ria
Eur·asia
Eu·ro·cur·ren·cy
  -ren·cies
Eu·ro·dol·lar
Eu·ro·mar·ket
Eu·rope
Eu·ro·pe·an
eu·tha·na·sia
eu·tro·phi·ca·tion
evac·u·ate
  -at·ed, -at·ing,
  -a·tive
evac·u·a·tion
evade
  evad·ed, evad·ing,
  evad·er
eval·u·ate
  -a·tion, -at·ed,
  -at·ing
ev·a·nes·cence
evan·gel·i·cal
evan·ge·lism
evan·ge·list
evan·ge·lize
  -lized, -liz·ing,
  -li·za·tion
evap·o·rate
  -rat·ed, -rat·ing,
  -ra·tion
eva·sion
eva·sive

even
 evened, even·er
even·hand·ed
eve·ning (n)(time)
even·ing (v)
 (smoothing)
event
event·ful
even·tide
even·tu·al
even·tu·al·i·ty
 -ties
even·tu·al·ly
even·tu·ate
 -at·ed, -at·ing
ev·er·green
ev·er·last·ing
ev·er·more
ev·ery·body
ev·ery·day
ev·ery·place
ev·ery·thing
ev·ery·where
evict
 evic·tion, evic·tor
ev·i·dence
 -denced,
 -denc·ing
ev·i·dent
ev·i·den·tial
ev·i·den·tia·ry

evince
 evinced,
 evinc·ing,
 evinc·ible
evis·cer·ate
 -at·ed, -at·ing,
 -a·tion
evo·ca·ble
evo·ca·tion
evoc·a·tive
evoke
 evoked, evok·ing
evo·lu·tion
 -tion·ary,
 -tion·ari·ly,
 -tion·ism
evolve
 evolved,
 evolv·ing,
 evolv·able
ewe (sheep; cf. *yew*,
 you)
ex·ac·er·bate
 -bat·ed, -bat·ing,
 -ba·tion
ex·act
ex·act·ing
ex·ac·ti·tude
ex·act·ly
ex·ag·ger·ate
 -at·ed, -at·ing,
 -a·tion
ex·alt

ex·al·ta·tion
ex·am·i·na·tion
ex·am·ine
 -ined, -in·ing,
 -in·er
ex·am·ple
 -pled, -pling
ex·as·per·ate
 -at·ed, -at·ing,
 -at·ing·ly
ex·as·per·a·tion
ex·ca·vate
 -vat·ed, -vat·ing
ex·ca·va·tion
ex·ca·va·tor
ex·ceed (surpass; cf.
 accede)
ex·ceed·ing
ex·cel
 -celled, -cel·ling
ex·cel·lence
ex·cel·len·cy
ex·cel·lent
ex·cept (exclude; cf.
 accept)
ex·cep·tion
ex·cep·tion·al
ex·cerpt
ex·cess (surplus; cf.
 access)
ex·ces·sive

ex·change
  -changed,
  -chang·ing,
  -change·abil·i·ty
ex·che·quer
ex·cis·able
ex·cise
  -cised, -cis·ing
ex·cit·able
  -able·ness,
  -abil·i·ty
ex·ci·ta·tion
ex·cite
  -cit·ed, -cit·ing,
  -cit·ed·ly
ex·cite·ment
ex·claim
ex·cla·ma·tion
ex·clam·a·to·ry
ex·clude
  -clud·ed,
  -clud·ing, -clud·er
ex·clu·sion
ex·clu·sive
ex·com·mu·ni·cate
ex·com·mu·ni·ca·tion
ex·co·ri·ate
  -at·ed, -at·ing,
  -a·tion
ex·crete
  -cret·ed, -cret·ing,
  -cret·er
ex·cre·tion

ex·cru·ci·ate
  -at·ed, -at·ing
ex·cul·pate
  -pat·ed, -pat·ing,
  -pa·tion
ex·cul·pa·to·ry
ex·cur·sion
ex·cur·sive
ex·cu·sa·to·ry
ex·cuse
  -cused, -cus·ing,
  -cus·able
ex·e·cute
  -cut·ed, -cut·ing,
  -cut·able
ex·e·cu·tion
ex·e·cu·tion·er
ex·ec·u·tive
ex·ec·u·tor
ex·ec·u·trix (fem)
  -tri·ces (pl)
ex·e·ge·sis
  -ge·ses (pl)
ex·em·plar
ex·em·pla·ry
ex·em·pli·fi·ca·tion
ex·em·pli·fy
  -fied, -fy·ing
ex·empt
ex·emp·tion
ex·er·cise (exertion;
  cf. *exorcise*)
  -cised, -cis·ing,
  -cis·able

ex·ert (exercise; cf.
  exsert)
ex·er·tion
ex·e·unt
ex·hal·ant
ex·ha·la·tion
ex·hale
  -haled, -hal·ing
ex·haust
  -haust·er,
  -haust·ible
ex·haus·tion
ex·haus·tive
ex·hib·it
  -i·tive, -i·to·ry,
  -i·tor
ex·hi·bi·tion
ex·hi·bi·tion·er
ex·hil·a·rate
  -rat·ed, -rat·ing,
  -rat·ing·ly
ex·hil·a·ra·tion
ex·hil·a·ra·tive
ex·hort
ex·hume
  -humed,
  -hum·ing,
  -hu·ma·tion
ex·i·gen·cy
  -cies
ex·ile
  -iled, -il·ing
ex·ist

ex·ists
ex·is·tence
ex·is·tent
ex·is·ten·tial·ism
ex·it
ex·o·dus
ex of·fi·cio
ex·on·er·ate
  -at·ed, -at·ing,
  -a·tion
ex·or·bi·tant
ex·or·cise (expel; cf.
  exercise)
  -cised, -cis·ing
ex·o·ter·ic
ex·ot·ic
ex·pand
ex·panse
ex·pan·si·ble
ex·pan·sion
ex·pan·sive
ex par·te
ex·pa·ti·ate
  -at·ed, -at·ing
ex·pa·tri·ate
  -at·ed, -at·ing,
  -a·tion
ex·pect
ex·pec·tan·cy
  -cies
ex·pec·tant
ex·pec·ta·tion
ex·pec·to·rant

ex·pec·to·rate
  -rat·ed, -rat·ing,
  -ra·tion
ex·pe·di·en·cy
  -en·cies, -en·tial
ex·pe·di·ent
  -ent·ly
ex·pe·dite
  -dit·ed, -dit·ing
ex·pe·di·tion
ex·pe·di·tion·ary
ex·pe·di·tious
ex·pel
  -pelled, -pel·ling,
  -pel·la·ble
ex·pend·able
ex·pen·di·ture
ex·pense
  -penses, -pensed,
  -pen·sing
ex·pen·sive
ex·pe·ri·ence
  -enced, -enc·ing
ex·pe·ri·en·tial
ex·per·i·ment
ex·per·i·men·tal
ex·pert
  -pert·ly, -pert·ness
ex·per·tise
ex·pi·ate
  -at·ed, -at·ing,
  -a·ble
ex·pi·a·tion

ex·pi·a·to·ry
ex·pi·ra·tion
ex·pire
  -pired, -pir·ing
ex·plain
  -plain·able,
  -plain·er
ex·pla·na·tion
ex·plan·a·to·ry
ex·ple·tive
ex·pli·ca·ble
ex·plic·it
ex·plode
  -plod·ed,
  -plod·ing, -plod·er
ex·ploit
ex·ploi·ta·tion
ex·plo·ra·tion
ex·plor·a·to·ry
ex·plore
  -plored, -plor·ing
ex·plor·er
ex·plos·i·me·ter
ex·plo·sion
ex·plo·sive
ex·po·nent
ex·port
  -port·able,
  -port·abil·i·ty
ex·por·ta·tion
ex·port·er
ex·pose (v)
  -posed, -pos·ing,
  -pos·er

ex·po·sé (n)
ex·po·si·tion
ex·pos·i·to·ry
ex post fac·to
ex·po·sure
ex·pound
ex·press
  -press·er,
  -press·ible
ex·pres·sion
ex·pres·sive
ex·press·ly
ex·press·way
ex·pro·pri·ate
ex·pul·sion
  -pul·sive
ex·punge
  -punged,
  -pung·ing,
  -pung·er
ex·pur·gate
  -gated, -gat·ing,
  -ga·tion
ex·pur·ga·to·ry
ex·qui·site
ex·sert (protrude; cf.
  exert)
ex·sert·ed
ex·tant (existing; cf.
  extent)
ex·tem·po·ra·ne·ous
ex·tem·po·rary
ex·tem·po·re

ex·tem·po·rize
  -rized, -riz·ing,
  -riz·er
ex·tend
ex·ten·si·ble
ex·ten·sion
ex·ten·sive
ex·tent (degree; cf.
  extant)
ex·ten·u·ate
  -at·ed, -at·ing,
  -a·to·ry
ex·ten·u·a·tion
ex·te·ri·or
ex·ter·mi·nate
  -nat·ed, -nat·ing,
  -na·tion
ex·ter·nal
ex·ter·nal·ize
  -ized, -iz·ing
ex·tinct
ex·tinc·tion
ex·tin·guish
  -guish·able,
  -guish·er
ex·tir·pate
  -pat·ed, -pat·ing,
  -pa·tion
ex·tol
  -tolled, -tol·ling,
  -tol·ler
ex·tort
ex·tor·tion

ex·tra
ex·tract
  -tract·abil·i·ty,
  -tract·able
ex·trac·tion
ex·trac·tive
ex·trac·tor
ex·tra·cur·ric·u·lar
ex·tra·dit·able
ex·tra·dite
  -dit·ed, -dit·ing
ex·tra·di·tion
ex·tral·i·ty
ex·tra·mar·i·tal
ex·tra·mu·ral
ex·tra·ne·ous
ex·tra·net
ex·traor·di·nary
  -nar·i·ly,
  -nari·ness
ex·trap·o·late
  -lated, -lat·ing,
  -la·tion
ex·tra·sen·so·ry
ex·trav·a·gance
ex·trav·a·gant
ex·trav·a·gan·za
ex·treme
ex·treme·ly
ex·trem·i·ty
  -ties
ex·tri·cate
  -cat·ed, -cat·ing,
  -ca·tion

ex·trin·sic
ex·tro·vert
ex·trude
  -trud·ed, -trud·ing,
  -trud·er
ex·tru·sion
ex·u·ber·ance
ex·u·ber·ant
ex·ude
  -ud·ed, -ud·ing
ex·ult
ex·ul·ta·tion
eye·ball
eye·brow
eyed
eye·drop·per
eye·ful
eye·glass
eye·hole
eye·lash
eye·let
eye·lid
eye-open·er
eye·piece
eye·sight
eye·sore
eye·spot
eye·strain
eye·tooth
eye·wash
eye·wink
eye·wit·ness
ey·rie (var. of *aerie*)

fa·ble
  -bled, -bling, -bler
fab·ric
fab·ri·cant
fab·ri·cate
  -cat·ed, -cat·ing,
  -ca·tor
fab·ri·ca·tion
fab·u·lous
fa·cade
face·down
face-lift·ing
fac·et (of diamond;
  cf. *faucet*)
fa·ce·tious
face-to-face
fa·cial
fac·ile
fa·cil·i·tate
  -tat·ed, -tat·ing,
  -ta·tor
fa·cil·i·ty
  -ties
fac·ing
fac·sim·i·le
fact find·er

fac·tion
  -tion·al,
  -tion·al·ism,
  -tion·al·ly
fac·tious (partisan;
  cf. *factitious,
  fictitious*)
fac·ti·tious (artifi-
  cial; cf. *factious,
  fictitious*)
fac·tor
  -tored, -tor·ing
fac·to·ri·al
fac·to·ry
  -ries
fac·tu·al
fac·ul·ta·tive
fac·ul·ty
  -ties
fad
fade
  fad·ed, fad·ing,
  fad·er
Fahr·en·heit
fail-safe
fail·ure
faint (weak; cf.
  feint)
  faint·ish, faint·ly

faint·heart·ed
fair (just; cf. *fare*)
fair·ground
fair·ly
fair-mind·ed
fair play
fair-spo·ken
fair trade (n)
fair-trade (v)
fair·way
fair-weath·er (adj)
fairy
  fairies, fairy·like
fairy tale (n)
fairy-tale (adj)
faith·ful
  -ful (pl), -ful·ly,
  -ful·ness
faith·less
fa·ji·ta
fake
  faked, fak·ing,
  fak·er
fa·kir
fal·con
Falk·land Is·lands
fal·la·cious
fal·la·cy
  -cies

fal·li·bil·i·ty
fal·li·ble
fall·ing-out
  fallings-out (pl)
fall out (v)
fall·out (n)
fal·low
false·hood
false
  false·ly, false·ness,
  fals·er
fal·set·to
  -tos
fal·si·fy
  -fied, -fy·ing,
  -fi·ca·tion
fal·si·ty
  -ties
fal·ter
  -tered, -ter·ing,
  -ter·er
fa·mil·ial
fa·mil·iar
fa·mil·iar·i·ty
  -ties
fa·mil·iar·ize
  -ized, -iz·ing,
  -iza·tion
fam·i·ly
  -lies
fam·ine
fam·ish
fa·mous

fa·nat·ic
  -i·cal, -i·cal·ly
fa·nat·i·cism
fan·ci·ful
fan·cy
  -cies, -cied, -cy·ing
fan·cy-free
fan·cy·work
fan·fare
fan·tail
fan·ta·sia
fan·ta·size
  -sized, -siz·ing,
  -siz·er
fan·tas·tic
  -ti·cal, -ti·cal·ly
fan·ta·sy
  -sies, -sied, -sy·ing
far·a·day
far·a·way
farce
  farced, farc·ing
far·ci·cal
fare (price; cf. *fair*)
  fared, far·ing
fare·well
far·fetched
fa·ri·na
farm·er
farm·hand
farm·house
farm·ing
farm·land

farm·stead
farm·yard
far-off
far-out
far-reach·ing
far·row
far·see·ing
far·sight·ed
far·ther (at greater
  distance; cf.
  further)
far·ther·most
far·thest
far·thing
fas·cia
  -ci·ae (pl)
fas·ci·nate
  -nat·ed, -nat·ing
fas·ci·na·tion
fas·ci·na·tor
fas·cism
fash·ion
  -ioned, -ion·ing
fash·ion·able
fas·ten·ing
fast-for·ward
fas·tid·i·ous
fast·ness
fast track (n)
fast-track (adj, v)
fa·tal·i·ty
  -ties
fa·tal·ly

fate (destiny; cf.
    fete)
    fat·ed, fat·ing
fate·ful
fa·ther
    -ther·hood,
    -ther·less, -thered
fa·ther-in-law
    fa·thers-in-law (pl)
fa·ther·land
fa·ther·like
fa·ther·ly
fath·om
fath·om·able
fath·om·less
fa·tigue
    -tigued, -tigu·ing
fat·ten
    -tened, -ten·ing,
    -ten·ed
fat·ty
    -ti·er, -ti·est,
    -ti·ness
fa·tu·ity
fat·u·ous
fau·cet (for water;
    cf. *facet*)
fault·less
faulty
    fault·i·er, fault·i·ly,
    fault·i·ness
faun (deity; cf.
    fawn)

faux pas
    faux pas (pl)
fa·vor·able
fa·vored
fa·vor·ite
fa·vor·it·ism
fawn (deer; cf. *faun*)
fax
faze
    fazed, faz·ing
fear·ful
fear·less
fear·some
fea·si·ble
    -bly, -bil·i·ty
feat (deed; cf. *feet*)
feath·er·bed·ding
feath·er·stitch
feath·er·weight
feath·ery
fea·ture
    -tured, -tur·ing,
    -ture·less
Feb·ru·ary
fe·cund
    -cun·di·ty
fed·er·al·ism
fed·er·al·ist
fed·er·al·iza·tion
fed·er·al·ize
    -ized, -iz·ing
fed·er·ate
    -at·ed, -at·ing

fed·er·a·tion
fee·ble
    -bler, -blest,
    -ble·ness
fee·ble·mind·ed
feed·back
feed·er
feed·stuff
feel·er
feel·ing
feet (pl. of *foot*; cf.
    feat)
feign
feigned
feint (trick; cf. *faint*)
feld·spar
fe·lic·i·tate
    -tat·ed, -tat·ing,
    -ta·tion
fe·lic·i·ty
    -ties
fe·line
fel·low
fel·low·ship
fel·on
fe·lo·ni·ous
fel·o·ny
    -nies
fe·male
fem·i·nine
fem·i·nin·i·ty
fem·i·nism

fe·mur
  fe·murs (pl)
fence
  fenced, fenc·ing,
  fenc·er
fend·er
fer·ment
  -able
fer·men·ta·tion
fe·ro·cious
fe·roc·i·ty
fer·ret
Fer·ris wheel
fer·rous
fer·ry·boat
fer·tile
fer·til·i·ty
fer·til·iza·tion
fer·til·ize
  -ized, -iz·ing,
  -iz·able
fer·til·iz·er
fer·vent
fer·vid
fer·vor
fes·ter
  -tered, -ter·ing
fes·ti·val
fes·tive
fes·tiv·i·ty
  -ties
fes·toon

fetch·ing
  -ing·ly
fete (festival; cf.
  fate)
  fet·ed, fet·ing
fe·tish
fet·lock
fet·ter
fet·tle
fe·tus
feu·dal·ism
feu·dal·ize
  -ized, -iz·ing
feud·ist
fe·ver
  -vered, -ver·ing
fe·ver·ish
fey
fi·an·cé (masc)
fi·an·cée (fem)
fi·as·co
  -coes
fi·at
fi·ber·board
fi·ber·glass
fi·ber-op·tic (adj)
fi·ber op·tics (n)
fi·brous
fib·u·la
  -lae (pl)
fiche (microfilm; cf.
  fish)
  fiche (pl)

fick·le
fic·tion
  -tion·al, -tion·al·ly
fic·ti·tious (imagi-
  nary; cf. *factious,
  factitious*)
fid·dle
  -dled, -dling,
  -dler
fid·dle·stick
fi·del·i·ty
  -ties
fidg·ety
fi·do·net
fi·du·cia·ry
  -ries
field
field day
field·er
field goal
field house
fiend
fierce
  fierc·er, fierc·est,
  fierce·ly
fi·ery
fi·es·ta
fif·teen
  -teenth
fifth
  fifths
fif·ty
  -ties, -ti·eth

fif·ty-fif·ty
fig·ment
fig·u·ra·tive
fig·ure
fig·ure·head
fig·u·rine
Fi·ji
fil·a·ment
fil·bert
file
   fil·ing
filed
file trans·fer
   pro·to·col (FTP)
fil·ial
fil·i·bus·ter
   -tered, -ter·ing,
   -ter·er
fil·i·gree
   -greed, -gree·ing
fil·ing
Fil·i·pi·no
   Fil·i·pi·nos (pl)
fill·er
   fill·ers
fil·let
fill·ing
film·mak·er
film·strip
fil·ter (strainer; cf.
   philter)
   -tered, -ter·ing

filthy
   filth·i·er,
   filth·i·est, filth·i·ly
fil·tra·tion
fi·na·gle
fi·nal
   -nal·ly
fi·na·le
fi·nal·ist
fi·nal·i·ty
   -ties
fi·nal·ize
   -ized, -iz·ing
fi·nance
   -nanced,
   -nanc·ing
fi·nan·cial
fi·nan·cier
find·er
find·ing
fine
   fined, fin·er,
   fin·est
fine·ly
fine·ness
fin·ery
   -er·ies
fi·nesse
   -nessed, -ness·ing
fine-tune
fin·ger
   -gered, -ger·ing
fin·ger bowl

fin·ger·print
fin·ger·tip
fin·icky
fi·nis
fin·ish
fin·ished
fi·nite
Fin·land
fir (tree; cf. *fur*)
fire·arm
fire·ball
fire·boat
fire·box
fire·break
fire·bug
fire·crack·er
fire-eat·er
fire fight·er
fire·fly
fire·house
fire·light
fire·man
fire·place
fire·plug
fire·pow·er
fire·proof
fire·side
fire tow·er
fire·trap
fire wall
fire·wood
fir·ing

firm
    firm·ly, firm·ness
firm·ware
first
first·born
first class (n)
first-class (adj, adv)
first-hand
first-rate
fis·cal (financial; cf. *physical*)
fish (aquatic animal; cf. *fiche*)
fish·er
fish·er·man
fish·ery
    -er·ies
fish·hook
fish·ing
fish stick
fish·tail
fishy
    fish·i·er, fish·i·est
fis·sion
    -sioned, -sion·ing
fis·sion·able
fis·sure
    -sured, -sur·ing
fit
    fit·ted, fit·ting,
    fit·ness
fit·ful
five·fold

fix·ate
    -at·ed, -at·ing
fix·a·tion
fix·a·tive
fixed
fix·ing
fix·ture
fiz·zle
    -zled, -zling
flab·ber·gast
flab·by
    -bi·er, -bi·est,
    -bi·ly
flac·cid
flag·ging
flag·pole
fla·gran·cy
fla·grant
flag·ship
flag·staff
flag·stone
flail
flair (aptitude; cf. *flare*)
flaky
    flak·i·er, flak·i·est,
    flak·i·ness
flam·boy·ant
flame·out
flame·proof
fla·min·go
    -gos
flam·ma·ble

flan·nel
flap
    flapped, flap·ping
flap·jack
flap·per
flare (torch; cf. *flair*)
    flared, flar·ing
flare-up
flash·back
flash·bulb
flash card
flash flood
flash·ing
flash·light
flash point
flashy
    flash·i·er,
    flash·i·est,
    flash·i·ly
flat·bed
flat·car
flat·iron
flat·ten
    -tened, -ten·ing,
    -ten·er
flat·ter
    -ter·er, -ter·ing·ly
flat·tery
    -ter·ies
flat·top
flat·ware
flat·work
flaunt

fla·vor·ful

fla·vor
 -vored, -vor·ing

flax·seed

flaxy
 flax·i·er, flax·i·est

flea (insect; cf. *flee*)

flea·bite

flea-bit·ten

flea mar·ket

fledg·ling

flee (escape; cf. *flea*)
 fled, flee·ing

fleece

flesh

flesh·i·ness

flesh·ly

fleshy
 flesh·i·er,
 flesh·i·est

fleu·ry

flew (did fly; cf. *flu, flue*)

flex·dol·lars

flex·i·ble
 -bly, -bil·i·ty

flex·time

flick·er
 -ered, -er·ing

fli·er

flight at·ten·dant

flight deck

flight pay

flight plan

flim·flam
 -flammed,
 -flam·ming,
 -flam·mer

flim·sy
 -si·er, -si·est,
 -si·ly

flinch

flint glass

flinty
 flint·i·er,
 flint·i·est, flint·i·ly

flip
 flipped, flip·ping

flip-flop

flip·pan·cy
 -cies

flip·pant

flip·per

flip side

flir·ta·tious

flit·ter

float·ing

floe (ice; cf. *flow*)

flood·gate

flood·light

flood·plain

flood·wa·ter

floor·board

floor·ing

floor lamp

floor·walk·er

flop·py
 -pies, -pi·er, -pi·ly

flop·py disk

flo·ral

flo·res·cence

flo·res·cent

flo·ri·cul·ture

flor·id

flo·rist

flo·ta·tion

flo·til·la

flot·sam

flounce
 flounced, flouncy,
 flounc·ing

floun·der
 -der (pl), -dered,
 -der·ing

flour (bread; cf.
 flower)

flour·ish

flow (of water; cf.
 floe)

flow·chart

flow·er (blossom; cf.
 flour)

flow·er·pot

flow·ery

flown

flu (influenza; cf.
 flew, flue)

fluc·tu·ate
 -at·ed, -at·ing,
 -a·tion

flue (chimney; cf.
  flew, flu)
flu·en·cy
flu·ent
fluffy
  fluff·i·er,
  fluff·i·est,
  fluff·i·ness
flu·id
flu·id·ex·tract
flu·id·i·ty
flu·id·ounce
flu·o·res·cent
flu·o·ri·date
  -dat·ed, -dat·ing,
  -da·tion
flu·o·ride
flu·o·ro·scope
flur·ry
  -ries, -ried, -ry·ing
flut·ter
flux
fly·by
  fly·bys (pl)
fly-by-night
fly·catch·er
fly·er
fly·ing
fly·wheel
foamy
  foam·i·er,
  foam·i·est,
  foam·i·ness

fo·cal
fo·cal·ize
  -ized, -iz·ing,
  -iza·tion
fo·cus (sing)
  fo·ci (pl)
fo·cus
  -cused, -cus·ing,
  -cus·able
fod·der
fog·bound
fog·gy (weather; cf.
  fogy)
  -gi·er, -gi·est,
  -gi·ness
fog·horn
fo·gy (person; cf.
  foggy)
  -gies, -gy·ish,
  -gy·ism
foi·ble
fold·er
fo·liage
fo·li·ate
fo·li·at·ed
fo·li·a·tion
fo·lio
  -li·os
folk·lore
folksy
  folks·i·er,
  folks·i·est
folk·tale

folk·way
fol·li·cle
fol·low
fol·low·er
fol·low·ing
fol·low through (v)
fol·low-through (n)
fol·low up (v)
fol·low-up (n, adj)
fol·ly
  -lies
fon·dant
fon·dle
  -dled, -dling, -dler
fond·ly
fond·ness
fon·due
font
food·ie
fool·ery
  -er·ies
fool·har·dy
  -har·di·ly,
  -har·di·ness
fool·ish
fool·proof
fools·cap
foot·ball
foot·bath
foot·board
foot·bridge
foot·can·dle
foot·ed

119

foot·er
foot·fall
foot fault (n)
foot·fault (v)
foot·gear
foot·hill
foot·hold
foot·ing
foot·lights
foot·lock·er
foot·loose
foot·mark
foot·note
foot·path
foot·print
foot·race
foot·rest
foot·sore
foot·step
foot·stool
foot·way
foot·wear
foot·work
for (function word;
  cf. *fore*)
for·age
  -aged, -ag·ing,
  -ag·er
for·ay
for·bear (be patient;
  cf. *forebear*)
  -borne, -bear·ing,
  -bear·er

for·bear·ance
for·bid
  -bade, -bid·den,
  -bid·ding
forced
force·ful
for·ceps
  -ceps (pl),
  -ceps·like
forc·ible
fore (front; cf. *for*)
fore·arm
fore·bear (ancestor;
  cf. *forbear*)
fore·bode
fore·bod·ing
fore·cast
  -cast·ing,
  -cast·able, -cast·er
fore·close
fore·clo·sure
fore·fa·ther
fore·fin·ger
fore·foot
fore·front
fore·go
  -went, -gone,
  -go·ing
fore·ground
fore·hand
fore·hand·ed
fore·head
for·eign

for·eign·er
fore·judge
fore·lock
fore·man
fore·mast
fore·most
fore·name
fore·noon
fo·ren·sic
fore·or·dain
fore·part
fore·quar·ter
fore·run
  -ran, -run,
  -run·ning
fore·run·ner
fore·see
  -saw, -seen,
  -see·ing
fore·shad·ow
fore·short·en
fore·sight
for·est
  -est·al, -est·ed,
  -es·ta·tion
fore·stall
for·est·er
for·est·ry
fore·tell
  -told, -tell·ing,
  -tell·er
fore·thought
for·ev·er

fore·warn
fore·word (preface;
  cf. *forward*)
for·feit
for·feit·er
for·fei·ture
forg·er
forg·ery
  -er·ies
for·get
  -got, -got·ten,
  -get·ting
for·get·ful
for·get-me-not
for·get·ta·ble
for·give·ness
for·giv·ing
for·go
  -went, -gone,
  -go·ing
for·lorn
form
for·mal
  -mal·ly (ceremoni-
  ally; cf. *formerly*),
  -mal·ness
form·al·de·hyde
for·mal·i·ty
  -ties
for·mal·ize
  -ized, -iz·ing,
  -iza·tion

for·mat
  -mat·ted,
  -mat·ting
for·ma·tion
for·ma·tive
for·mer (adj)
form·er (n)
for·mer·ly (previ-
  ously; cf.
  formally)
For·mi·ca
for·mi·da·ble
form·less
for·mu·la
  -las
for·mu·la·rize
  -rized, -riz·ing,
  -ri·za·tion
for·mu·late
  -lat·ed, -lat·ing,
  -la·tor
for·mu·la·tion
for·sake
  -sook, -saken,
  -sak·ing
for·swear
  -swore, -sworn,
  -swear·ing
for·syth·ia
fort (stronghold; cf.
  forte)
forte (talent; cf. *fort*)

forth (forward; cf.
  fourth)
forth·com·ing
forth·right
for·ti·fi·ca·tion
for·ti·fi·er
for·ti·fy
  -fied, -fy·ing
for·tis·si·mo
  -mos
for·ti·tude
fort·night
FOR·TRAN
for·tress
for·tu·itous
for·tu·ity
  -ities
for·tu·nate
for·tune
  -tuned, -tun·ing
for·tune-tell·er
for·ty
  -ties, -ti·eth
for·ty-nin·er
fo·rum
  fo·rums
for·ward (ahead; cf.
  foreword)
  -ward·ly,
  -ward·ness
for·ward·er
for·ward·ing
for·wards

fos·sil
fos·sil·if·er·ous
fos·ter
  -tered, -ter·ing,
  -ter·er
foul (bad; cf. *fowl*)
foul·mouthed
foun·da·tion
found·er (n)
  -der·ing, -dered
foun·der (v)
found·ling
found·ry
  -ries
foun·tain
foun·tain·head
four·score
four·some
four·teen
  -teenth
fourth (next after
  third; cf. *forth*)
  fourths, fourth·ly
fowl (poultry; cf.
  foul)
  fowl (pl), fowl·er
fox·hole
fox·hound
fox ter·ri·er
fox-trot
foy·er
fra·cas
  -cas·es (pl)

frac·tion
frac·tion·al
frac·tious
frac·ture
  -tured, -tur·ing
frag·ile
fra·gil·i·ty
frag·ment
frag·men·tar·y
fra·grance
fra·grant
frail·ty
  -ties
frame-up
frame·work
fram·ing
franc (money; cf.
  frank)
France
fran·chise
  -chised, -chis·ing
Fran·cis·can
frank (candid; cf.
  franc)
Frank·furt
frank·furt·er
frank·in·cense
frank·ly
fran·tic
fra·ter·nal
fra·ter·ni·ty
  -ties

frat·er·nize
  -niz·ed, -niz·ing,
  -ni·za·tion
fraud·u·lence
fraud·u·lent
freak·ish
freck·le
  -led, -ling
free·board
free·born
free·dom
free-for-all
free-form
free·hand
free·hold
free lance (n)
free-lance (adj, v)
free on board
  (FOB)
free·stand·ing
free·stone
free·style
free·think·er
free·ware
free·way
freeze (from cold; cf.
  frieze)
  froze, fro·zen,
  freez·ing
freeze-dry
freez·er
freight
freight·er

French Gui·a·na
fre·net·ic
fren·zy
  -zies, -zied,
  -zy·ing
Fre·on
fre·quen·cy
  -cies
fre·quent
fresh
  fresh·ly,
  fresh·ness
fres·co
  fres·coes
fresh·en
  -ened, -en·ing,
  -en·er
fresh·wa·ter
fret·ful
Freud·ian
fri·ar
fric·as·see
  -seed, -see·ing
fric·tion
fric·tion·al
Fri·day
friend
  friend·less,
  friend·less·ness
friend·ly
  -li·er, -li·est,
  -li·ness
friend·ship

frieze (ornament; cf.
  freeze)
frig·ate
fright
fright·en
  -ened, -en·ing,
  -en·ing·ly
fright·ful
frig·id
fri·gid·i·ty
frit·ter
fri·vol·i·ty
  -ties
friv·o·lous
frog·man
frol·ic
  -icked, -ick·ing
frol·ic·some
front·age
fron·tal
fron·tier
fron·tis·piece
front·less
front man
front mat·ter
front-run·ner
frost·bite
  -bit, -bit·ing,
  -bit·ten
frost·ing
froze
fro·zen
fruc·tose

fru·gal
  -gal·i·ty, -gal·ly
fruit
fruit·cake
fruit·ful
fru·ition
fruit·less
frus·trate
  -trat·ed, -trat·ing
frus·tra·tion
fud·dy-dud·dy
  -dies
fu·el
  -eled, -el·ing
fu·el cell
fu·gi·tive
Fu·ji
ful·crum
  -crums
ful·fill
  -filled, -fill·ing,
  -fill·ment
full
  full·ness
full·back
full-blood·ed
full-blown
full-bod·ied
full dress (n)
full-dress (adj)
full-fledged
full-length
full-scale

full-size
full time (n)
full-time (adj)
ful·ly
fum·ble
  -bled, -bling, -bler
fu·mi·gate
  -gat·ed, -gat·ing,
  -ga·tion
func·tion
  -tioned, -tion·ing
func·tion·al
fun·da·men·tal
  -tal·ly
fun·da·men·tal·ism
fund-rais·ing
fu·ner·al (burial; cf.
  funereal)
fu·ner·ary
fu·ne·re·al (solemn;
  cf. *funeral*)
fun·gi·cide
fun·gous (adj)
fun·gus (n)(sing)
  fun·gi (pl)
fu·nic·u·lar
fun·nel
  -neled, -nel·ing
fun·ny
  -ni·er, -ni·est,
  -ni·ly
fur (hair; cf. *fir*)
  furred, fur·ring

fur·be·low
fur·bish
fur·ri·ous
fur·long
fur·lough
fur·nace
fur·nish
fur·ni·ture
fu·ror
fur·ri·er
fur·ring
fur·row
fur·ry (with fur; cf.
  fury)
  -ri·er, -ri·est
fur·ther (in addi-
  tion; cf. *farther*)
  -thered, -ther·ing,
  -ther·er
fur·ther·ance
fur·ther·more
fur·ther·most
fur·thest
fur·tive
fu·ry (rage; cf. *furry*)
  -ries
fu·se·lage
fus·ible
fu·sion
fussy
  fuss·i·er,
  fuss·i·est,
  fuss·i·ness

fu·tile
fu·til·i·ty
fu·ture
fu·tu·ri·ty
fuzzy
  fuzz·i·er,
  fuzz·i·est,
  fuzz·i·ness

G

ga·ble
Ga·bon
gad·fly
gad·get
Gael·ic
gaffe
gai·ety
  -eties
gain
  gain·er
gain·ful
gait (manner of
  walking; cf. *gate*)
gal·axy
  -ax·ies
gal·lant
gal·lant·ry
  -ries
gal·le·on
gal·le·ria
gal·lery
  -ler·ies
gal·ley
  -leys
gal·lon
gal·lop
gal·lop·ing
gal·lows
  -lows (pl)

gall·stone
gal·va·nize
  -nized, -niz·ing,
  -ni·za·tion
gam·bit
Gam·bia
gam·ble
  -bled, -bling,
  -bler
gam·brel
game·keep·er
games·man·ship
gan·gli·on
  -glia (pl)
gang·plank
gan·grene
gang·ster
ga·rage
  -raged, -rag·ing
gar·bage
gar·den
  -den·ed, -den·ing,
  -den·er
gar·de·nia
gar·gle
  -gled, -gling
gar·goyle
gar·land
gar·lic

gar·ment
gar·ner
  nered, -ner·ing
gar·net
gar·nish
gar·nish·ee
  -eed, -ee·ing
gar·nish·ment
gar·ri·son
  -soned, -son·ing
gar·ru·lous
gar·ter
gas·eous
gas·ket
gas·light
gas·o·hol
gas·o·line
gas·sy
  -si·er, -si·est,
  -si·ness
gas·tric
gas·tri·tis
gas·tro·in·tes·ti·nal
gas·tron·o·my
  -tro·nom·ic,
  -tro·nom·i·cal,
  -tro·nom·i·cal·ly
gate (door; cf. *gait*)
  gat·ed, gat·ing

125

gate·way

gau·dy
  gaud·i·er,
  gaud·i·est,
  gaud·i·ness

gauge
  gauged, gaug·ing,
  gauge·able

gaunt·let

gauze

gav·el
  -eled, -el·ing

gay·ness

ga·ze·bo
  -bos

ga·zelle
  -zelles

ga·zette
  -zett·ed, -zett·ing

ga·zil·lion

gaz·pa·cho

Gdansk

gear·ing

gear·shift

ge·la·ti

gel·a·tin

ge·lat·i·nous

gem·ol·o·gist

gem·stone

gen·darme

gen·der
  -dered, -der·ing

ge·ne·al·o·gy
  -al·o·gies,
  -a·log·i·cal,
  -a·log·i·cal·ly

gen·er·al

Gen·er·al
  Agree·ment on
  Tar·iffs and
  Trade (GATT)

gen·er·al·i·ty
  -ties

gen·er·al·iza·tion

gen·er·al·ize
  -ized, -iz·ing,
  -iz·able

gen·er·al·ly

gen·er·al·ship

gen·er·ate
  -at·ed, -at·ing

gen·er·a·tion

Gen·er·a·tion X

gen·er·a·tive

gen·er·a·tor

ge·ner·ic

gen·er·os·i·ty
  -ties

gen·er·ous

gen·e·sis
  -e·ses (pl)

ge·net·ic

Ge·ne·va

ge·nial
  -nial·i·ty, -nial·ly

gen·i·tal

gen·i·tive

ge·nius (greatly
  gifted; cf. *genus*)
  -nius·es (pl)

geno·cide

genre

gen·tile

gen·til·i·ty
  -ties

gen·tle
  gen·tler, gen·tlest,
  gent·ly

gen·tle·ness

gen·try
  -tries

gen·u·flect
  -flec·tion

gen·u·ine

ge·nus (classifica-
  tion; cf. *genius*)
  gen·era (pl)

geo·cen·tric

ge·og·ra·pher

geo·graph·ic

ge·og·ra·phy
  -phies

geo·log·ic

ge·ol·o·gy
  -gies, -gist

ge·om·e·ter

geo·met·ric

geo·me·tri·cian

ge·om·e·try
-tries
geo·ther·mal
ge·ra·ni·um
ge·ri·at·rics
Ger·man
ger·mane
Ger·ma·ny
ger·mi·cide
ger·mi·nate
-nat·ed, -nat·ing,
-na·tion
germ·proof
ger·ry·man·der
-dered, -der·ing
ger·und
ge·stalt
ge·sta·po
-pos
ges·tate
-tat·ed, -tat·ing
ges·ta·tion
ges·tic·u·late
-lat·ed, -lat·ing,
-la·tory
ges·tic·u·la·tion
ges·ture
-tured, -tur·ing
get
got, get·ting
get·away (n)
get-to·geth·er (n)
Get·tys·burg

get up (v)
get·up (n)
gey·ser
Gha·na
ghast·ly
-li·er, -li·est,
-li·ness
gher·kin
ghet·to
-tos
ghost·ly
-li·er, -li·est,
-li·ness
ghoul (demon; cf.
goal)
gi·ant
gib·ber·ish
gibe (taunt; cf. *jib,
jibe*)
gibed, gib·ing
Gi·bral·tar
gid·dy
-di·er, -di·est,
-di·ness
giga·bit
giga·bit net·work
giga·byte
giga·hertz
gi·gan·tic
gig·gle
-gled, -gling
gig·o·lo
-los

gild (decorate with
gold; cf. *guild*)
gild·ed, gild·ing
gilt (gold-colored; cf.
guilt)
gilt-edged
gim·let
gim·mick
gin·ger
-gered, -ger·ing
gin·ger ale
gin·ger·bread
gin·ger·ly
ging·ham
gink·go
-goes
gin·seng
gi·raffe
-raffes
gird·er
gir·dle
-dled, -dling
girl·ish
girth
gist (essence; cf. *jest*)
give-and-take
give away (v)
give·away (n)
giv·en
give up
giz·zard
gla·cial
-cial·ly

gla·cier (ice; cf.
  glazier)
glad
  glad·ly, glad·ness
glad·den
  -dened, -den·ing
glad·i·a·tor
glad·i·o·lus
  -o·li (pl)
glam·or·ize
  -ized, -iz·ing,
  -iza·tion
glam·or·ous
glam·our
glance
  glanced, glanc·ing
glan·du·lar
glar·ing
glas·nost
glass·ware
glassy
  glass·i·er,
  glass·i·ness
glaze
  glazed, glaz·ing,
  glaz·er
gla·zier (glass-
  worker; cf.
  glacier)
glean·ings
glee·ful
glid·er

glim·mer
  -mered, -mer·ing
glimpse
  glimpsed,
  glimps·ing
glis·ten
  -tened, -ten·ing
glitch
glit·ter
glob·al
  -al·ly
glob·al·ize
  -al·i·za·tion
globe
glob·u·lar
glock·en·spiel
gloomy
  gloom·i·er,
  gloom·i·ly,
  gloom·i·ness
glo·ri·fy
  -fied, -fy·ing,
  -fi·ca·tion
glo·ri·ous
glo·ry
glos·sa·ry
  -ries
glossy
  gloss·i·er,
  gloss·i·est,
  gloss·i·ness
glow·er
glow·worm

glu·cose
glue
  glu·ey, glued,
  glu·ing
glum·ness
glu·ten
  -ten·ous
glu·ti·nous
glut·ton
glut·ton·ous
glut·tony
  -ton·ies
glyc·er·in
gnarl
gnarled
gnash
gnat
gnaw
gneiss
gnome
gnu (animal; cf.
  knew, new)
  gnu (pl)
go
  goes, went,
  go·ing, gone
go-ahead
goal (objective; cf.
  ghoul)
goal·post
gob·ble
  -bled, -bling
gob·bler

gob·let
gob·lin
go-cart
god·child
god·daugh·ter
god·dess
god·fa·ther
god·less
god·like
god·ly
  -li·er, -li·est,
  -li·ness
god·moth·er
god·par·ent
god·send
god·son
go-get·ter
gog·gle
  -gled, -gling
goi·ter
Go·lan Heights
gold·brick
gold·en
gold·en·rod
gold-filled
gold·fish
gold·smith
golf
Go·li·ath
gon·do·la
gon·do·lier
goo
  goo·ey

good-bye or
  good-by
good-heart·ed
good-hu·mored
good·ly
  -li·er, -li·est
good-na·tured
good·ness
good-tem·pered
good·will
goo·gol
goose·ber·ry
goose·flesh
goose·neck
go·pher
gorge
  gorged, gorg·ing,
  gorg·er
gor·geous
Gor·gon·zo·la
go·ril·la (animal; cf.
  guerrilla)
gos·pel
gos·sa·mer
gos·sip
Goth·ic
gou·lash
gourd
gour·met
gout
gov·ern
  -ern·able
gov·er·nance

gov·ern·ess
gov·ern·ment
  -men·tal,
  -men·tal·ize,
  -men·tal·ly
gov·er·nor
gov·er·nor·ship
grab
  grabbed,
  grab·bing,
  grab·ber
grace·ful
grace·less
gra·cious
gra·da·tion
gra·di·ent
grad·u·al
grad·u·ate
  -at·ed, -at·ing
grad·u·a·tion
graf·fi·ti (pl)
  -to (sing), -tist
gram·mar
  -mar·i·an
gram·mat·i·cal
Gra·na·da
gra·na·ry
  -ries
grand·child
grand·daugh·ter
gran·deur
grand·fa·ther
gran·di·ose

grand·moth·er
grand·son
grand·stand
grang·er
gran·ite
gran·ite·ware
grant·ee
grant-in-aid
  grants-in-aid (pl)
gran·u·lar
gran·u·late
  -lat·ed, -lat·ing
gran·u·la·tion
grape·fruit
grape·vine
graph
graph·ic
graph·i·cal
graph·i·cal user
  in·ter·face(GUI)
graph·ite
grap·nel
grap·ple
  -pled, -pling, -pler
grasp
grassy
  grass·i·er
grate (irritate; cf.
  great)
  grat·ed, grat·ing,
  grat·er
grate·ful
grat·i·fi·ca·tion

grat·i·fy
  -fied, -fy·ing
grat·ing

gra·tis
grat·i·tude
gra·tu·itous
gra·tu·ity
  -ities
grav·el
  -eled, -el·ing
grave·stone
grave·yard
grav·i·tate
  -tat·ed, -tat·ing,
  -ta·tive
grav·i·ta·tion
grav·i·ty
  -ties
gra·vy
  -vies
gray·beard
gray·ish
grease
  greased, greas·ing
greas·er
grease·wood
greasy
  greas·i·er,
  greas·i·ness
great (large; cf.
  grate)
Gre·cian

Greece
greedy
  greed·i·er,
  greed·i·est,
  greed·i·ness
Greek
green·back
green·ery
  -er·ies
green-eyed
green·horn
green·house
green·ing
green·mail
Green·wich
greet·ing
gre·gar·i·ous
Gre·go·ri·an
grem·lin
Gre·na·da
gre·nade
gren·a·dier
gren·a·dine
grey·hound
grid·dle
grid·iron
grid·lock
griev·ance
griev·ous
grif·fin
grill (broil; cf, *grille*)
grille (grating; cf.
  grill)

grill·work

gri·mace

grin
grinned,
grin·ning,
grin·ning·ly

grind·stone

grip (grasp; cf.
gripe, grippe)
gripped,
grip·ping, grip·per

gripe (complain; cf.
grip, grippe)

grippe (sickness; cf.
grip, gripe)

gris·ly (ghastly; cf.
gristly, grizzly)
-li·er, -li·est,
-li·ness

gris·tle

gris·tly (full of
gristle; cf. *grisly,
grizzly*)
-tli·er, -tli·est,
-tli·ness

grist·mill

grit
grit·ted, grit·ting

grit·ty
-ti·er, -ti·est,
-ti·ness

griz·zle
-zled, -zling

griz·zly (bear; cf.
grisly, gristly)
-zli·er, -zli·est

groan (moan; cf.
grown)

gro·cery
-cer·ies

grog·gy
-gi·er, -gi·est,
-gi·ness

grok

grooms·man

groove (rut; cf.
grove)
grooved,
groov·ing

gross
gross·ly,
gross·ness

gro·tesque

ground·break·ing

ground·hog

ground·less

ground·ling

ground·wa·ter

ground·work

group·ware

grove (trees; cf.
groove)

grov·el
-eled, -el·ing

grow
grow·ing, grow·er

growl·er

grown (matured; cf.
groan)

growth

Groz·ny

grub
grubbed,
grub·bing

grub·stake

grudge
grudg·ing,
grudg·ing·ly

gru·el

gru·el·ing

grue·some

grum·ble
-bled, -bling, -bler

grumpy
grump·i·er,
grump·i·est,
grump·i·ness

Guam

guar·an·tee (n, v)
(secure; cf.
guaranty)
-teed, -tee·ing

guar·an·tor

guar·an·ty (n, v)
(a pledge; cf.
guarantee)
-ties, -tied, -ty·ing

guard·ian
-ian·ship

guards·man
Gua·te·ma·la
gu·ber·na·to·ri·al
guern·sey
  -seys
guer·ril·la (soldier;
  cf. *gorilla*)
guess
guess·ti·mate
guess·work
guest
guid·ance
guide·book
guide·line
guild (association;
  cf. *gild*)
guil·lo·tine
guilt (deserving
  blame; cf. *gilt*)
guilt·less
guilty
  guilt·i·er,
  guilt·i·est,
  guilt·i·ness
guin·ea
Guin·ea
gui·tar
gull·ible
  -ibly, -ibil·i·ty
gul·ly
  -lies, -lied, -ly·ing
gum·drop

gum·my
  -mi·er, -mi·est,
  -mi·ness
gump·tion
gun·boat
gun·fire
gun·man
gun·nery
gun·pow·der
gun·shot
gun·wale
gup·py
  -pies
gur·gle
  -gled, -gling
gush·er
gus·to
  -toes
gut·ter
gut·tur·al
Guy·ana
guz·zle
  -zled, -zling, -zler
gym·na·si·um
  -si·ums
gym·nast
gym·nas·tic
gy·ne·col·o·gy
gyp·sum
gyp·sy
  -sies, -sied, -sy·ing

gy·rate
  -rat·ed, -rat·ing,
  -ra·tor
gy·ra·tion
gy·ro·com·pass
gy·ro·scope
gy·ro·sta·bi·liz·er

ha·be·as cor·pus
hab·er·dash·er
hab·ile
ha·bil·i·tate
 -tat·ed, -tat·ing
hab·it
hab·it·able
ha·bi·tant
hab·i·tat
hab·i·ta·tion
ha·bit·u·al
ha·bit·u·ate
 -at·ed, -at·ing
ha·ci·en·da
hack·er
hack·ney
 -neys, -neyed,
 -ney·ing
hack·saw
had·dock
hag·gard
hag·gle
 -gled, -gling
Hague, The
hail (ice; cf. *hale*)
hail·stone
hail·storm
hair (fur; cf. *hare*)
hair·brush

hair·cut
hair·dress·er
hair·line
hair·piece
hair·rais·ing
hairy
 hair·i·er,
 hair·i·ness
Hai·ti
Hai·tian
hale (healthy; cf.
 hail)
 haled, hal·ing
half
 halves (pl)
half-and-half
half·back
half broth·er
half·heart·ed
half hour
half-moon
half note
half-pint
half sis·ter
half step
half·time
half-truth
half·way
hal·i·but

hall (room; cf. *haul*)
hal·le·lu·jah
hall·mark
hal·low
Hal·low·een
hal·lu·ci·nate
 -nat·ed, -nat·ing
hal·lu·ci·na·tion
hal·lu·ci·na·to·ry
hal·lu·ci·no·gen
 -gen·ic
hall·way
hal·ter
halve (v)(divide in
 half; cf. *have*)
 halved, halv·ing
ham·burg·er
ham·let
ham·mer
 -mered, -mer·ing
ham·mock
ham·per
 -pered, -per·ing
ham·ster
ham·string
 -strung
hand·bag
hand·ball
hand·bill

133

hand·book
hand·cuff
hand·ed·ness
hand·ful
  -fuls
hand·gun
hand·held
hand·i·cap
  -cap·ping
hand·i·capped
hand·i·craft
hand·i·ly
hand·i·work
hand·ker·chief
  -chiefs
han·dle
  -dled, -dling
han·dle·bar
han·dler
hand·made
hand-me-down
hand·out
hand·rail
hand·shake
hand·some
  -some·ly
hands-on
hand·stand
hand·wo·ven
hand·write
  -wrote, -writ·ten
han·gar (shed; cf.
  hanger)

hang·er (for clothes;
  cf. *hangar*)
hang·ing
hang·nail
hang out (v)
hang·out (n)
han·ky-pan·ky
Ha·noi
Ha·nuk·kah
hap·haz·ard
hap·less
hap·pen
  -pened, -pen·ing
hap·pen·stance
hap·pi·ly
hap·pi·ness
hap·py
  -pi·er, -pi·est
hap·py-go-lucky
ha·rangue
  -rangued,
  -rangu·ing
ha·rass
har·bin·ger
har·bor
  -bored, -bor·ing
hard-and-fast
hard·back
hard-boiled
hard copy
hard·cov·er
hard disk
hard drive

hard·en
  -ened, -en·ing
hard-fist·ed
hard-head·ed
hard-heart·ed
hard·ly
hard·ness
hard-nosed
hard-of-hear·ing
hard-pressed
hard·ship
hard·top
hard·ware
hard-wired
hard·wood
hard·work·ing
har·dy
  -di·er, -di·est,
  -di·ness
hare (rabbit; cf.
  hair)
  hares
hare·brained
hare·lip
har·em
har·le·quin
harm·ful
harm·less
har·mon·ic
har·mon·i·ca
har·mo·ni·ous
har·mo·nize
  -nized, -niz·ing

har·mo·ny
  -nies
har·ness
har·poon
harp·si·chord
har·ri·er
Har·ris·burg
har·row
har·ry
  -ried, -ry·ing
hart (deer; cf. *heart*)
Hart·ford
har·vest
has-been (n)
ha·sen·pfef·fer
hash·ish
hash mark
has·sle
  -sled, -sling
has·ten
  -tened, -ten·ing
hast·i·ly
hasty
  hast·i·er,
  hast·i·est,
  hast·i·ness
hatch·ery
  -er·ies
hatch·et
hatch·ing
hate·ful
ha·tred
hat·ter

haugh·ty
  -ti·er, -ti·est
haul (pull; cf. *hall*)
haunt
have (possess; cf.
  halve)
ha·ven
have-not (n)
hav·oc
Ha·wai·ian
haw·thorn
hay fe·ver
hay·rack
hay·seed
haz·ard
haz·ard·ous
haze
  hazed, haz·ing
ha·zel
hazy
  haz·i·er, haz·i·est,
  haz·i·ness
H-bomb
head·ache
head·band
head·cheese
head cold
head·er
head·first
head·hunt·er
head·ing
head·less
head·light

head·line
head·lock
head·long
head-on (adj)
head·phone
head·quar·ters
head·rest
head·room
head·set
head·strong
head·wait·er
head·way
head wind
heal (cure; cf. *heel*)
health
health·ful
healthy
  health·i·er,
  health·i·est
hear (listen; cf. *here*)
  heard (past tense
  of hear, cf. *herd*),
  hear·ing
hear·ken
  -kened, -ken·ing
hear·say
hearse
heart (in body; cf.
  hart)
heart·ache
heart·beat
heart·break
heart·bro·ken

heart·burn
heart·en
  -ened, -en·ing
heart·felt
hearth
hearth·stone
heart·i·ly
heart·land
heart·less
heart·sick
heart·warm·ing
hearty
  heart·i·er,
  heart·i·est
heat·er
hea·then
heath·er
heat·stroke
heave
  heaved, heav·ing
heav·en
heav·en·ly
heav·en·ward
heavi·ly
heavy
  heavi·er, heavi·est
heavy-du·ty
heavy-foot·ed
heavy-hand·ed
heavy·heart·ed
heavy·set
heavy·weight
He·brew

hec·tic
hec·to·me·ter
hedge
  hedg·ing
hedge·hog
hedge·row
heed·ful
heed·less
heel (of foot; cf. *heal*)
heif·er
height
height·en
  -ened, -en·ing
Heim·lich
  ma·neu·ver
hei·nous
heir (inheritor; cf. *air*)
heir·ess (fem)
heir·loom
Hel·e·na
he·li·cop·ter
he·lio·graph
he·lio·trope
he·li·pad
he·li·port
he·li·um
hel·lion
hel·met
helms·man
help·er
help·ful

help·less
help·mate
Hel·sin·ki
hel·ter-skel·ter
hemi·ple·gia
hemi·sphere
  -spher·ic
hem·line
hem·lock
he·mo·glo·bin
he·mo·phil·ia
hem·or·rhage
  -rhaged, -rhag·ing
hem·or·rhoid
hem·stitch
hence·forth
hence·for·ward
hep·a·ti·tis
hep·ta·gon
hep·tath·lon
her·ald
he·ral·dic
her·ald·ry
  -ries
herb·age
herb·al
her·bi·cide
her·biv·o·rous
Her·cu·le·an
herd (group of animals; cf. *heard*)
herd·er
here (place; cf. *hear*)

here·abouts
here·af·ter
here·by
he·red·i·tary
he·red·i·ty
here·in
here·in·af·ter
here·in·be·fore
here·on
her·e·sy
-sies
her·e·tic
he·ret·i·cal
here·to·fore
here·with
her·i·ta·ble
her·i·tage
her·mit
her·mit·age
her·nia
he·ro
-roes
he·ro·ic
her·o·in (drug; cf. *heroine*)
her·o·ine (woman; cf. *heroin*)
her·o·ism
her·on
her·ring
her·ring·bone
her·self
Her·ze·go·vi·na

hes·i·tan·cy
-cies
hes·i·tant
hes·i·tate
-tated, -tat·ing, -tat·ing·ly
hes·i·ta·tion
het·er·o·ge·ne·i·ty
het·er·o·ge·neous
het·ero·sex·u·al
heu·ris·tic
hew (chop; cf. *hue*)
hewed, hew·ing
hexa·gon
hex·ag·o·nal
hey·day
hi·a·tus
hi·ber·nate
-nat·ed, -nat·ing, -na·tion
hi·bis·cus
hic·cup
hick·o·ry
-ries
hid·den
hide·away
hid·eous
hide·out
hi·er·arch
hi·er·ar·chi·cal
hi·er·ar·chy
-chies
hi·ero·glyph·ic

high chair
high-class
high fi·del·i·ty
high five
high-grade
high·land
high lev·el
high·light
-light·ed, -light·ing
high·ness
high-pitched
high-pow·ered
high-pres·sure
high-rise
high school
high-strung
high tech·nol·o·gy
high-ten·sion
high-test
high·way
hi·jack
hi·lar·i·ous
hi·lar·i·ty
hill·bil·ly
-lies
hill·side
hilly
hill·i·er, hill·i·est
him (pronoun; cf. *hymn*)
Hi·ma·la·yan
him·self

137

hin·der (v)
   -dered, -der·ing
hin·drance
hind·sight
Hin·du
hinge
   hinged, hing·ing
hip·bone
hip-hop
hip·pie
   -pies
hip·po·pot·a·mus
   -mus·es (pl)
hire
   hired, hir·ing
Hi·ro·shi·ma
His·pan·ic
his·ta·mine
his·to·ri·an
his·tor·ic
his·tor·i·cal
his·to·ry
   -ries
his·tri·on·ic
hit
   hit·ting, hit·less
hit-and-miss
hit-and-run
hitch·hike
hith·er
hith·er·to
HIV

hoard (amass; cf.
   horde)
hoard·ing
hoarse (voice; cf.
   horse)
   hoars·er, hoars·est
hoax
hob·ble
   -bled, -bling
hob·by·horse
hob·gob·lin
hob·nob
   -nobbed,
   -nob·bing
ho·bo
   -boes
Ho Chi Minh City
hock·ey
ho·cus-po·cus
hodge·podge
hoe
   hoed, hoe·ing
hoe·down
hog
   hogs, hogged,
   hog·ging
hog·wash
hold·er
hold·fast
hold·ing
hold over (v)
hold·over (n)
hold up (v)

hold·up (n)
hole (cavity; cf.
   whole)
hol·ey (full of holes;
   cf. *holly, holy,
   wholly*)
hol·i·day
ho·li·ness
ho·lis·tic
Hol·land
hol·lan·daise sauce
hol·low
   -low·er, -low·est
hol·ly (shrub; cf.
   *holey, holy,
   wholly*)
ho·lo·caust
ho·lo·graph
hol·ster
ho·ly (sacred; cf.
   *holey, holly,
   wholly*)
   -li·er, -li·est
hom·age
hom·burg
home·body
home·bound
home·com·ing
home·grown
home·land
home·less
home·like

home·ly (plain; cf.
  homey)
  -li·er, -li·est,
  -li·ness
home·made
home plate
home·room
home rule
home run
home·school·ing
home·sick
home·site
home·spun
home·stead
home·stretch
home·town
home·ward
home·work
hom·ey (homelike;
  cf. *homely*)
  hom·ey·ness,
  hom·i·er,
  hom·i·est
ho·mi·cide
hom·i·ly
  -lies
ho·mo·ge·ne·ity
ho·mo·ge·neous
  (alike; cf.
  homogenous)
ho·mog·e·nize
  -nized, -niz·ing

ho·mog·e·nous
  (from same
  source; cf.
  homogeneous)
ho·mol·o·gous
hom·onym
ho·mo·phone
ho·mo·sex·u·al
Hon·du·ras
hon·est
hon·es·ty
  -ties
hon·ey
hon·ey·bee
hon·ey·comb
hon·ey·dew
hon·ey·moon
hon·ey·suck·le
Hong Kong
hon·ky-tonk
Ho·no·lu·lu
hon·or
  -ored, -or·ing
hon·or·able
hon·o·rar·i·um
  -ia (pl)
hon·or·ary
hood·ed
hood·lum
hoof·er
hook up (v)
hook·up (n)

hook·worm
hooky
Hoo·sier
hope
  hoped, hop·ing
hope·ful
  -ful·ly
hope·less
hop·per
hop·scotch
horde (crowd; cf.
  hoard)
hore·hound
ho·ri·zon
hor·i·zon·tal
hor·mone
hor·net
horny
horo·scope
hor·ri·ble
hor·rid
hor·ri·fy
  -fied, -fy·ing
hor·ror
hors d'oeuvre
  hors d'oeuvres (pl)
horse (animal; cf.
  hoarse)
horse·back
horse·fly
horse·hair
horse·play

horse·pow·er
horse·rad·ish
horse·shoe
hor·ti·cul·ture
  -tur·al
ho·siery
hos·pice
hos·pi·ta·ble
hos·pi·tal
hos·pi·tal·i·ty
  -ties
hos·pi·tal·ize
  -ized, -iz·ing
hos·tage
hos·tel·ry
  -ries
host·ess
hos·tile
hos·til·i·ty
  -ties
hos·tler
hot
  hot·ter, hot·test
hot air
hot·bed
hot-blood·ed
hot-but·ton
hot-desk·ing
hot dog
ho·tel
hot·head
hot·house
hot·link

hot-look·ing
hot plate
hot rod
hot·shot
hot tub
hot-wire
hour (60 minutes;
  cf. *our*)
hour·glass
hour-long
hour·ly
house
  housed, hous·ing
house·break
  -broke, -broken,
  -break·ing
house·clean
house·hold
house·keep·er
house·lights
house·moth·er
house·plant
house sit·ter
house·wares
house·warm·ing
house·wife
  -wives (pl)
house·work
hov·el
hov·er
how·ev·er
how·it·zer
howl·er

how·so·ev·er
how-to
hua·ra·che
hub-and-spoke
hub·bub
huck·le·ber·ry
huck·ster
hud·dle
  -dled, -dling
hue (color; cf. *hew*)
huffy
  huff·i·er,
  huff·i·est,
  huff·i·ness
huge
  hug·er, hug·est
hu·man
hu·mane
hu·man·ism
hu·man·i·tar·i·an
hu·man·i·ty
  -ties
hu·man·ize
  -ized, -iz·ing
hu·man·kind
hu·man·ly
hum·ble
  -ble·ness, -bly,
  -bled
hum·bug
hum·drum
hu·mer·us (bone; cf.
  humorous)
  hu·mer·i (pl)

hu·mid
hu·mid·i·fi·er
hu·mid·i·fy
  -fied, -fy·ing
hu·mid·i·ty
  -ties
hu·mi·dor
hu·mil·i·ate
  -at·ed, -at·ing,
  -a·tion
hu·mil·i·ty
hum·ming·bird
hu·mor
  -mored, -mor·ing
hu·mor·ist
hu·mor·ous (funny;
  cf. *humerus*)
hump·back
Hum·vee
hunch·back
hun·dred
  hun·dredth
hun·dred·weight
Hun·gar·i·an
Hun·ga·ry
hun·ger
  -gered, -ger·ing
hun·gry
  -gri·er, gri·est,
  -gri·ly
hunt·er
hunts·man
hur·dle
  -dled, -dling, -dler

Hu·ron
hur·rah
hur·ri·cane
hur·ry
  -ried, -ry·ing
hurt
hus·band
hus·band·ry
hus·ky
  -ki·er, -ki·est
hus·tle
  -tled, -tling
hy·a·cinth
hy·brid
hy·dran·gea
hy·drant
hy·drate
  -drat·ed, -drat·ing
hy·drau·lic
hy·dro·car·bon
hy·dro·chlo·ric acid
hy·dro·chlo·ride
hy·dro·dy·nam·ics
hy·dro·elec·tric
hy·dro·gen
hy·drol·o·gy
hy·drom·e·ter
hy·dro·pho·bia
hy·dro·plane
hy·dro·pon·ics
hy·dro·stat·ic
hy·drous
hy·e·na

hy·giene
  -gien·ic, -gien·ist
hymn (song; cf. *him*)
hym·nal
hym·nol·o·gy
hy·per·bo·la (curve;
  cf. *hyperbole*)
hy·per·bo·le (exag-
  geration; cf.
  hyperbola)
hy·per·crit·i·cal
  (overcritical; cf.
  hypocritical)
hy·per·ki·net·ic
hy·per·link
hy·per·me·dia
hy·per·sen·si·tive
hy·per·ten·sion
hy·per·text
Hy·per·text
  Mark·up
  Lan·guage
  (HTML)
hy·per·text trans·fer
  pro·to·col (HTTP)
hy·per·ther·mia
hy·phen
hy·phen·ate
  -at·ed, -at·ing
hyp·no·sis
hyp·not·ic
hyp·no·tism
  -tist

141

hyp·no·tize
   -tized, -tiz·ing
hy·po·chon·dria
hy·po·chon·dri·ac
hy·poc·ri·sy
hyp·o·crite
hyp·o·crit·i·cal
   (deceitful; cf.
   hypercritical)
hy·po·der·mal
hy·po·der·mic
hy·po·der·mis
hy·pot·e·nuse
hy·poth·e·cate
   -cat·ed, -cat·ing
hy·poth·e·sis (sing)
   -e·ses (pl)
hy·po·thet·i·cal
   -cal·ly
hys·te·ria
   -ter·ic, -ter·i·cal
hys·ter·ics

Ibe·ri·an
ibis (bird)
  ibis (pl)
ibu·pro·fen
ice
  iced, ic·ing
ice age
ice bag
ice·berg
ice·bound
ice-cold
ice cream
ice floe
Ice·land
ice pick
ice wa·ter
ici·cle
ic·ing
icon
icy
  ic·i·er, ic·i·est,
  ic·i·ness
idea
ide·al (perfect; cf.
  idle, idol, idyll)
ide·al·ism
ide·al·ist
ide·al·is·tic

ide·al·ize
  -ized, -iz·ing
ide·al·ly
iden·ti·cal
iden·ti·fi·ca·tion
iden·ti·fy
  -fied, -fy·ing,
  -fi·able
iden·ti·ty
ideo·log·i·cal
ide·ol·o·gy
  -gies
id·i·o·cy
  -cies
id·i·om
id·i·om·at·ic
id·io·syn·cra·sy
  -sies
id·i·ot
id·i·ot·ic
idle (inactive; cf.
  ideal, idol, idyll)
  idle·ness, idly,
  idling
idol (object of wor-
  ship; cf. *ideal,*
  idle, idyll)
idol·a·try
  -tries

idol·ize
  -ized, -iz·ing, -iz·er
idyll (of rustic life;
  cf. *ideal, idle,*
  idol)
idyl·lic
if·fy
ig·loo
  -loos
ig·ne·ous
ig·nite
  -nit·ed, -nit·ing,
  -nit·able
ig·ni·tion
ig·no·ble
ig·no·min·i·ous
ig·no·mi·ny
  -nies
ig·no·ra·mus
  -mus·es
ig·no·rance
ig·no·rant
ig·nore
  -nored, -nor·ing
igua·na
il·e·um (intestine;
  cf. *ilium*)
  il·ea (pl)

il·i·um (pelvic bone;
    cf. *ileum*)
    il·ia (pl)
ilk
ill-ad·vised
ill-bred
il·le·gal
    -gal·i·ty, -gal·ly
il·leg·i·ble (unread-
    able; cf. *eligible,
    ineligible*)
    -bly, -bil·i·ty
il·le·git·i·ma·cy
il·le·git·i·mate
ill-fat·ed
ill-fa·vored
il·lib·er·al
il·lic·it (unlawful; cf.
    elicit)
il·lim·it·able
il·lit·er·a·cy
    -cies
il·lit·er·ate
    -ate·ly, -ate·ness
ill-man·nered
ill-na·tured
ill·ness
il·log·i·cal
ill-starred
ill-treat
il·lu·mi·nate
    -nat·ed, -nat·ing
il·lu·mi·na·tion
il·lu·mi·na·tive
144

il·lu·mine
    -mined, -min·ing
il·lu·sion
il·lu·sion·ist
il·lu·sive (mislead-
    ing; cf. *elusive*)
    -sive·ly,
    -sive·ness
il·lu·so·ry
il·lus·trate
    -trat·ed, -trat·ing,
    -tra·tor
il·lus·tra·tion
il·lus·tra·tive
il·lus·tri·ous
ill will
im·age
    -aged, -ag·ing,
    -ag·er
im·ag·ery
    -er·ies
imag·in·able
imag·i·nary
imag·i·na·tion
imag·i·na·tive
imag·ine
    -ined, -in·ing
im·bal·ance
im·be·cile
im·be·cil·i·ty
im·bibe
    -bibed, -bib·ing
im·bri·cate
    -cat·ed, -cat·ing

im·bue
    -bued, -bu·ing
im·i·ta·ble
im·i·tate
    -tat·ed, -tat·ing,
    -ta·tor
im·i·ta·tion
im·i·ta·tive
im·mac·u·late
im·ma·nent (within
    the mind; cf. *emi-
    nent, imminent*)
im·ma·te·ri·al
im·ma·ture
im·mea·sur·able
im·me·di·a·cy
    -cies
im·me·di·ate
im·me·di·ate·ly
im·me·mo·ri·al
im·mense
im·men·si·ty
    -ties
im·merge
    -merged,
    -merg·ing,
    -mer·gence
im·merse
    -mersed,
    -mers·ing
im·mer·sion
im·mi·grant
    (incoming; cf.
    emigrant)

im·mi·grate
-grat·ed, -grat·ing,
-gra·tion
im·mi·nence
im·mi·nent
(impending; cf.
*eminent,
immanent*)
im·mo·bile
im·mo·bi·lize
-li·za·tion, -liz·er
im·mod·er·ate
-ate·ly, -ate·ness,
-a·tion
im·mod·est
im·mo·late
-lat·ed, -lat·ing
im·mor·al
im·mo·ral·i·ty
im·mor·tal
im·mor·tal·i·ty
im·mor·tal·ize
-ized, -iz·ing
im·mov·able
im·mune
im·mu·ni·ty
-ties
im·mu·nize
-nized, -niz·ing,
-ni·za·tion
im·mu·nol·o·gy
im·mu·ta·ble
-ble·ness, -bil·i·ty
im·pact

im·pair
-pair·er,
-pair·ment
im·pal·pa·ble
im·pan·el
im·part
im·par·tial
-tial·i·ty, -tial·ly
im·par·ti·ble
im·pass·able
(cannot be passed;
cf. *impassible*)
im·passe
im·pas·si·ble (inca-
pable of pain; cf.
impassable)
im·pas·sion
-sioned, -sion·ing
im·pas·sive
im·pa·tience
im·pa·tient
im·peach
-peach·able,
-peach·ment
im·pec·ca·ble
-bly, -bil·i·ty
im·pede
-ped·ed, -ped·ing,
-ped·er
im·ped·i·ment
im·pel
-pelled, -pel·ling
im·pend
im·pen·e·tra·bil·i·ty

im·pen·e·tra·ble
im·per·a·tive
-tive·ly, -tive·ness
im·per·cep·ti·ble
im·per·fect
-fect·ly, -fect·ness
im·per·fec·tion
im·pe·ri·al
-al·ly
im·pe·ri·al·ism
-al·ist, -al·is·tic
im·per·il
-iled, -il·ing,
-il·ment
im·pe·ri·ous
im·per·ish·able
im·per·ma·nence
im·per·me·able
im·per·son·al
im·per·son·ate
-at·ed, -at·ing,
-ator
im·per·ti·nence
im·per·ti·nen·cy
-cies
im·per·ti·nent
im·per·turb·able
-ably, -abil·i·ty
im·per·vi·ous
im·pe·ti·go
im·pet·u·os·i·ty
-ties
im·pet·u·ous
im·pe·tus

im·pi·ety
  -eties
im·pinge
  -pinged,
  -ping·ing,
  -pinge·ment
im·pi·ous
imp·ish
im·pla·ca·ble
im·plant
im·plau·si·ble
  -bil·i·ty
im·ple·ment
  -men·ta·tion
im·pli·cate
  -cat·ed, -cat·ing
im·pli·ca·tion
im·plic·it
im·plode
im·plore
  -plored,
  -plor·ing,
  -plor·ing·ly
im·plo·sion
im·ply
  -plied, -ply·ing
im·po·lite
im·pol·i·tic
im·pon·der·a·ble
im·port
  -port·er
im·por·tance
im·por·tant

im·por·ta·tion
im·por·tu·nate
im·por·tune
  -tuned, -tun·ing
im·por·tu·ni·ty
  -ties
im·pose
  -posed, -pos·ing,
  -pos·er
im·po·si·tion
im·pos·si·bil·i·ty
im·pos·si·ble
im·pos·tor
  (pretender; cf.
  imposture)
im·pos·ture (fraud;
  cf. *impostor*)
im·po·tence
im·po·tent
im·pound
im·pov·er·ish
im·prac·ti·ca·ble
  -bly, -bil·i·ty
im·prac·ti·cal
im·preg·na·ble
im·preg·nate
  -nat·ed, -nat·ing
im·pre·sa·rio
  -ri·os
im·press (influence;
  cf. *empress*)
im·press·ible
im·pres·sion

im·pres·sion·able
im·pres·sive
im·pri·mis
im·print
im·pris·on
  -on·ment
im·prob·a·ble
im·promp·tu
im·prop·er
im·pro·pri·ety
  -eties
im·prov·able
im·prove
  -proved,
  -prov·ing
im·prove·ment
im·prov·i·dence
im·prov·i·dent
im·pro·vi·sa·tion
im·pro·vise
  -vised, -vis·ing,
  -vis·er
im·pru·dence
im·pru·dent
im·pu·dence
im·pu·dent
im·pugn
im·pulse
im·pul·sion
im·pul·sive
im·pu·ni·ty
im·pure

im·pu·ri·ty
-ties
im·pu·ta·tion
im·pute
-put·ed, -put·ing,
-put·able
in·abil·i·ty
in·ac·ces·si·ble
-bly, -bil·i·ty
in·ac·cu·ra·cy
-cies
in·ac·cu·rate
in·ac·tion
in·ac·tive
-tive·ly, -tiv·i·ty
in·ad·e·qua·cy
-cies
in·ad·e·quate
in·ad·mis·si·ble
in·ad·ver·tence
in·ad·ver·tent
in·ad·vis·able
in·alien·able
in·al·ter·able
inane
inane·ly,
inane·ness
in·an·i·mate
in·ap·peas·able
in·ap·pli·ca·ble
in·ap·po·site
in·ap·pre·cia·ble
in·ap·pre·cia·tive

in·ap·pro·pri·ate
in·apt
in·ar·tic·u·late
in·ar·tis·tic
in·as·much as
in·at·ten·tion
in·at·ten·tive
in·au·di·ble
in·au·gu·ral
in·au·gu·rate
-rat·ed, -rat·ing
in·au·gu·ra·tion
in·aus·pi·cious
in·born
in·bound
in·bred
in·cal·cu·la·ble
in·can·desce
-desced, -desc·ing
in·can·des·cence
in·can·des·cent
in·can·ta·tion
in·ca·pa·ble
-bly, -bil·i·ty
in·ca·pac·i·tate
-tat·ed, -tat·ing
in·ca·pac·i·ty
-ties
in·car·cer·ate
-at·ed, -at·ing,
-a·tion
in·car·nate
in·car·na·tion

in·cen·di·ary
-ar·ies
in·cense
-censed, -cens·ing
in·cen·tive
in·cep·tion
in·ces·sant
in·cest
in·ces·tu·ous
in·cho·ate
inch·worm
in·ci·dence
in·ci·dent
in·ci·den·tal
in·ci·den·tal·ly
in·cin·er·ate
-at·ed, -at·ing,
-a·tion
in·cin·er·a·tor
in·cip·i·ent
in·cise
-cised, -cis·ing
in·ci·sion
in·ci·sive
-sive·ly,
-sive·ness
in·ci·sor
in·ci·ta·tion
in·cite (stir up; cf.
insight)
-cit·ed, -cit·ing,
-cite·ment
in·clem·en·cy

in·clem·ent
in·cli·na·tion
in·cline
  -clined, -clin·ing
in·clude
in·clud·ed
  -clud·ing
in·clu·sion
in·clu·sive
in·cog·ni·to
in·co·her·ence
in·co·her·ent
in·com·bus·ti·ble
in·come
in·com·ing
in·com·men·su·rate
in·com·mu·ni·ca·ble
in·com·pa·ra·ble
in·com·pat·i·bil·i·ty
  -ties
in·com·pat·i·ble
in·com·pe·tence
in·com·pe·tent
in·com·plete
in·com·pre·hen·si·ble
in·com·press·ible
in·con·ceiv·able
in·con·clu·sive
in·con·gru·i·ty
  -ities
in·con·gru·ous
in·con·se·quent
in·con·se·quen·tial
in·con·sid·er·able

in·con·sid·er·ate
in·con·sis·ten·cy
in·con·sis·tent
in·con·sol·able
in·con·spic·u·ous
in·con·stant
in·con·test·able
in·con·ti·nence
in·con·tro·vert·ible
in·con·ve·nience
in·con·ve·nient
in·con·vert·ible
in·cor·po·rate
  -rat·ing, -ra·tion
in·cor·po·rat·ed
in·cor·po·re·al
in·cor·rect
in·cor·ri·gi·ble
  -ble·ness, -bly,
  -bil·i·ty
in·cor·rupt
in·cor·rupt·ible
in·co·terms
in·crease
  -creased,
  -creas·ing,
  -creas·able
in·creas·ing·ly
in·cred·i·ble (unbe-
  lievable; cf.
  incredulous)
  -i·ble·ness, -i·bly,
  -ibil·i·ty
in·cre·du·li·ty

in·cred·u·lous
  (unbelieving; cf.
  incredible)
in·cre·ment
  -men·tal,
  -men·tal·ly
in·crim·i·nate
  -nat·ed, -nat·ing
in·cu·bate
  -bat·ed, -bat·ing
in·cu·ba·tion
in·cul·cate
in·cum·ben·cy
  -cies
in·cum·bent
in·cur
  -curred, -cur·ring
in·cur·able
in·cur·sion
in·cur·vate
  -vat·ed, -vat·ing,
  -va·ture
in·debt·ed·ness
in·de·cen·cy
in·de·cent
in·de·ci·pher·able
in·de·ci·sion
in·de·ci·sive
in·de·co·rum
in·deed
in·de·fat·i·ga·ble
in·de·fen·si·ble
in·de·fin·able
in·def·i·nite

in·del·i·ble
in·del·i·ca·cy
in·del·i·cate
in·dem·ni·fi·ca·tion
in·dem·ni·fy
  -fied, -fy·ing, -fi·er
in·dem·ni·ty
  -ties
in·dent
in·den·ta·tion
in·den·tion
in·den·ture
  -tured, -tur·ing
in·de·pen·dence
in·de·pen·dent
in·de·scrib·able
in·de·struc·ti·ble
in·de·ter·min·able
in·de·ter·mi·nate
  -nate·ly,
  -nate·ness,
  -na·tion
in·dex
  in·dex·es or
  in·di·ces (pl),
  in·dex·er
in·dex·ing
In·dia
in·dia ink
In·di·an
In·di·an·ap·o·lis
in·di·cate
  -cat·ed, -cat·ing

in·di·ca·tion
in·dic·a·tive
in·di·ca·tor
in·dict (charge with
  a crime; cf. *indite*)
in·dict·able
in·dict·ment
in·dif·fer·ence
in·dif·fer·ent
in·di·gence
in·dig·e·nous
  (native to; cf.
  indigent)
in·di·gent (poor; cf.
  indigenous)
in·di·gest·ible
in·di·ges·tion
in·dig·nant
in·dig·na·tion
in·dig·ni·ty
  -ties
in·di·go
  -gos
in·di·rect
  -rect·ly, -rect·ness
in·di·rec·tion
in·dis·cern·ible
in·dis·creet (using
  poor judgment;
  cf. *indiscrete*)
in·dis·crete (not
  separate; cf.
  indiscreet)

in·dis·cre·tion
in·dis·crim·i·nate
in·dis·crim·i·na·tion
in·dis·pens·able
in·dis·posed
in·dis·po·si·tion
in·dis·put·able
in·dis·sol·u·ble
in·dis·tinct
in·dis·tin·guish·able
in·dite (write; cf.
  indict)
  -dit·ed, -dit·ing
in·di·vid·u·al
in·di·vid·u·al·ism
in·di·vid·u·al·ist
in·di·vid·u·al·i·ty
  -ties
in·di·vid·u·al·ize
  -ized, -iz·ing,
  -iza·tion
in·di·vis·i·ble
In·do·chi·na
In·do-Chi·nese
in·doc·tri·nate
  -nat·ed, -nat·ing
  -na·tion
in·do·lence
in·do·lent
in·dom·i·ta·ble
In·do·ne·sia
in·door
in·drawn

in·du·bi·ta·ble
in·duce
   -duced, -duc·ing,
   -duc·ible
in·duce·ment
in·duct
in·duct·ee
in·duc·tion
in·duc·tive
in·duc·tor
in·dulge
   -dulged,
   -dulg·ing,
   -dulg·er
in·dul·gence
   -genced,
   -genc·ing
in·dul·gent
in·du·rate
in·dus·tri·al
in·dus·tri·al·ism
in·dus·tri·al·ist
in·dus·tri·al·ize
   -ized, -iz·ing,
   -iza·tion
in·dus·tri·ous
in·dus·try
ine·bri·ate
   -at·ed, -at·ing,
   -a·tion
in·ebri·ety
in·ed·i·ble
in·ef·fa·ble

in·ef·fec·tive
in·ef·fec·tu·al
in·ef·fi·ca·cious
in·ef·fi·ca·cy
in·ef·fi·cien·cy
   -cies
in·ef·fi·cient
in·el·e·gance
in·el·e·gant
in·el·i·gi·ble (not
   qualified; cf.
   eligible, illegible)
   -bil·i·ty
in·el·o·quent
in·ept
   -ep·ti·tude, -ept·ly,
   -ept·ness
in·equal·i·ty
in·eq·ui·ta·ble
in·eq·ui·ty (unfair-
   ness; cf. *iniquity*)
in·erad·i·ca·ble
in·ert
in·er·tia
in·es·cap·able
   -ably
in·es·sen·tial
in·es·ti·ma·ble
in·ev·i·ta·ble
   -ble·ness, -bly,
   -bil·i·ty
in·ex·act
   -ac·ti·tude, -act·ly,
   -act·ness

in·ex·cus·able
in·ex·haust·ible
   -ible·ness, -ibly,
   -ibil·i·ty
in·ex·o·ra·ble
in·ex·pe·di·ent
in·ex·pen·sive
in·ex·pe·ri·ence
in·ex·pert
in·ex·pi·a·ble
in·ex·plain·able
in·ex·pli·ca·ble
in·ex·plic·it
in·ex·press·ible
in·ex·pres·sive
in·ex·tin·guish·able
in·ex·tri·ca·ble
in·fal·li·ble
   -bly, -bil·i·ty
in·fa·mous
in·fa·my
   -mies
in·fan·cy
   -cies
in·fant
in·fan·tile
in·fan·try
   -tries
in·fat·u·ate
   -at·ed, -at·ing,
   -a·tion
in·fect
in·fec·tion

in·fec·tious
in·fec·tive
in·fe·lic·i·ty
  -ties
in·fer
  -ferred, -fer·ring,
  -fer·able
in·fer·ence
in·fer·en·tial
in·fe·ri·or
  -or·i·ty
in·fer·nal
in·fer·no
  -nos
in·fest
  -fes·ta·tion
in·fi·del
in·fi·del·i·ty
  -ties
in·field
in·fil·trate
  -trat·ed, -trat·ing,
  -tra·tion
in·fi·nite
in·fin·i·tes·i·mal
in·fin·i·tive
in·fin·i·ty
  -ties
in·firm
in·fir·ma·ry
  -ries
in·fir·mi·ty
  -ties

in·flame
  -flamed, -flam·ing
in·flam·ma·ble
in·flam·ma·tion
in·flam·ma·to·ry
in·flate
  -flat·ed, -flat·ing
in·fla·tion
in·fla·tion·ary
in·flect
in·flec·tion
in·flex·i·ble
in·flict
in·flic·tion
in·flow
in·flu·ence
  -enced, -enc·ing
in·flu·en·tial
in·flu·en·za
in·flux
in·fo·bot
in·fo·mer·cial
in·fo·pre·neur
in·form
in·for·mal
  -mal·i·ty, -mal·ly
in·for·mant
in·for·ma·tion
in·for·ma·tion
  su·per·high·way
in·for·ma·tive
in·form·er
in·fo·tain·ment

in·fract
  -frac·tion
in·fra·red
in·fra·struc·ture
in·fre·quent
in·fringe
  -fringed,
  -fring·ing
in·fringe·ment
in·fu·ri·ate
  -at·ed, -at·ing
in·fuse
  -fused, -fus·ing
in·fu·sion
in·ge·nious
  (inventive; cf.
  ingenuous)
in·ge·nue
in·ge·nu·i·ty
  -ties
in·gen·u·ous (can-
  did; cf. *ingenious*)
in·glo·ri·ous
in·got
in·grained
in·grate
in·gra·ti·ate
  -at·ed, -at·ing,
  -a·tion
in·grat·i·tude
in·gre·di·ent
in·gress
in·grown

in·hab·it
in·hab·it·ant
in·hale
  -haled, -hal·ing
in·hal·er
in·har·mo·ni·ous
in·her·ence
in·her·ent
in·her·it
in·her·i·tance
in·hib·it
in·hi·bi·tion
in·hib·i·tor
in·hos·pi·ta·ble
in·house
in·hu·man (lacking kindness; cf. *inhumane*)
in·hu·mane (not considerate; cf. *inhuman*)
in·hu·man·i·ty
  -ties
in·im·i·cal
in·im·i·ta·ble
in·iq·ui·tous
in·iq·ui·ty (wickedness; cf. *inequity*)
  -ties
ini·tial
  -tialed, -tial·ing,
  -tial·ly

ini·tial·ize
  -ized,
  -iz·ing
ini·ti·ate (v)
  -at·ed, -at·ing,
  -a·tor
ini·ti·a·tion
ini·tia·tive
in·ject
in·jec·tion
in·ju·di·cious
in·junc·tion
in·jure
  -jured, -jur·ing
in·ju·ri·ous
in·ju·ry
  -ries
in·jus·tice
ink-jet
in·kling
in·laid
in·land
in·lay
in·let
in-line skates
in lo·co pa·ren·tis
in·mate
in·most
in·nate
in·ner
in·ning
in·no·cence
in·no·cent

in·noc·u·ous
in·no·vate
  -vat·ed, -vat·ing,
  -va·tor
in·no·va·tion
in·no·va·tive
in·nu·en·do
  -dos
in·nu·mer·a·ble
in·oc·u·late
  -lat·ed, -lat·ing
in·oc·u·la·tion
in·of·fen·sive
in·op·er·a·ble
in·op·por·tune
in·or·di·nate
in·or·gan·ic
in·put
  -put·ted, -put·ting
in·quest
in·quire
  -quired, -quir·ing
in·qui·ry
  -ries
in·qui·si·tion
in·quis·i·tive
in·quis·i·tor
in·road
ins and outs
in·sane
in·san·i·tary
in·san·i·ty
  -ties

in·sa·tia·ble
in·scribe
in·scrip·tion
in·scru·ta·ble
in·sect
in·sec·ti·cide
in·se·cure
  -cur·i·ty
in·sen·sate
in·sen·si·ble
in·sen·si·tive
in·sep·a·ra·ble
in·sert
in·ser·tion
in·ser·vice (adj)
in·side
in·sid·i·ous
in·sight (under-
  standing; cf.
  incite)
in·sig·nia
in·sig·nif·i·cance
in·sig·nif·i·cant
in·sin·cere
in·sin·u·ate
  -at·ed, -at·ing
in·sin·u·a·tion
in·sist
in·sis·tence
in·sis·tent
in·so·far
in·sole
in·so·lence

in·so·lent
in·sol·u·ble
in·sol·vent
  -ven·cy
in·som·nia
in·spect
in·spec·tion
in·spec·tor
in·spi·ra·tion
in·spire
  -spired, -spir·ing,
  -spir·er
in·sta·bil·i·ty
in·stall
  -stalled, -stall·ing,
  -stall·er
in·stal·la·tion
in·stall·ment
in·stance
  -stanced,
  -stanc·ing
in·stan·ta·neous
in·stant·ly
in·stead
in·step
in·sti·gate
  -gat·ed, -gat·ing,
  -ga·tor
in·still
  -stilled, -still·ing
in·stinct
in·stinc·tive

in·sti·tute
  -tut·ed, -tut·ing
in·sti·tu·tion
  -tion·al, -tion·al·ly
in·struct
in·struc·tion
  -tion·al
in·struc·tive
in·struc·tor
in·stru·ment
in·stru·men·tal
in·stru·men·tal·i·ty
in·stru·men·ta·tion
in·sub·or·di·nate
  -nate·ly, -na·tion
in·suf·fer·able
in·suf·fi·cient
in·su·lar
in·su·late
  -lat·ed, -lat·ing
in·su·la·tion
in·su·la·tor
in·su·lin
in·sult
in·su·per·a·ble
in·sup·port·able
in·sup·press·ible
in·sur·able
  -abil·i·ty
in·sur·ance
in·sure
  -sured, -sur·ing
in·sur·er

in·sur·gent
in·sur·rec·tion
in·tact
in·take
in·tan·gi·ble
in·te·ger
in·te·gral
in·te·grate
 -grat·ed, -grat·ing
in·te·grat·ed
 ser·vic·es dig·i·tal
 net·work (ISDN)
in·te·gra·tion
in·te·gra·tor
in·teg·ri·ty
in·tel·lect
in·tel·lec·tu·al
 -al·i·ty, -al·ly,
 -al·ness
in·tel·li·gence
in·tel·li·gent
in·tel·li·gi·ble
 -ble·ness, -bly,
 -bil·i·ty
in·tem·per·ance
in·tem·per·ate
 -ate·ly, -ate·ness
in·tend
in·tend·ing
in·tense
 -tense·ly,
 -tense·ness

in·ten·si·fy
 -fied, -fy·ing,
 -fi·ca·tion
in·ten·si·ty
 -ties
in·ten·sive
 -sive·ly, -sive·ness
in·tent
 -tent·ness
in·ten·tion
in·ten·tion·al
 -al·i·ty, -al·ly
in·ter
 -terred, -ter·ring
in·ter·ac·tion
in·ter·ac·tive
in·ter·cede
 -ced·ed, -ced·ing
in·ter·cept
in·ter·cep·tor
in·ter·ces·sion
in·ter·change
in·ter·change·able
 -able·ness, -ably
in·ter·col·le·giate
in·ter·com
in·ter·com·mu·ni·ca·tion
in·ter·con·nect
 -nec·tion
in·ter·course
in·ter·de·nom·i·na·tion·al
in·ter·de·part·men·tal
 -tal·ly

in·ter·de·pen·dent
in·ter·dict
 -dic·tion, -dic·tive,
 -dic·to·ry
in·ter·dis·ci·plin·ary
in·ter·est
in·ter·face
in·ter·fere
 -fered, -fer·ing
in·ter·fer·ence
in·ter·ga·lac·tic
in·ter·im
in·te·ri·or
in·ter·ject
 -jec·tor, -jec·to·ry
in·ter·jec·tion
in·ter·lock
in·ter·loc·u·tor
in·ter·lope
 -lop·er
in·ter·lude
in·ter·mar·riage
in·ter·me·di·ary
 -ar·ies
in·ter·me·di·ate
 -ate·ly, -ate·ness
in·ter·ment
in·ter·mi·na·ble
 -ble·ness, -bly
in·ter·min·gle
in·ter·mis·sion
in·ter·mit
 -mit·ted, -mit·ting

in·ter·mit·tent
in·tern
  -tern·ship
in·ter·nal
in·ter·na·tion·al
in·ter·na·tion·al·ize
  -iza·tion
In·ter·net
in·ter·nist
in·ter·per·son·al
in·ter·po·late
  (insert; cf.
  interpret)
  -lat·ed, -lat·ing
in·ter·pose
  -posed, -pos·ing
in·ter·pret (trans-
  late; cf.
  interpolate)
in·ter·pre·ta·tion
in·ter·pret·er
in·ter·ra·cial
  -cial·ly
in·ter·re·late
  -la·tion,
  -la·tion·ship
in·ter·ro·gate
  -gat·ed, -gat·ing,
  -ga·tion
in·ter·rog·a·tive
  -tive·ly
in·ter·rupt
  -rup·tion,
  -rup·tive

in·ter·sect
in·ter·sec·tion
in·ter·sperse
  -spersed,
  -spers·ing,
  -sper·sion
in·ter·state
  (between states;
  cf. *intrastate*)
in·ter·twine
in·ter·ur·ban
in·ter·val
in·ter·vene
  -vened, -ven·ing,
  -ven·tion
in·ter·view
  -view·er
in·tes·ti·nal
  -nal·ly
in·tes·tine
in·ti·fa·da
in·ti·ma·cy
in·ti·mate
  -mat·ed, -mat·ing,
  -mate·ly
in·ti·ma·tion
in·tim·i·date
  -dat·ed, -dat·ing,
  -da·tion
in·tol·er·a·ble
  -a·bly, -a·bil·i·ty
in·tol·er·ance
in·tol·er·ant

in·to·na·tion
in·tone
  -toned, -ton·ing
in·tox·i·cant
in·tox·i·cate
  -cat·ed, -cat·ing
in·tra·mu·ral
in·tra·net
in·tran·si·gent
in·tran·si·tive
  -tive·ly
in·tra·pre·neur
in·tra·state (within
  the state; cf.
  interstate)
in·trep·id
  -trep·id·ly,
  -trep·id·ness
in·tri·ca·cy
in·tri·cate
  -cate·ly,
  -cate·ness
in·trigue
  -trigued,
  -trigu·ing
in·trin·sic
  -si·cal·ly
in·tro·duce
  -duced, -duc·ing,
  -duc·er
in·tro·duc·tion
in·tro·duc·to·ry

in·tro·spect
  -spec·tive·ly,
  -spec·tive·ness
in·tro·vert
in·trude
  -trud·ed, -trud·ing,
  -trud·er
in·tru·sion
in·tu·ition
in·tu·i·tive
  -tive·ly, -tive·ness
in·un·date
  -dat·ed, -dat·ing,
  -da·tion
in·ure
  -ured, -ur·ing
in·vade
  -vad·ed, -vad·ing,
  -vad·er
in·val·id (adj)
in·va·lid (n)
in·val·i·date
  -da·tion, -da·tor
in·val·id·i·ty
  -ties
in·valu·able
  -ably
in·vari·able
  -ably, -abil·i·ty
in·va·sion
in·va·sive

in·vent
  -ven·tor,
  -ven·tress
in·ven·tion
in·ven·tive
  -tive·ness
in·ven·to·ry
in·ven·to·ries
in·verse
  -verse·ly
in·ver·sion
in·vert
in·ver·te·brate
in·vest
in·ves·ti·gate
  -ga·tion,
  -ga·tion·al, -ga·tor
in·ves·ti·ture
in·vest·ment
in·vig·o·rate
  -rat·ed, -rat·ing,
  -ra·tion
in·vin·ci·ble
  -ble·ness, -bly,
  -bil·i·ty
in·vis·i·ble
  -ble·ness, -bly,
  -bil·i·ty
in·vi·ta·tion
in·vite
  -vit·ed, -vit·ing
in vi·tro
in·vo·ca·tion

in·voice
  -voiced, -voic·ing
in·voke
  -voked, -vok·ing
in·vol·un·tary
  -tari·ly, -tari·ness
in·volve
  -volve·ment
in·vul·ner·a·ble
  -bly, -bil·i·ty
in·ward
in-your-face
io·dine
ion·o·sphere
io·ta
ip·so fac·to
Iran
Ira·ni·an
Iraq
Iraqi
iras·ci·ble (quick to
  anger; cf. *erasable*)
  -ble·ness, -bly,
  -bil·i·ty
irate
  irate·ly, irate·ness
Ire·land
ir·i·des·cence
ir·i·des·cent
iron·clad
iron·ic
  iron·i·cal·ly
iron·ing

iro·ny
  -nies
ir·ra·di·ate
  -at·ed, -at·ing
ir·ra·tio·nal
  -nal·ly
ir·rec·on·cil·able
  -ably, -abil·i·ty
ir·re·duc·ible
ir·re·fut·able
  -ably, -abil·i·ty
ir·reg·u·lar
  -lar·ly
ir·rel·e·vance
ir·rel·e·vant
ir·re·li·gious
ir·rep·a·ra·ble
  -bly
ir·re·press·ible
  -ibly, -ibil·i·ty
ir·re·proach·able
  -ably, -abil·i·ty
ir·re·sist·ible
  -ible·ness, -ibly
ir·re·spec·tive
ir·re·spon·si·ble
  -ble·ness, -bly
ir·re·triev·able
  -ably, -abil·i·ty
ir·rev·er·ent
ir·re·vers·ible
  -ibly, -ibil·i·ty

ir·re·vo·ca·ble
  -bly
ir·ri·gate
  -gat·ed, -gat·ing,
  -ga·tion
ir·ri·ta·bil·i·ty
ir·ri·ta·ble
  -ble·ness, -bly
ir·ri·tant
ir·ri·tate
  -tat·ed, -tat·ing,
  -tat·ing·ly
ir·ri·ta·tion
ir·rupt (break in; cf.
  erupt)
  -rup·tion
isin·glass
Is·lam
  -lam·ic
is·land
isle (small island; cf.
  aisle)
iso·bar
iso·late
  -lat·ed, -lat·ing
iso·la·tion·ism
  -ist
iso·met·rics
isos·ce·les
iso·therm
iso·tope
Is·ra·el
Is·rae·li

is·sue
  -sued, -su·ing
isth·mus
Ital·ian
ital·ic
ital·i·cize
  -cized, -ciz·ing
It·a·ly
item
item·iza·tion
item·ize
  -ized, -iz·ing
itin·er·ant
itin·er·ary
  -ar·ies
itin·er·ate
its (possessive)
it's (it is or it has)
it·self
ivo·ry
  -ries
ivy
  ivies

jack·et
jack·ham·mer
jack-in-the-box
jack-in-the-pul·pit
   -pits
jack·knife
jack-of-all-trades
jack-o'-lan·tern
jack·pot
jack·rab·bit
Ja·cuz·zi
jag·uar
jai alai
jail·break
Ja·kar·ta
ja·la·pe·no
ja·lopy
   -lop·ies
jam (food; cf. *jamb*)
   jammed,
   jam·ming
Ja·mai·ca
jamb (of a door; cf.
   jam)
jam·bo·ree
jan·i·tor
   -to·rial
Jan·u·ary
ja·pan (varnish)

Ja·pan (country)
Jap·a·nese
   Jap·a·nese (pl)
jar
jar·gon
jas·mine
jaun·dice
jav·e·lin
jaw·bone
jaw·break·er
jazz·er·cize
jeal·ous
   -ous·ness
jeal·ou·sy
Jef·fer·son
Je·ho·vah
jel·ly
   jel·lies, jel·lied,
   jel·lying
jel·ly·fish
jeop·ar·dize
   -dized, -diz·ing
jeop·ar·dy
Jer·i·cho
jer·ky
   -i·er, -i·est
jer·sey
jest (joke; cf. *gist*)
Je·su·it

jet
   jet·ted, jet·ting
jet·ti·son
jet·ty
   -ties
jew·el
   -eled, -el·ing
jew·el·er
jew·el·ry
jib (sail; cf. *gibe,
   jibe*)
jibe (agree; cf. *gibe,
   jib*)
jig·gle
   -gled, -gling
jig·saw
jinx
jit·ter·bug
job
   jobbed, job·bing
job·ber
job·less
   -less·ness
job lot
jock·ey
   -eys, -eyed,
   -ey·ing
joc·u·lar
   -lar·i·ty

158

Jodh·pur
jog
    jogged, jog·ging
join·der
join·er
joint
    joint·ed·ly
join·ture
joke
    joked, jok·ing,
    jok·ing·ly
jok·er
jol·ly
    -li·er, -li·est
jon·quil
Jor·dan
josh
jos·tle
jour·nal
jour·nal·ism
jour·nal·ist
jour·nal·is·tic
    -ti·cal·ly
jour·nal·ize
    -ized, -iz·ing
jour·ney
    -neys, -neyed,
    -ney·ing
jo·vial
jowl
joy·ful
    -ful·ly, -ful·ness
joy·ous
    -ous·ness

joy·stick
ju·bi·lant
ju·bi·la·tion
ju·bi·lee
Ju·da·ism
Ju·dea
Ju·de·an
judge
    judged, judg·ing
judg·ment
    -men·tal,
    -men·tal·ly
ju·di·cial (of a
    judge; cf.
    judicious)
ju·di·cia·ry
ju·di·cious (of a
    judgment; cf.
    judicial)
ju·do
jug·ger·naut
jug·gle
    -gled, -gling
jug·u·lar
juice
    juiced, juic·ing
ju·lep
Jul·ian cal·en·dar
ju·li·enne
Ju·ly
jum·ble
    -bled, -bling
jum·bo
    -bos

jump·er
jump·ing jack
jump seat
junc·tion (joining;
    cf. *juncture*)
junc·ture (crisis; cf.
    junction)
June
Ju·neau
jun·gle
ju·nior
ju·ni·per
jun·ket
junk·ie
    -ies
jun·ta
ju·ris·dic·tion
ju·ris·pru·dence
ju·rist
ju·ror
ju·ry
    -ries
jus·tice
jus·ti·fi·able
    -ably
jus·ti·fi·ca·tion
jus·ti·fi·er
jus·ti·fy
    -fied, -fy·ing, -fi·er
ju·ve·nile
jux·ta·pose
    -posed, -pos·ing

kaf·fee·klatsch
kai·ser
ka·lei·do·scope
ka·mi·ka·ze
kan·ga·roo
kar·a·o·ke
kar·at or car·at
(weight; cf. *caret,*
carrot)
ka·ra·te
Kash·mir
kay·ak
Ka·zakh·stan
keen
keen·ness,
keen·er
keep
kept, keep·ing
keep·sake
ken·nel
kelp
Ken·ya
kern
ker·nel (seed; cf.
colonel)
ker·o·sene
ketch·up (tomato
sauce; var. of
catsup)

key (to a door; cf.
quay)
keyed, key·less
key·board
key·hole
key·note
key·stroke
key word
kha·ki
kick·back
kick off (v)
kick·off (n)
kick·stand
kid
kid·ded, kid·ding,
kid·ding·ly
kid·nap
-napped,
-nap·ping,
-nap·per
kid·ney
-neys
kill (slay; cf. *kiln*)
kill·er
kill·ing
kill·joy
kiln (oven; cf. *kill*)
ki·lo·byte

kilo·cy·cle
ki·lo·gram
ki·lo·me·ter
kilo·watt
ki·mo·no
-nos
kin·der·gar·ten
kind·heart·ed
kin·dle
-dled, -dling
kind·li·ness
kin·dling
kind·ly
kind·ness
kin·dred
ki·ne·sics
kin·es·the·sia
-thet·ic,
-thet·i·cal·ly
ki·net·ic
king·dom
king·fish
king·ly
king-size
kins·folk
kin·ship
ki·osk
kitch·en

kitch·en·ette
kitch·en·ware
kit·ten
ki·wi·fruit
kluge
klutz
knack
knap·sack
knave (rogue; cf. *nave)*
knav·ery
knead (dough; cf. *need)*
knee·cap
knee-deep
knee-high
knew (did know; cf. *gnu, new)*
knick·knack
knife
   knives (pl)
knight (title; cf. *night)*
knight·hood
knit
   knit·ted, knit·ting, knit·ter
knock down (v)
knock·down (n,adj)
knock out (v)
knock·out (n)
knock·wurst

knot (tied; cf. *not)*
   knot·ted,
   knot·ting
knot·hole
know
   knew, known,
   know·ing
know·bot
know-how (n)
know-it-all
knowl·edge
knowl·edge·able
   -able·ness, -ably
knuck·le
   knuck·led,
   knuck·ling
Ko·rea
ko·sher
kryp·ton
ku·dos
kud·zu
kum·quat
Ku·wait

la·bel
-beled, -bel·ing
la·bor
-bored, -bor·ing
lab·o·ra·to·ry (sci-
ence; cf. *lavatory*)
-ries
la·bor·er
la·bo·ri·ous
lab·y·rinth
lace
laced, lac·ing
lac·er·ate
-at·ed, -at·ing
lac·er·a·tion
lack·a·dai·si·cal
la·con·ic
-con·i·cal·ly
lac·quer
-quered, -quer·ing
la·crosse
lac·tate
-tat·ed, -tat·ing,
-ta·tion
lac·tose
lad·der
lad·ing
lad·le

la·dy
-dies
la·dy·bug
la·dy·like
lag
lagged, lag·ging
la·goon
laid-back (adj)
lain (rested; cf. *lane*)
lais·sez-faire
la·ity
La·maze
lamb·skin
lame (weak; cf.
lamé)
lam·er, lam·est,
lame·ness
la·mé (brocaded fab-
ric; cf. *lame*)
la·ment
la·men·ta·ble
-bly
lam·en·ta·tion
lam·i·nate
-nat·ed, -nat·ing
lam·poon
lamp·post
lam·prey
land·fill

land·ing craft
land·la·dy
land·locked
land·lord
land·mark
land·own·er
land·scape
-scaped, -scap·ing,
-scap·er
land·slide
lane (path; cf. *lain*)
lan·guage
lan·guid
-guid·ness
lan·guish
lanky
lank·i·er,
lank·i·est,
lank·i·ness
lan·o·lin
Lan·sing
lan·tern
lao·gai
Laos
lap
lapped, lap·ping
lap·dog
la·pel

lap·i·dary
  -dar·ies
lapse (terminate; cf. *elapse*)
  lapsed, laps·ing
lap·top
lar·ce·nous
lar·ce·ny
  -nies
lar·ghet·to
  -tos
lar·i·at
lark·spur
lar·va (sing)
  -vae (pl)
lar·yn·gi·tis
lar·ynx
la·sa·gna
las·civ·i·ous
  -ous·ness
la·ser
la·ser disc
last min·ute
latch·key
latch·string
late
  lat·er (afterward; cf. *latter*), lat·est, late·ness
la·ten·cy
la·tent
lat·er·al
  -al·ly

la·tex
lat·i·tude
lat·te
lat·ter (subsequent; cf. *later*)
lat·tice
lat·tice·work
Lat·via
laud·able
lau·da·to·ry
laugh·able
  -ably
laugh·ing·stock
laugh·ter
launch
laun·der
  -dered, -der·ing
laun·der·ette
Laun·dro·mat
laun·dry
  -dries
lau·re·ate
lau·rel
lav·a·to·ry (for washing; cf. *laboratory*)
lav·en·der
lav·ish
  -ish·ness
law-abid·ing
law·ful
  -ful·ly, -ful·ness

law·less
  -less·ness
law·mak·er
lawn mow·er
law·suit
law·yer
lax·a·tive
lax·ity
lay·away (n)
lay·er
lay·man
lay off (v)
lay·off (n)
lay out (v)
lay·out (n)
lay over (v)
lay·over (n)
lay·per·son
lay up (v)
lay-up (n)
lay·wom·an
lazy
  -zi·er, -zi·est, -zi·ly
lead (v)(guide)
lead (n)(metal; cf. *led*)
lead·en
lead·er
lead-in (n, adj)
lead off (v)
lead·off (n, adj)
lead time
lead up (v)

163

lead·up (n)
leaf
  leaves (pl)
leaf mold
league
leak·age
leak·proof
lean (thin; cf. *lien*)
lean-to
  lean-tos (pl)
leap
  leaped, leap·ing
leap year
learn
  learned, learn·ing,
  learn·er
lease
  leased (past tense
  of *lease*; cf. *least*),
  leas·ing
least (smallest; cf.
  leased)
leath·er
  -ered, -er·ing
leath·er·neck
leave
  leav·ing
leav·en
  -ened, -en·ing
Leb·a·nese
Leb·a·non
lec·tern
lec·tor

lec·ture
  -tured, -tur·ing,
  -tur·er
led (guided; cf. *lead*)
led·ger
lee·ward
lee·way
left-hand·ed
left·over
leg·a·cy
  -cies
le·gal
  -gal·ly
le·gal·ism
le·gal·i·ty
le·gal·ize
  -ized, -iz·ing
leg·end
leg·end·ary
  -en·dari·ly
leg·ging
leg·i·ble
  -bly, -bil·i·ty
le·gion
leg·is·late
  -lat·ed, -lat·ing
leg·is·la·tion
leg·is·la·tive
  -tive·ly
leg·is·la·tor
leg·is·la·ture
le·git·i·ma·cy

le·git·i·mate
  -mate·ly
leg·room
le·gume
leg·work
lei·sure
lei·sure·ly
lem·on·ade
le·mur
length
length·en
  -ened, -en·ing
lengthy
  length·i·er,
  length·i·ly,
  length·i·ness
le·nien·cy
le·nient
Len·in·grad
len·til
leop·ard
le·o·tard
lep·re·chaun
lep·ro·sy
le·sion
les·see
less·en (decrease; cf.
  lesson)
  -ened, -en·ing
less·er
les·son (study; cf.
  lessen)
les·sor

let
  let or let·ted,
    let·ting
le·thal
le·thar·gic
  -gi·cal·ly
leth·ar·gy
let's (let us)
let·tered
let·ter·head
let·ter·per·fect
let·tuce
let up (v)
let·up (n)
leu·ke·mia
lev·ee (embank-
  ment; cf. *levy*)
  -eed, -ee·ing
lev·el
  -eled, -el·ing,
    -el·ness
le·ver·age
le·vi·a·than
lev·i·ta·tion
lev·i·ty
levy (tax; cf. *levee*)
  lev·ies
lex·i·cog·ra·pher
li·a·bil·i·ty
  -ties
li·a·ble (obligated;
  cf. *libel*)
li·ai·son

li·ar
li·ba·tion
li·bel (defame; cf.
  liable)
  -beled, -bel·ing
li·bel·ous
lib·er·al
  -al·ly
lib·er·al·ism
lib·er·al·i·ty
  -ties
lib·er·al·ize
  -ized, -iz·ing,
  -iza·tion
lib·er·ate
  -at·ed, -at·ing,
  -a·tor
lib·er·a·tion
Li·be·ria
lib·er·ty
li·brar·i·an
li·brary
li·bret·to
Lib·ya
li·cense
  -censed, -cens·ing,
  -cens·er
li·cen·tious
  -tious·ness
li·chen
lic·o·rice
lie (untruth; cf. *lye*)
Liech·ten·stein

lien (claim; cf. *lean*)
lieu
lieu·ten·an·cy
lieu·ten·ant
life
  lives (pl)
life·blood
life·boat
life·guard
life jack·et
life·less
  -less·ness
life·long
life·sav·er
life-size
life span
life-style
life·time
lift-off (n)
lig·a·ment
lig·a·ture
light·en
  -ened, -en·ing
  (becoming light;
  cf. *lightning)*
light-fin·gered
light-head·ed
light·heart·ed
light·house
light·ning (electrical
  discharge; cf.
  lightening)
light pen

light·proof
lights-out
light·weight
light-year
lik·able
  -able·ness,
  -abil·i·ty
like·li·hood
like·ly
  like·li·er, like·li·est
like·ness
like·wise
li·lac
Li·ma
limb
lim·ber
  -bered, -ber·ing
lim·bo
  -bos
lime·light
lim·er·ick
lim·it
  -it·less, -it·less·ly,
  -it·less·ness
lim·i·ta·tion
Lim·ou·sin
  (cattle)
lim·ou·sine
lim·pid
lin·age (number of
  lines; cf. *lineage*)
Lin·coln

lin·eage (family; cf.
  linage)
lin·eal (ancestral
  line; cf. *linear*)
lin·ear (of lines; cf.
  lineal)
line·man
lin·en
line print·er
line up (v)
line·up (n)
lin·ger
  -gered, -ger·ing
lin·ge·rie
lin·go
  -goes
lin·guist
lin·i·ment
lin·ing
link·age
links (of chain; cf.
  lynx)
li·no·le·um
Li·no·type
lin·seed
li·on·ess
li·on·heart·ed
lip·o·suc·tion
lip-read
  lip-read·ing
lip·stick
lip-synch
liq·ue·fac·tion

liq·ue·fy
  -fied, -fy·ing,
  -fi·able
li·queur
liq·uid
  -uid·i·ty, -uid·ly
liq·ui·date
  -dat·ed, -dat·ing,
  -da·tion
liq·uid crys·tal
  dis·play (LCD)
li·quor
Lis·bon
lis·ten
  -tened, -ten·ing,
  -ten·er
list·less
list price
List·serv
list·serv·er
li·ter
lit·er·a·cy
lit·er·al
lit·er·al·ly
lit·er·ary
lit·er·ate
lit·er·a·ture
lite·ware
lithe
litho·graph
  -gra·pher
li·thog·ra·phy
Lith·u·a·nia

lit·i·gant
lit·i·gate
  -gated, -gat·ing,
  -ga·tion
lit·ter
lit·ter·bag
lit·tle
  -tler, -tlest
Lit·tle Rock
li·tur·gi·cal
lit·ur·gy
  -gies
liv·able
live
  lived, liv·ing
live-in (adj)
live·li·hood
live·long
live·ly
  live·li·er,
  live·li·est
live·stock
liv·id
liz·ard
lla·ma
load (burden; cf.
  lode)
loan (for temporary
  use; cf. *lone*)
loath·some
lob·by
  -bies, -bied,
  -by·ing

lob·ster
lo·cal (nearby; cf.
  locale)
lo·cal ar·ea
  net·work (LAN)
lo·cale (locality; cf.
  local)
lo·cal·i·ty
  -ties
lo·cal·ize
  -ized, -iz·ing
lo·cate
  -cat·ed, -cat·ing
lo·ca·tion
lock·jaw
lock·nut
lock out (v)
lock·out (n)
lock·smith
lock·step
lock·stitch
lock·up (n)
lo·co·mo·tion
lo·co·mo·tive
lo·cust
lo·cu·tion
lode (ore; cf. *load*)
lodge (n, v)(shelter;
  cf. *loge*)
  lodged, lodg·ing
log
  logged, log·ging
log·a·rithm

loge (theater level;
  cf. *lodge*)
log·ic
log·i·cal
  -cal·ly, -cal·ness
log in (v)
log-in (n)
lo·gis·tic
logo
log on (v)
log-on (n)
loi·ter
lol·li·pop
lone (solitary; cf.
  loan)
lone·li·ness
lone·ly
lone·some
long-dis·tance (adj,
  adv)
lon·gev·i·ty
long·hand
long·horn
lon·gi·tude
lon·gi·tu·di·nal
long-range
long run
long·shore·man
long shot
long-stand·ing
long-suf·fer·ing
long suit
long-term

long-wind·ed
look-alike (n, adj)
look·out (n)
loop
loop·hole
loose (adj, v) (unat-
    tached; cf. *lose,
    loss*)
    loose·ly,
    loose·ness, loosed
loose-leaf
loos·en
    -ened, -en·ing
lop·sid·ed
lo·qua·cious
    -cious·ness
lose (misplace; cf.
    loose, loss)
    lost, los·ing
loss (something lost;
    cf. *loose, lose*)
lo·tion
lot·tery
lot·to
lo·tus
loud·mouthed
loud·speak·er
lounge
lou·ver
lov·able
    -able·ness, -ably
lo·va·stat·in
love·ly
    -li·er, -li·ness

love seat
love·sick
low-down (n)
low·down (adj)
low·er·case
    -cased, -cas·ing
low-key
    low-keyed
low-lev·el
low·ly
    low·li·ness
low-mind·ed
low-pres·sure
low-pro·file
low-ten·sion
lox
loy·al·ty
loz·enge
lu·bri·cant
lu·bri·cate
    -ca·tion
lu·cid
lu·cid·i·ty
lucky
    luck·i·ly
lu·cra·tive
lu·di·crous
lug
    lugged, lug·ging
lug·gage
lu·gu·bri·ous
luke·warm
lul·la·by
    -bies, -bied

lum·ba·go
lum·bar (adj)(nerve;
    cf. *lumber*)
lum·ber (n, v)
    (wood or to move
    heavily; cf.
    lumbar)
    -bered, -ber·ing
lum·ber·yard
lu·mi·nary
    -nar·ies
lu·mi·nous
lu·na·cy
    -cies
lu·nar
lu·na·tic
lun·cheon
lun·cheon·ette
lunch·room
lurch
lure
    lured, lur·ing
lu·rid
lurk
lus·cious
    -cious·ness
lus·ter
    -tered, -ter·ing
lust·ful
    -ful·ly, -ful·ness
lus·trous
lusty
Lux·em·bourg
lux·u·ri·ous

lux·u·ry
  -ries
ly·ce·um
Ly·cra
lye (chemical; cf. *lie*)
ly·ing
lymph
lym·phat·ic
lym·pho·ma
lynch
lynx (animal; cf.
  links)
  lynx (pl)
lyr·ic
lyr·i·cal
lyr·i·cism

ma·ca·bre
mac·ad·am
ma·ca·re·na
mac·a·ro·ni
mac·a·roon
Ma·chi·a·vel·lian
ma·chine
ma·chine-read·able
ma·chin·ery
  -er·ies
ma·chin·ist
ma·chis·mo
mack·er·el
Mack·i·nac
mack·in·tosh (rain-
  coat; cf. *McIntosh*)
mac·ro
  -ros
mac·ro·cosm
mac·ro·eco·nom·ics
ma·cron
Mad·a·gas·car
mad·am
mad·den
  -dened, -den·ing
made (did make; cf.
  maid)
Ma·dei·ra
made-up (adj)

Mad·i·son
mad·ness
mad·ri·gal
mag·a·zine
ma·gen·ta
mag·got
mag·ic
  -i·cal, -i·cal·ly
ma·gi·cian
mag·is·te·ri·al
mag·is·tra·cy
  -cies
mag·is·trate
mag·na cum lau·de
mag·na·nim·i·ty
  -ties
mag·nan·i·mous
mag·nate (rich per-
  son; cf. *magnet*)
mag·ne·sia
mag·ne·sium
mag·net (attracts
  iron; cf. *magnate*)
mag·net·ic
mag·ne·tism
mag·ne·tite
mag·ne·tize
  -tized, -tiz·ing
mag·ni·fi·ca·tion

mag·nif·i·cence
mag·nif·i·cent
  (splendid; cf.
  munificent)
mag·nif·i·co
mag·ni·fi·er
mag·ni·fy
  -fied, -fy·ing
mag·ni·tude
mag·no·lia
mag·num
mag·pie
ma·ha·ra·ja
ma·hat·ma
ma·hog·a·ny
  -nies
maid (girl; cf. *made*)
maid·en
maid·en·ly
maid·en name
mail (letters; cf.
  male)
  mailed, mail·able,
  mail·abil·i·ty
mail·bag
mail bomb
mail·box
mail·er
mail or·der (n)

mail room
main (chief; cf.
  mane)
main·frame
main·land
main·ly
main·sail
main·spring
main·stay
main stem
main·stream
main·tain
main·te·nance
maize (corn; cf.
  maze)
ma·jes·tic
maj·es·ty
  -ties
ma·jor
  -jored, -jor·ing
ma·jor·do·mo
ma·jor·i·ty
  -ties
make-be·lieve
make·shift
make up (v)
make·up (n)
mak·ing
mal·ad·just·ment
mal·ad·min·is·tra·tion
mal·adroit
mal·a·dy
  -dies

mal·aise
mal·a·prop·ism
mal·ap·ro·pos
ma·lar·ia
Ma·lay
Ma·lay·sia
mal·con·tent
male (masculine; cf.
  mail)
male·dic·tion
ma·lev·o·lent
mal·fea·sance
mal·for·ma·tion
mal·formed
mal·func·tion
mal·ice
ma·li·cious
  (harmful)
ma·lign
ma·lig·nan·cy
  -cies
ma·lig·nant
ma·lig·ni·ty
ma·lin·ger
  -gered, -ger·ing
mal·lard
mal·lea·ble
mal·let
mal·nu·tri·tion
mal·odor
mal·odor·ous
mal·po·si·tion
mal·prac·tice

Mal·tese
mal·treat
mam·mal
mam·moth
man·a·cle
  -cled, -cling
man·age
  -aged, -ag·ing
man·age·able
man·age·ment
man·ag·er
  -a·ge·ri·al,
  -a·ge·ri·al·ly
man·a·tee
man·da·mus
man·da·rin
man·da·tary (agent;
  cf. *mandatory*)
  -tar·ies
man·date
  -dat·ed, -dat·ing
man·da·to·ry
  (compelling; cf.
  mandatary)
  -ries
man·di·ble
man·do·lin
mane (hair; cf.
  main)
man-eat·er
ma·nège

ma·neu·ver
  -vered, -ver·ing,
  -ver·er
man·ga·nese
man·ger
man·gle
man·go
  -goes
man·grove
mangy
  mang·i·er,
  mang·i·est
man·han·dle
man·hood
man·hour
man·hunt
ma·nia
ma·ni·ac
ma·ni·a·cal
man·ic
man·i·cot·ti
man·i·cure
  -cured, -cur·ing
man·i·cur·ist
man·i·fest
man·i·fes·ta·tion
man·i·fes·to
  -tos
man·i·fold
man·i·kin
ma·nila
ma·nip·u·late
  -lat·ed, -lat·ing,
  -la·tion

172

man·i·tou
man·kind
man·ly
  -li·er, -li·est,
  -li·ness
man-made
man·na
manned
man·ne·quin
man·ner (mode; cf.
  manor)
man·ner·ism
man·nish
man-of-war
  men-of-war (pl)
ma·nom·e·ter
man·or (estate; cf.
  manner)
man·pow·er (per-
  sonnel available)
man·sion
man·slaugh·ter
man·tel (shelf; cf.
  mantle)
man·tel·piece
man·til·la
man·tle (cloak; cf.
  mantel)
man·u·al
man·u·fac·ture
  -tur·ing, -tured
man·u·fac·tur·er
ma·nure
manu·script

many
many·fold
many-sid·ed
ma·ple
map·ping
mar·a·schi·no
  -nos (pl)
mar·a·thon
ma·raud
ma·raud·er
mar·ble
  -bled, -bling
mar·ble·ize
  -ized, -iz·ing
March
mar·che·sa (fem)
  -che·se (pl)
mar·che·se (masc)
  -che·si (pl)
mar·chio·ness (fem)
Mar·di Gras
mar·ga·rine
mar·ga·ri·ta
mar·gin
mar·gin·al
mar·gi·na·lia
mari·gold
mar·i·jua·na
mar·i·nade
  -nad·ed, -nad·ing
ma·rine
mar·i·ner
mar·i·o·nette

mar·i·tal (marriage;
   cf. *martial*)
mar·i·time
mark down (v)
mark·down (n)
mar·ket
mar·ket·able
mar·ket·ing
mar·ket·place
marks·man
marks·wom·an
mark up (v)
mark·up (n)
mar·ma·lade
mar·mo·set
ma·roon
mar·quee (canopy;
   cf. *marquise*)
mar·que·try
mar·quise (gem
   setting; cf.
   marquee)
mar·riage
mar·row
mar·row·bone
mar·ry
  -ried, -ry·ing
mar·shal (officer; cf.
   martial)
  -shaled, -shal·ing
marsh·mal·low
marshy
  marsh·i·er,
  marsh·i·est

mar·su·pi·al
mar·ten (furbearing
   animal; cf.
   martin)
mar·tial (warlike; cf.
   marital, marshal)
  -tial·ly
mar·tian
mar·tin (bird; cf.
   marten)
mar·tyr
mar·tyr·dom
mar·vel
  -veled, -vel·ing
mar·vel·ous
mas·cot
mas·cu·line
  -line·ly, -lin·i·ty
mas·och·ism
  -och·ist
  -och·is·tic
ma·son
  -soned, -son·ing
Ma·son·ic
Ma·son·ite
ma·son·ry
  -ries
mas·quer·ade
  -ad·ed, -ad·ing
mas·sa·cre
  -sa·cred, -sa·cring
mas·sage
mas·seur (masc)

mas·seuse (fem)
mas·sif
mas·sive
mass media (pl)
  medium (sing)
mass-pro·duce
mas·ter
  -tered, -ter·ing
mas·ter·ful
mas·ter key
mas·ter·mind
mas·ter of
  cer·e·mo·nies
mas·ter·piece
mas·ter plan
mas·ter ser·geant
mas·tery
mast·head
mas·ti·cate
  -cat·ed, -cat·ing
mas·tiff
mast·odon
mat·a·dor
match·book
match·less
match play
ma·te·ri·al
  (substance; cf.
   matériel)
  -al·ly, -al·ness
ma·te·ri·al·ism
  -ist, -is·tic
ma·te·ri·al·i·ty
  -ties

173

ma·te·ri·al·iza·tion
ma·te·ri·al·ize
  -ized, -iz·ing
ma·te·ria med·i·ca
ma·té·ri·el (equip-
  ment; cf.
  material)
ma·ter·nal
ma·ter·ni·ty
  -ties
math·e·mat·i·cal
math·e·ma·ti·cian
math·e·mat·ics
mat·i·nee
ma·tri·arch
ma·tri·ar·chy
  -chies
ma·tri·cide
ma·tric·u·late
  -lat·ed, -lat·ing
mat·ri·mo·nial
mat·ri·mo·ny
ma·trix
  -tri·ces (pl)
ma·tron
ma·tron·ly
mat·ter
mat·ter-of-fact
mat·ting
mat·tock
mat·tress
mat·u·rate
  -rat·ed, -rat·ing

mat·u·ra·tion
ma·ture
  -tured
ma·tu·ri·ty
ma·tu·ti·nal
mat·zo
  mat·zoth (pl)
maud·lin
mau·so·le·um
  -leums
mauve
mav·er·ick
mawk·ish
max·im
max·i·mal
max·i·mize
  -mized, -miz·ing,
  -mi·za·tion
max·i·mum
may·be
May Day (May 1; cf.
  Mayday)
May·day (signal; cf.
  May Day)
may·flow·er
may·hem
may·on·naise
may·or
may·or·al·ty
may·pole
maze (puzzle; cf.
  maize)
  mazed, maz·ing

ma·zur·ka
mazy
Mc·In·tosh (apple;
  cf. *mackintosh*)
McJob
mead·ow
mead·ow·lark
mea·ger
meal·time
mean (stingy; cf.
  mien)
  mean·ing,
  mean·er,
  mean·ness
me·an·der
  -dered, -der·ing
mean·ing·less
mean·ly
mean·time
mean·while
mea·sles
mea·sly
mea·sure
  -sured, -sur·ing,
  -sur·able
mea·sure·less
mea·sure·ment
meat (food; cf. *meet,*
  mete)
me·chan·ic
me·chan·i·cal
me·chan·ics
mech·a·nism

mech·a·nist

med·al (award; cf. *meddle*)

med·al·ist

me·dal·lion

med·dle (interfere; cf. *medal*)
-dled, -dling, -dler

med·dle·some

me·dia (pl)
me·di·um (sing)

me·di·al

me·di·an

me·di·ate
-at·ed, -at·ing

me·di·a·tion

me·di·a·tor

med·ic·aid

med·i·cal

medi·care

med·i·cate
-cat·ed, -cat·ing

med·i·ca·tion

med·i·cide

me·dic·i·nal

med·i·cine

me·di·eval

me·di·eval·ism

me·di·o·cre

me·di·oc·ri·ty
-ties

med·i·tate
-tat·ed, -tat·ing, -ta·tor

med·i·ta·tion

med·i·ta·tive

Med·i·ter·ra·nean

me·di·um (sing)
me·dia (pl)

med·ley
-leys

meet (encounter; cf. *meat, mete*)

meet·ing

meet·ing·house

mega·bit

mega·byte

mega·cy·cle

mega·deal

mega·flops

mega·hertz

mega·hit

mega·phone

mega·serv·er

mehn·di

mel·an·cho·lia

mel·an·chol·ic

mel·an·choly
-chol·ies

mé·lange

mel·a·no·ma

me·lee

me·lio·rate
-rat·ed, -rat·ing, -ra·tion

me·lio·rism

mel·lif·lu·ous

mel·low

me·lo·de·on

me·lod·ic

me·lo·di·ous

mel·o·dist

mel·o·dize
-dized, -diz·ing

melo·dra·ma

melo·dra·mat·ic

mel·o·dy
-dies

mel·on

melt·down

mem·ber

mem·ber·ship

mem·brane

mem·bra·nous

me·men·to
-tos

mem·oir

mem·o·ra·bil·ia

mem·o·ra·ble

mem·o·ran·dum (sing)
-dums or -da (pl)

me·mo·ri·al

me·mo·ri·al·ist

me·mo·ri·al·ize
-ized

mem·o·rize
-rized, -riz·ing, -ri·za·tion

mem·o·ry
  -ries
men·ace
  -aced, -ac·ing,
  -ac·ing·ly
mé·nage
me·nag·er·ie
men·da·cious
men·dac·i·ty
  -ties
men·di·can·cy
men·di·cant
me·nial
men·in·gi·tis
  -git·i·des (pl)
Men·no·nite
men·stru·ate
men·tal
men·tal·i·ty
  -ties
men·thol
men·tion
  -tion·ing,
  -tion·able
men·tioned
men·tor
menu
menu bar
menu-driv·en
mer·can·tile
mer·can·til·ism
mer·ce·nary
  -nar·ies

mer·cer·ize
  -ized, -iz·ing
mer·chan·dise
  -dised, -dis·ing,
  -dis·er
mer·chant
mer·chant·able
mer·chant·man
mer·ci·ful
mer·ci·less
mer·cu·ri·al
mer·cu·ric
mer·cu·rous
mer·cu·ry
  -ries
mer·cy
  -cies
mere·ly
merge
  merged, merg·ing
merg·er
me·rid·i·an
me·ringue
me·ri·no
  -nos
mer·it
mer·i·to·ri·ous
mer·maid
mer·ri·ment
merry
  -ri·er, -ri·est, -ri·ly
mer·ry-go-round
mer·ry-mak·ing

me·sa
mes·mer·ism
mes·mer·ize
me·so·mor·phic
mes·quite
mes·sage
  -saged, -sag·ing
mes·sen·ger
mes·si·ah
Messrs. (pl)
  Mr. (sing)
messy
  mess·i·er,
  mess·i·est
met·a·bol·ic
me·tab·o·lism
meta·car·pal
met·al (iron; cf.
  mettle)
  -aled, -al·ing
meta·lan·guage
me·tal·lic
met·al·log·ra·phy
met·al·loid
met·al·lur·gy
  -gi·cal, -gist
met·al·work
meta·mor·phic
meta·mor·phism
meta·mor·phose
  -phosed, -phos·ing
meta·mor·pho·sis
  -pho·ses (pl)

met·a·phor
meta·phys·ic
meta·phys·i·cal
meta·phy·si·cian
meta·phys·ics
meta·tar·sal
meta·tar·sus
mete (measure; cf.
   meat, meet)
   met·ed, met·ing
me·te·or
me·te·or·ic
me·te·or·ite
me·te·or·oid
me·te·o·rol·o·gy
   -ro·log·ic,
   -ro·log·i·cal,
   -ro·log·i·cal·ly
me·ter
me·ter maid
meth·a·done
meth·ane
meth·od
me·thod·i·cal
meth·od·ist
meth·od·ize
   -ized, -iz·ing
meth·od·ol·o·gy
   -gies
me·tic·u·lous
met·ric
met·ri·cal
me·trol·o·gy

met·ro·nome
me·trop·o·lis
met·ro·pol·i·tan
met·tle (spirit; cf.
   metal)
met·tle·some
Mex·i·can
Mex·i·co
mez·za·nine
mez·zo·so·pra·no
mez·zo·tint
mi·as·ma
   -mas (pl), -mal,
   -mat·ic
mi·crobe
mi·cro·bi·ol·o·gy
mi·cro·brew·er·y
mi·cro·ceph·a·ly
mi·cro·chip
mi·cro·com·put·er
mi·cro·cosm
mi·cro·eco·nom·ics
mi·cro·fib·er
mi·cro·fiche
   -fiche (pl)
mi·cro·film
mi·cro·form
mi·cro·graph
mi·cro·man·age
mi·crom·e·ter
mi·cron
Mi·cro·ne·sia
mi·cro·or·gan·ism

mi·cro·phone
mi·cro·pro·ces·sor
mi·cro·scope
mi·cro·scop·ic
   -scop·i·cal·ly
mi·cro·sec·ond
mi·cro·wave
mid·air
mid·brain
mid·day
mid·dle
mid·dle-aged
mid·dle class (n)
mid·dle-class (adj)
mid·dle·man
mid·dle·ware
mid·dle·weight
mid·dling
midg·et
mid·land
mid·life
mid·night
mid·riff
mid·ship·man
mid·size
mid·sum·mer
mid·term
mid·way
mid·week
mid·wife
mid·win·ter
mid·year

mien (bearing; cf. *mean*)

miff

might (strength; cf. *mite*)

might·i·ly

might·i·ness

mighty
might·i·er,
might·i·est

mi·graine

mi·grate
-grat·ed, -grat·ing,
-gra·tion

mi·gra·to·ry

mi·ka·do

mi·la·dy

mil·dew

mile·age

mile·post

mile·stone

mil·i·tance

mil·i·tan·cy

mil·i·tant

mil·i·ta·rism
-rist, -ris·tic,
-ris·ti·cal·ly

mil·i·ta·rize
-rized, -riz·ing,
-ri·za·tion

mil·i·tary

mil·i·tate
-tat·ed, -tat·ing

mi·li·tia

milk glass

milk shake

milk snake

milk·weed

milky
milk·i·er,
milk·i·est,
milk·i·ness

mill·age

mil·le·na·ry (1000th anniversary; cf. *millinery*)
-ries

mil·len·ni·um
-nia (pl)

mill·er

mil·let

mil·li·am·pere

mil·li·gram

mil·li·me·ter

mil·li·nery (hats; cf. *millenary*)

mill·ing

mil·lion
mil·lionth

mil·lion·aire

mil·li·sec·ond

mil·li·volt

mil·li·watt

mill·pond

mill·race

mill·stone

mill·stream

mill wheel

mill·wright

mim·eo·graph

mi·me·sis

mi·met·ic

mim·ic
-icked, -ick·ing

mim·ic·ry
-ries

mi·mo·sa

min·a·ret

mi·na·to·ry

mince
minced, minc·ing

mince·meat

mind (brain; cf. *mined*)

mind-bog·gling

mind·ful

mind read·er

mined (dug out; cf. *mind*)

mine
min·er (mine worker; cf. *minor*)

min·er·al

min·er·al·ize
-ized, -iz·ing

min·er·al·o·gy
-al·og·i·cal,
-al·o·gist

min·gle
  -gled, -gling
min·ia·ture
Mini·cam
mini·com·put·er
mini·course
min·i·mal
min·i·mize
  -mized, -miz·ing
min·i·mum
  -i·ma (pl)
min·ing
mini·se·ries
mini·site
mini·state
min·is·ter (clergy-
  man; cf. *minster*)
  -tered, -ter·ing
min·is·te·ri·al
min·is·trant
min·is·tra·tion
min·is·try
  -tries
min·i·tow·er
mini·van
min·now
mi·nor (underage;
  cf. *miner*)
mi·nor·i·ty
min·ster (church; cf.
  minister)
min·strel
mint·age

min·u·end
min·u·et
mi·nus
mi·nus·cule
min·ute (n)(60 sec-
  onds; cf. *mi·nute*)
mi·nute (adj)(very
  small; cf. *min·ute*)
min·ute hand
mi·nute·ly (in
  detail)
min·ute·man
mi·o·sis
  -ses (pl)
mir·a·cle
mi·rac·u·lous
mi·rage
mir·ror
mirth
  mirth·ful,
  mirth·ful·ly,
  mirth·ful·ness
mis·ad·ven·ture
mis·align
mis·al·li·ance
mis·an·thrope
mis·an·throp·ic
mis·an·thro·py
mis·ap·pre·hend
  -hen·sion
mis·ap·pro·pri·ate
mis·be·lief
mis·car·riage

mis·car·ry
mis·cel·la·nea
mis·cel·la·neous
mis·cel·la·ny
  -nies
mis·chance
mis·chief
mis·chie·vous
mis·com·mu·ni·ca·tion
mis·con·ceive
  -cep·tion
mis·con·duct
mis·con·strue
mis·cue
mis·deal
  -dealt, -dealing
mis·de·mean·or
mis·di·rect
mi·ser
mis·er·a·ble
mi·ser·ly
  -li·ness
mis·ery
  -er·ies
mis·fea·sance
mis·fire
mis·fit
mis·for·tune
mis·give
  -gave, -giv·en
mis·guide
mis·hap
mis·in·ter·pret

179

mis·join·der
mis·judge
mis·lay
  -laid, -lay·ing
mis·lead
  -led
mis·man·age
mis·no·mer
mi·sog·y·nist
mis·place
mis·print
mis·pri·sion
mis·pro·nounce
mis·quote
mis·read
  -read, -read·ing
mis·rep·re·sent
  -sen·ta·tion,
  -sen·ta·tive
mis·rule
mis·sal (book; cf.
  missile, missive)
mis·sile (weapon; cf.
  missal, missive)
miss·ing
mis·sion
  -sioned,
  -sion·ing
mis·sion·ary
  -ar·ies
mis·sive (letter; cf.
  missal, missile)
mis·speak

mis·spell
mis·state
  -state·ment
mis·tak·able
mis·take
  -took, -tak·en,
  -tak·ing
mis·tle·toe
mis·tral
mis·treat
  -treat·ment
mis·tress
mis·tri·al
mis·trust
misty
  mist·i·er,
  mist·i·est,
  mist·i·ness
mis·un·der·stand
  -stood, -stand·ing
mis·us·age
mis·use
mite (something
  tiny; cf. *might*)
mi·ter
  -tered, -ter·ing,
  -ter·er
mit·i·gate
  -gat·ed, -gat·ing
mit·ten
mit·ti·mus
mix·er
mix·ture

mix-up
mne·mon·ic (adj)
mne·mon·ics (n)
moan
moat (ditch; cf.
  mote)
mob
  mobbed,
  mob·bing
mo·bile
  -bil·i·ty
mo·bi·li·za·tion
mo·bi·lize
  -lized, -liz·ing
moc·ca·sin
mo·cha
mock·ery
  -er·ies
mock·ing·bird
mod·al (of a mode;
  cf. *model*)
  -al·ly
mo·dal·i·ty
  -ties
mode (fashion; cf.
  mood)
mod·el (pattern; cf.
  modal)
  -eled, -el·ing
mod·el·er
mo·dem
mod·er·ate
  -at·ed, -at·ing

mod·er·a·tor
mod·ern
mod·ern·ism
mod·ern·iza·tion
mod·ern·ize
  -ized, -iz·ing
mod·est
mod·es·ty
mo·di·cum
mod·i·fi·ca·tion
mod·i·fi·er
mod·i·fy
  -fied, -fy·ing
mod·ish
mod·u·lar
mod·u·late
  -lat·ed, -lat·ing,
  -la·tor
mod·u·la·tion
mod·ule
mod·u·lus
mo·dus ope·ran·di
Mog·a·di·shu
mo·hair
Mo·hawk
moist
moist·en
  -ened, -en·ing
mois·ture
mo·lar
mo·las·ses
mold

moldy
  mold·i·er,
  mold·i·est
mo·lec·u·lar
mol·e·cule
mole·hill
mole·skin
mo·lest
  -les·ta·tion,
  -les·ter
mol·li·fy
  -fied, -fy·ing
mol·lusk
mol·ly·cod·dle
  -dled, -dling
mol·ten
mo·ment
mo·men·tari·ly
mo·men·tary
mo·ment·ly
mo·men·tous
mo·men·tum
Mo·na·co
mon·arch
mon·ar·chism
  -chist
mon·ar·chy
mon·as·tery
  -ter·ies
mo·nas·tic
Mon·day
mon·e·tary

mon·e·tize
  -tized, -tiz·ing
mon·ey
  mon·eys
mon·ey·bags
mon·eyed
mon·ey·lend·er
mon·ey·mak·er
mon·ey mar·ket
mon·ey or·der
mon·ger
  -gered, -ger·ing
Mon·go·lia
Mon·go·lian
mon·grel
mo·ni·tion
mon·i·tor
  -tor·ing, -tored
mon·i·to·ry
  -ries
monk·ery
  -er·ies
mon·key
  -keys, -keyed,
  -key·ing
mon·key wrench
mono·chro·mat·ic
mono·chrome
mon·o·cle
mo·nog·a·my
  -a·mous

mono·gram
-grammed,
-gram·ming
mono·graph
mono·lith
mono·logue
mo·nop·o·list
mo·nop·o·lis·tic
mo·nop·o·lize
-lized, -liz·ing
mo·nop·o·ly
-lies
mono·rail
mono·syl·lab·ic
mono·syl·la·ble
mono·tone
mo·not·o·nous
mo·not·o·ny
Mono·type
mon·ox·ide
mon·sieur
mon·si·gnor
-gnors
mon·soon
mon·ster
mon·stros·i·ty
-ties
mon·strous
mon·tage
-taged, -tag·ing
Mont·gom·ery
month
month·ly

Mont·pe·lier
mon·u·ment
mon·u·men·tal
mood (feeling; cf. *mode*)
moody
mood·i·er,
mood·i·est
moon·beam
moon·light
-lighted,
-light·ing, -light·er
moon·lit
moon·rise
moon·shine
moon·stone
moon·struck
moor·age
moor·ing
moose (large ani-mal; cf. *mouse, mousse*)
moose (pl)
mo·raine
mor·al (ethical; cf. *morale*)
mo·rale (attitude; cf. *moral*)
mor·al·ism
mor·al·ist
mo·ral·i·ty (virtue; cf. *mortality*)
-ties

mor·al·ize
-ized, -iz·ing,
-iza·tion
mo·rass
mor·a·to·ri·um
Mo·ra·vi·an
mor·bid
mor·bid·i·ty
mor·dant (dyeing term; cf. *mordent*)
mor·dent (musical term; cf. *mordant*)
more or less
more·over
mo·res
Mor·mon
morn·ing (forenoon; cf. *mourning*)
mo·roc·co (leather)
Mo·roc·co
mo·ron
-ron·ic
mo·rose
mor·phine
mor·phol·o·gy
mor·row
mor·sel
-seled, -sel·ing
mor·tal
mor·tal·i·ty (death rate; cf. *morality*)
mor·tar
mor·tar·board

mort·gage
mort·gag·ee
mort·gag·or
mor·ti·cian
mor·ti·fi·ca·tion
mor·ti·fy
  -fied, -fy·ing
mor·tise
mor·tu·ary
  -ar·ies
mo·sa·ic
Mos·cow
Mo·ses
mo·sey
  -seyed, -sey·ing
Mos·lem
mos·qui·to
  -toes
moss·back
mote (speck; cf.
  moat)
mo·tel
moth·ball
moth-eat·en
moth·er
  -ered, -er·ing
moth·er·board
moth·er-in-law
  moth·ers-in-law
  (pl)
moth·er·land
moth·er·ly
  -li·ness

moth·er-of-pearl
moth·proof
mo·tif
mo·tion
  -tioned, -tion·ing,
  -tion·less
mo·ti·vate
  -vat·ed, -vat·ing
mo·ti·va·tion
mo·tive
mot·ley
mo·tor
mo·tor·bike
mo·tor·boat
mo·tor·cade
mo·tor·car
mo·tor·cy·cle
  -cy·clist
mo·tor·drome
mo·tor·ist
mo·tor·ize
  -ized, -iz·ing
mot·tle
  -tled, -tling
mot·to
  -toes
moun·tain
moun·tain·eer
moun·tain·ous
moun·tain·side
Mount·ie
mount·ing

mourn
  mourn·er
mourn·ing (griev-
  ing; cf. *morning*)
mouse (small ani-
  mal; cf. *moose,
  mousse*)
mice (pl), moused,
  mous·ing
mouse pad
mouse·trap
mousse (food; cf.
  moose, mouse)
mouth·ful
mouth·piece
mouth-to-mouth
mouth·wash
mov·able
move
  moved, mov·ing
move·ment
mov·ie
mow
  mowed, mow·ing
Mo·zam·bique
moz·za·rel·la
Mr.
  Messrs. (pl)
Mrs.
  Mes·dames (pl)
Ms.
  Mses. or Mss. (pl)
MS DOS

much
mu·ci·lage
muck·rake
mu·cous (adj)
mu·cus (n)
mud·dle
-dled, -dling
mud·dy
-died, -dy·ing,
-di·ness
mud·guard
mud·sling·er
muf·fin
muf·fle
-fled, -fling
muf·fler
mug
mugged,
mug·ging
mug·ger
mu·lat·to
-toes
mul·ber·ry
mul·ish
mull·er
mul·ti·cast
mul·ti·cul·tur·al
mul·ti·dis·ci·pli·nary
mul·ti·fac·et·ed
mul·ti·far·i·ous
mul·ti·form
mul·ti·lat·er·al
mul·ti·me·dia

mul·ti·mil·lion·aire
mul·ti·na·tion·al
mul·ti·ple
mul·ti·ple-choice
mul·ti·ple
scle·ro·sis
mul·ti·plex
mul·ti·pli·cand
mul·ti·pli·ca·tion
mul·ti·plic·i·ty
-ties
mul·ti·pli·er
mul·ti·ply
-plied, -ply·ing
mul·ti·pro·cess·ing
mul·ti·pro·gram·ming
mul·ti·task·ing
mul·ti·tude
mul·ti·tu·di·nous
mum·mi·fy
-fied, -fy·ing
mum·my
-mies
mun·dane
munge
mu·nic·i·pal
mu·nic·i·pal·i·ty
mu·nif·i·cent
(generous; cf.
magnificent)
-cence
mu·ni·tion
mu·ral

mur·der
-dered, -der·ing
mur·der·er
mur·der·ous
murky
murk·i·er,
murk·i·est,
murk·i·ly
mur·mur
mus·ca·tel
mus·cle (of body; cf.
mussel, muzzle)
-cled, -cling
mus·cle-bound
mus·cu·lar
mus·cu·lar
dys·tro·phy
mus·cu·la·ture
muse
mused, mus·ing
mu·se·um
mush·room
mushy
mush·i·er,
mush·i·est
mu·sic
mu·si·cal (about
music; cf.
musicale)
mu·si·cale (enter-
tainment; cf.
musical)
mu·si·cian

mus·ket
mus·ke·teer
musk·mel·on
musk-ox
musk·rat
musky
  musk·i·er,
  musk·i·est
Mus·lim (religion)
mus·lin (cloth)
mus·sel (shellfish;
  cf. *muscle,*
  muzzle)
must
mus·tache
mus·tang
mus·tard (plant; cf.
  mustered)
mus·ter
  -tered (assembled;
  cf. *mustard*),
  -ter·ing
musty
  must·i·er,
  must·i·est,
  must·i·ness
mu·ta·ble
mu·tant
mu·tate
  -tat·ed, -tat·ing
mu·ta·tion
mute
mutex

mu·ti·late
  -lat·ed, -lat·ing,
  -la·tion
mu·ti·nous
mu·ti·ny
mut·ism
mut·ter
mut·ton
mu·tu·al
  -al·ly
mu·tu·al·ism
mu·tu·al·i·ty
muz·zle (mouth; cf.
  muscle, mussel)
  -zled, -zling
my·col·o·gy
my·o·pia
myr·i·ad
myrrh
my·self
mys·te·ri·ous
mys·tery
  -ter·ies
mys·tic
mys·ti·cal
mys·ti·cism
mys·ti·fi·ca·tion
mys·ti·fy
  -fied, -fy·ing
mys·tique
myth
myth·i·cal
myth·o·log·i·cal

my·thol·o·gy
  -gies

N

na·cho
  -chos
na·dir
nail
Nai·ro·bi
na·ive
na·ive·té
na·ked
name
  named, nam·ing
name·able
name·less
name·ly
name·plate
name·sake
nano·sec·ond
name·space
Na·mib·ia
nano·tech·nol·o·gy
nano·tube
nap
  napped,
  nap·ping
na·palm
naph·tha
nap·kin
Na·ples
nar·cis·sism
nar·cis·sus

  -cis·si (pl)
nar·co·sis
  -co·ses (pl)
nar·cot·ic
nar·co·tize
  -tized, -tiz·ing
nar·rate
  -rat·ed, -rat·ing
nar·ra·tion
nar·ra·tive
nar·row
  -row·ly, -row·ness
nar·row-mind·ed
na·sal
  -sal·i·ty, -sal·ly
na·scent
Nash·ville
Nas·sau
nas·tur·tium
nas·ty
  -ti·er, -ti·est, -ti·ly
na·tal
na·tant
na·ta·to·ri·um
na·tion
na·tion·al
na·tion·al·ism
na·tion·al·i·ty
  -ties

na·tion·al·ize
  -ized, -iz·ing
na·tion·wide
na·tive
  -tive·ly, -tive·ness
na·tiv·ism
  -tiv·ist
na·tiv·i·ty
  -ties
nat·u·ral
nat·u·ral·ism
nat·u·ral·ist
nat·u·ral·is·tic
nat·u·ral·ize
  -ized, -iz·ing,
  -iza·tion
nat·u·ral·ly
na·ture
nau·ga·hyde
naugh·ty
  -ti·er, -ti·est, -ti·ly
nau·sea
nau·seous
nau·ti·cal
nau·ti·lus
Na·va·ho
na·val (of navy; cf.
  navel)

nave (of church; cf. *knave*)

na·vel (of abdomen; cf. *naval*)

nav·i·ga·ble

nav·i·gate
-gat·ed, -gat·ing

nav·i·ga·tion

nav·i·ga·tor

na·vy
navies

na·vy yard

nay (no; cf. *née, neigh*)

Naz·a·rene

Na·zi

Ne·an·der·thal

Ne·a·pol·i·tan

near·by

near·ly

near·sight·ed

neat
neat·ness

neb·u·la
-las, -lar

neb·u·lize
-lized, -liz·ing

neb·u·lous

nec·es·sar·i·ly

nec·es·sary
-saries

ne·ces·si·tate
-tat·ed, -tat·ing

ne·ces·si·ty
-ties

neck·er·chief
-chiefs

neck·lace

neck·line

neck·tie

nec·rop·sy
-sies

nec·tar

nec·tar·ine

née (born; cf. *nay, neigh*)

need (require; cf. *knead*)

need·ful

nee·dle
-dled, -dling

nee·dle·point

need·less

nee·dle·work

needy
need·i·er,
need·i·est

ne·far·i·ous

ne·gate
-gat·ed, -gat·ing

neg·a·tive
-tive·ly, -tive·ness

ne·glect

ne·glect·ful

neg·li·gee

neg·li·gence

neg·li·gent

neg·li·gi·ble
-bil·i·ty

ne·go·tia·ble

ne·go·ti·ate
-at·ed, -at·ing,
-a·tor

ne·go·ti·a·tion

Ne·gro
-groes, -groid

neigh (of horse; cf. *nay, née*)

neigh·bor
-bored, -bor·ing

neigh·bor·hood

neigh·bor·ly

nei·ther

nem·a·tode

nem·e·sis
-e·ses (pl)

neo·con·ser·va·tive

ne·ol·o·gism
neon
neo·na·tal
neo·phyte
neo·plasm
Ne·pal
neph·ew
ne·phri·tis
  -phrit·i·des (pl)
nep·o·tism
Nep·tune
nerd
nerve
  nerved, nerv·ing
nerve·less
nerve-rack·ing
ner·vous
nervy
nes·tle
  -tled, -tling (v)
nest·ling (n)
Net·cast·er
Neth·er·lands
neth·er·most
net·i·quette
net·i·zen
net·split
net surf·ing
net·ting
net·tle
  -tled, -tling
Net·ware
net·work

net·work·ing
neu·ral
neu·ral·gia
neu·ral net·work
neur·as·the·nia
neu·ri·tis
  -rit·i·des (pl)
neu·rol·o·gist
neu·rol·o·gy
neu·ron
neu·ro·sis
  -ro·ses (pl)
neu·rot·ic
neu·ter
neu·tral
  -tral·ly
neu·tral·i·ty
neu·tral·iza·tion
neu·tral·ize
  -ized, -iz·ing
neu·tron
nev·er
nev·er·the·less
new (recent; cf. *gnu,*
    knew)
  new·ish, new·ness
New Ber·lin
new·bie
new·born
new·com·er
new·el
New·found·land
New Guin·ea

new·ly
news·break
news·cast
news·group
news·let·ter
news·mag·a·zine
news·mon·ger
news·pa·per
news·print
news·reader
news·reel
news·stand
news·wor·thy
  -wor·thi·ness
newsy
  news·i·er,
  news·i·est
New World Or·der
New Year
New Zea·land
next
next door (adv)
next-door (adj)
nib·ble
  -bled, -bling, -bler
Nic·a·ra·gua
nice·ty
  -ties
niche
  niched, nich·ing
nick
nick·el
  -eled, -el·ing

nick·el·ode·on
nick·name
nic·o·tine
niece
Ni·ger
Ni·ge·ria
nig·gard
nig·gard·ly
night (darkness; cf. *knight*)
night·cap
night·clothes
night·club
night·fall
night·gown
night·hawk
night·in·gale
night·ly
night·mare
  -mar·ish
night·stick
night·time
night·walk·er
ni·hil·ism
  -ist, -is·tic
nim·ble
  -bler, -blest
nin·com·poop
  -poop·ery
nine·pin
nine·teen
  -teenth

nine·ty
  -ties, -ti·eth
ninth
  ninths
nip·per
nip·ple
ni·sei
  ni·sei (pl)
ni·trate
ni·tric
ni·tride
ni·tri·fi·ca·tion
ni·tri·fy
  -fied, -fy·ing
ni·trite
ni·tro·gen
ni·tro·glyc·er·in
ni·trous
nit·ty-grit·ty
no·bil·i·ty
no·ble
  -bler, -blest, -bly
no·body
  -bod·ies
noc·tur·nal
noc·turne
nod
  nod·ded, nod·ding
node
nod·u·lar
nod·ule
no-fault

noise
  noise·less
noisy
  nois·i·er,
  nois·i·est, nois·i·ly
no·mad
nom de plume
no·men·cla·ture
nom·i·nal
  -nal·ly
nom·i·nate
  -nat·ed, -nat·ing
nom·i·na·tion
nom·i·na·tive
nom·i·nee
non·bio·de·grad·able
non·cha·lant
non·com·bat·ant
non·com·mit·tal
non·con·duc·tor
non·con·form·ist
non·con·for·mi·ty
non·co·op·er·a·tion
non·de·script
non·en·ti·ty
non·es·sen·tial
none·the·less
non·ex·empt
non·ex·is·tent
non·fea·sance
non·fic·tion
non·im·pact
  print·er

non·in·ter·ven·tion
non·me·tal·lic
non·par·ti·san
non·prof·it
non·res·i·dent
non·re·sis·tant
non·re·stric·tive
non·re·turn·able
non·sched·uled
non·sense
  -sen·si·cal
non·skid
non·stan·dard
non·stop
non·sup·port
non·union
non·ver·bal
non·vi·o·lence
non·vi·o·lent
non·vol·a·tile
non·vot·ing
noo·dle
  -dled, -dling
noon·day
noon·tide
noon·time
nor·mal
  -mal·i·ty, -mal·ly
nor·mal·ize
  -ized, iz·ing,
  -iza·tion
nor·ma·tive
Nor·plant

Norse
Norse·man
North Amer·i·can
  Free Trade
  Agree·ment
  (NAFTA)
north·east
north·east·ern
north·er·ly
  -lies
north·ern
North·ern·er
North Ko·rea
north·land
north·ward
north·west
north·west·er·ly
north·west·ern
Nor·way
Nor·we·gian
nose
  nosed, nos·ing
nose·dive (n)
nose·gay
nose·piece
nose·wheel
no-show
nos·tal·gia
  -gic, -gi·cal·ly
nos·tril
nos·trum
not (negative; cf.
  knot)

no·ta·bil·i·ty
  -ties
no·ta·ble
no·ta·bly
no·ta·rize
  -rized, -riz·ing
no·ta·tion
notch ba·by
note·book
not·ed
note·less
note·pad
note·wor·thy
  -wor·thi·ly
noth·ing
noth·ing·ness
no·tice
  -ticed, -tic·ing
no·tice·able
  -tice·ably
no·ti·fi·ca·tion
no·ti·fy
  -fied, -fy·ing
no·tion
no·to·ri·e·ty
  -eties
no·to·ri·ous
not·with·stand·ing
not·work
nour·ish
nour·ish·ment
nou·veau
nou·veau riche

nou·velle cui·sine
no·va·tion
nov·el
  -el·is·tic
nov·el·ette
nov·el·ist
nov·el·ize
  -ized, -iz·ing
no·vel·la
nov·el·ty
  -ties
No·vem·ber
no·ve·na
nov·ice
no·vi·tiate
No·vo·cain
now·a·days
no·way
no·where
no·win
nox·ious
noz·zle
nth
nu·ance
nu·cle·ar
nu·cle·ar win·ter
nu·cle·ate
  -at·ed, -at·ing,
  -ation
nu·cle·us
  nu·clei (pl)
nude
  nude·ly, nu·di·ty

nu·ga·to·ry
nug·get
nui·sance
nuke
  -nuked, nuk·ing
nul·li·fi·ca·tion
nul·li·fi·er
nul·li·fy
  -fied, -fy·ing
num·ber
num·ber crunch·er
num·ber
  chrunch·ing
num·ber·less
nu·mer·al
nu·mer·ate
  -at·ed, -at·ing
nu·mer·a·tion
nu·mer·a·tor
nu·mer·ic
nu·mer·i·cal
nu·mer·ic key·pad
  lo
nu·mer·ol·o·gy
  -ol·o·gist
nu·mer·ous
nu·mis·mat·ics
  -ma·tist
num·skull
nun·nery
  -ner·ies
nup·tial
nurse·maid

nurs·ery
  -er·ies
nur·ture
  -tured, -tur·ing,
  -tur·er
nut·crack·er
nut·meg
nut·pick
nu·tri·ent
nu·tri·ment
nu·tri·tion
nu·tri·tion·ist
nu·tri·tious
  -tious·ly,
  -tious·ness
nut·shell
nut·ty
  nut·ti·er, nut·ti·est
nuz·zle
  -zled, -zling
nye·work
ny·lon
nymph

O

oar (of a boat; cf. *or,*
    ore)
oar·lock
oars·man
oa·sis
    oa·ses (pl)
oat·cake
oath
oat·meal
ob·bli·ga·to
    -tos
obe·di·ence
obe·di·ent
obei·sance
obe·lisk
obese
obe·si·ty
obey
    obeyed, obey·ing
ob·fus·cate
    -cat·ed, -cat·ing,
    -ca·tion
obit·u·ary
    -ar·ies
ob·ject
ob·ject-ori·ent·ed
ob·jec·tion
ob·jec·tion·able

ob·jec·tive
    -tive·ly, -tive·ness,
    -tiv·i·ty
ob·la·tion
ob·li·gate
    -gat·ed, -gat·ing
ob·li·ga·tion
oblig·a·to·ry
oblige
    obliged, oblig·ing
oblique
oblit·er·ate
    -at·ed, -at·ing
obliv·i·on
obliv·i·ous
ob·long
ob·nox·ious
oboe
    obo·ist
ob·scene
ob·scen·i·ty
    -ties
ob·scur·ant
ob·scure
    -scured, -scure·ly,
    -scure·ness
ob·scu·ri·ty
    -ties

ob·se·qui·ous
ob·serv·able
ob·ser·vance
ob·ser·vant
ob·ser·va·tion
ob·ser·va·to·ry
    -ries
ob·serve
    -served, -serv·ing
ob·serv·er
ob·sess
ob·ses·sion
ob·ses·sive
ob·so·lesce
    -lesced, -lesc·ing
ob·so·les·cence
ob·so·les·cent
ob·so·lete
    -let·ed, -let·ing
ob·sta·cle
ob·stet·ric
ob·ste·tri·cian
ob·sti·na·cy
    -cies
ob·sti·nate
ob·strep·er·ous
ob·struct
ob·struc·tion

ob·tain
  -tain·able,
  -tain·abil·i·ty,
  -tain·ment
ob·trude
  -trud·ed, -trud·ing,
  -tru·sion
ob·tru·sive
ob·tuse
ob·verse
ob·vi·ate
  -at·ed, -at·ing,
  -a·tion
ob·vi·ous
oc·ca·sion
  -sioned, -sion·ing
oc·ca·sion·al
oc·ca·sion·al·ly
oc·ci·den·tal
  -tal·ly
oc·cip·i·tal
oc·clude
  -clud·ed,
  -clud·ing, -clu·sive
oc·clu·sion
oc·cult
oc·cult·ism
oc·cu·pan·cy
  -cies
oc·cu·pant
oc·cu·pa·tion
  -tion·al, -tion·al·ly

oc·cu·py
  -pied, -py·ing,
  -pi·er
oc·cur
  -curred, -cur·ring
oc·cur·rence
ocean·front
ocean·go·ing
oce·an·ic
ocean·og·ra·phy
  -og·ra·pher,
  -o·graph·ic
oce·lot
o'clock
oc·ta·gon
  -tag·o·nal,
  -tag·o·nal·ly
oc·tal
oc·tane
oc·tave
oc·ta·vo
oc·tet
Oc·to·ber
oc·to·ge·nar·i·an
oc·to·pus
  -pus·es (pl)
oc·u·lar
oc·u·list
odd·i·ty
  -ties
ode (poem; cf. *owed*)
odi·ous
odi·um

odor
  odored, odor·less
odor·if·er·ous
odor·ize
  -ized, -iz·ing
od·ys·sey
  -seys
off·beat
off·cast
off-col·or
of·fend
  -fend·er
of·fense
of·fen·sive
of·fer
  -fer·ing
of·fered
of·fer·to·ry
  -ries
off·hand
off-hour
of·fice
of·fice·hold·er
of·fi·cer
of·fi·cial (author-
  ized; cf. *officious*)
of·fi·cial·ism
of·fi·ci·ary
  -ar·ies
of·fi·ci·ate
  -at·ed, -at·ing,
  -a·tion

of·fi·cious (meddle-
  some; cf. *official*)
off·ing
off-key
off-lim·its
off-line
off-peak
off-print
off-screen
off-sea·son
off·set
  -set, -set·ting
off·shore
off·side
off·spring
off·stage
off-the-rec·ord
off-the-shelf
off-the-wall
off·track
off-white
off year
of·ten
of·ten·times
ohm
ohm·me·ter
oil·er
oil field
oil pan
oil·skin
oil slick
oil well

oily
  oil·i·er, oil·i·est,
  oil·i·ness
oint·ment
OK or okay
  OK'd or okayed,
  OK'ing or
  okay·ing
Oki·na·wa
Okla·ho·ma City
old·en
old-fash·ioned
old-line
old·ster
old-time (adj)
old-tim·er (n)
old-world (adj)
oleo·mar·ga·rine
oles·tra
ol·fac·tion
ol·fac·to·ry
oli·gar·chy
  -chies
ol·ive
Olym·pia
olym·pi·ad
Olym·pi·an
Olym·pic
om·buds·man
om·elet
om·i·nous
  -nous·ness
omis·si·ble

omis·sion
omit
  omit·ted,
  omit·ting
om·ni·bus
om·ni·di·rec·tion·al
om·nip·o·tence
om·nip·o·tent
om·ni·pres·ent
om·ni·science
om·ni·scient
om·niv·o·rous
on-again, off-again
once-over (n)
on·col·o·gy
on·com·ing
one (single thing; cf.
  won)
one-lin·er
one·ness
one-on-one
oner·ous
one·self
one-sid·ed
one·time
one-to-one
one-up·man·ship
one-way (adj)
on·go·ing
on·ion
on·ion·skin
on-line (adj, adv)
on·look·er

on·ly
on·rush
on·screen
on·set
on·slaught
on·to
on·tog·e·ny
on·tol·o·gy
onus
on·ward
on·yx
oozy
  ooz·i·er, ooz·i·est
opac·i·ty
  -ties
opal·es·cent
opaque
open
  opened, open·ing,
  open·er
open air (n)
open-air (adj)
open-end (adj)
open·hand·ed
open·heart·ed
open-hearth
open house
open-mind·ed
open·mouthed
open·work
op·era
  -er·at·ic
op·er·a·ble

op·er·and
op·er·ate
  -at·ed
op·er·at·ing
op·er·at·ing
  sys·tem (OS)
op·er·a·tion
op·er·a·tion·al
op·er·a·tive
op·er·a·tor
op·er·et·ta
oph·thal·mol·o·gist
oph·thal·mol·o·gy
oph·thal·mo·scope
opi·ate
opin·ion
opin·ion·at·ed
opi·um
op·po·nent
op·por·tune
  -tune·ly,
  -tune·ness
op·por·tun·ism
  -tun·ist, -tu·nis·tic
op·por·tu·ni·ty
  -ties
op·pose
  -posed, -pos·ing,
  -pos·er
op·po·site
  -site·ly
op·po·si·tion
op·press
  -pres·sor

op·pres·sion
op·pres·sive
  -sive·ness
op·ti·cal
op·ti·cal char·ac·ter
  rec·og·ni·tion
op·ti·cal fi·ber
op·ti·cal ma·ser
op·ti·cal scan·ning
op·ti·cian
op·tics
op·ti·mal
  -mal·ly
op·ti·mism
  -mist, -mis·tic,
  -mis·ti·cal·ly
op·ti·mize
  -mized, -mizing
op·ti·mum
  -ma (pl)
op·tion
op·tion·al
  -al·ly
op·to·e·lec·tron·ics
op·to·i·so·la·tor
op·tom·e·trist
op·tom·e·try
  -to·met·ric
op·u·lence
op·u·lent
or (conjunction; cf.
  oar, ore)
or·a·cle

oral (spoken; cf.
  aural)
  oral·ly
or·ange
or·ange·ade
orang·utan
ora·tion
or·a·tor
or·a·tor·i·cal
or·a·to·ry
  -ries
or·bit
  -bit·al
or·ca
or·chard
or·ches·tra
or·ches·tral
or·ches·trate
  -trat·ed, -trat·ing,
  -tra·tor
or·ches·tra·tion
or·chid
or·dain
  -dain·ment
or·deal
or·der
  -dered, -dering
or·der·li·ness
or·der·ly
  -lies
or·di·nal
or·di·nance (law;
  cf. *ordnance*)

or·di·nary
  -nar·ies, -nari·ly,
  -nari·ness
or·di·nate
or·di·na·tion
ord·nance
  (munitions; cf.
  ordinance)
ore (mineral; cf. *oar,
  or*)
or·gan
or·gan·ic
  -i·cal·ly
or·gan·ism
or·gan·ist
or·ga·ni·za·tion
or·ga·nize
  -ga·nized,
  -ga·niz·ing,
  -gan·iz·able
or·gy
  -gies
ori·ent
ori·en·tal
ori·en·tal·ism
ori·en·tate
  -tat·ed, -tat·ing
ori·en·ta·tion
or·i·fice
or·i·gin
orig·i·nal
orig·i·nal·i·ty
orig·i·nate

  -nat·ed, -nat·ing,
  -na·tion, -na·tor
ori·ole
or·na·ment
or·na·men·tal
or·na·men·ta·tion
or·nate
or·nery
or·ni·thol·o·gy
  -thol·o·gist,
  -tho·log·i·cal,
  -tho·log·i·cal·ly
or·phan
  -phaned,
  -phan·ing
or·phan·age
or·tho·don·tics
or·tho·dox
or·thog·ra·phy
or·tho·pe·dic
os·cil·late
  -lat·ed, -lat·ing
os·cil·la·tion
os·cil·la·tor
Os·lo
os·mo·sis
os·prey
os·si·fi·ca·tion
os·si·fy
  -fied, -fy·ing
os·ten·si·ble
  -bly

os·ten·sive
  -sive·ly
os·ten·ta·tion
os·ten·ta·tious
os·te·o·ar·thri·tis
os·teo·path
os·te·op·a·thy
  -teo·path·ic,
  -teo·path·i·cal·ly
os·teo·po·ro·sis
os·tra·cism
os·tra·cize
  -cized, -ciz·ing
os·trich
oth·er
oth·er·wise
oto·lar·yn·gol·o·gy
ot·to·man
ought (should; cf.
  aught)
our (possessive; cf.
  hour)
our·self
our·selves
oust·er
out
out-and-out
out·bal·ance
out·bid
out·bound
out·break
out·burst
out·cast

out·class
out·come
out·cry
out·dat·ed
out·dis·tance
out·do
out·door (adj)
out·doors (n, adv)
out·er
out·er·most
out·field
out·fit
  -fit·ted, -fit·ting
out·fit·ter
out·flank
out·fox
out·go
  -goes
out·go·ing
out·grow
  -grew, -grown,
  -grow·ing
out·growth
out·guess
out·ing
out·land·ish
out·lay
  -laid, -lay·ing
out·let
out·line
  -lined, lin·ing
out·live
out·look

out·ly·ing
out·ma·neu·ver
out·match
out·mode
  -mod·ed, -mod·ing
out·num·ber
out-of-date
out-of-door
out-of-the-way
out·pa·tient
out·place·ment
out·point
out·post
out·pour·ing
out·put
  -put·ted
out·rage
  -raged, -rag·ing
out·ra·geous
out·reach
out·rid·er
out·rig·ger
out·right
out·run
  -ran, -run,
  -run·ning
out·sell
  -sold, -sell·ing
out·set
out·side
out·sid·er
out·skirt
out·smart

out·soar
out·source
  -sourced,
  sourc·ing
out·speak
  -spoke, -spo·ken,
  -speak·ing
out·spread
  -spread,
  -spread·ing
out·stand·ing
out·stay
out·stretch
out·ward
out·ward·ly
out·wear
  -wore, -worn,
  -wear·ing
out·weigh
out·wit
out·work
oval
  oval·ness
ova·ry
  -ries
ova·tion
ov·en
over
over·abun·dance
over·achiev·er
over·all
over and over
over·arm

over·bal·ance
over·board
over·build
  -built, -build·ing
over·bur·den
over·cap·i·tal·ize
  -iza·tion
over·cast
  -cast, -cast·ing
over·charge
over·class
over·clock·ing
over·coat
over·come
  -came, -come,
  -com·ing
over·com·mit
over·com·pen·sate
over·con·fi·dence
over·crowd
over·do (too much;
  cf. *overdue*)
  -did, -do·ing, -does
over·dose
over·draft
over·draw
  -drew, -drawn,
  -draw·ing
over·due (past due;
  cf. *overdo*)
over·ea·ger
over·em·pha·size
over·es·ti·mate

over·ex·tend
over·flow
over·grow
  -grew, -grown,
  -grow·ing
over·hand
over·hang
  -hung, -hang·ing
over·haul
over·head
over·hear
  -heard, -hear·ing
over·heat
over·in·dulge
over·kill
over·land
over·lap
over·lay
  -laid, -lay·ing
over·load
over·look
over·ly
over·night
over·pass
over·pop·u·la·tion
over·pow·er
over·price
over·pro·tec·tive
over·qual·i·fied
over·rate
over·reach
over·re·act

over·ride
   -rode, -rid·den,
   -rid·ing
over·ripe
over·rule
over·run
   -ran, -run,
   -run·ning
over·seas
over·see
   -saw, -seen,
   -see·ing
over·seer
over·sen·si·tive
over·shad·ow
over·shoe
over·sight
over·sim·pli·fy
over·size
over·sleep
   -slept, -sleep·ing
over·spread
   -spread,
   -spread·ing
over·stay
over·step
over·sub·scribe
overt
   overt·ness
over·take
   -took, -tak·en,
   -tak·ing
over-the-count·er

over·throw
   -threw, -thrown,
   -throw·ing
over·time
over·tone
over·ture
   -tured, -tur·ing
over·turn
over·use
over·view
over·weigh
over·weight
over·whelm·ing
over·work
over·write
   -wrote, -writ·ten,
   writ·ing
over·zeal·ous
owe
   owed (indebted;
   cf. *ode*), ow·ing
owl·et
owl·ish
own
   own·er,
   own·er·ship
ox·al·ic ac·id
ox·bow
ox·ford
ox·heart
ox·i·dant
ox·i·da·tion
ox·ide

ox·i·dize
   -dized, -diz·ing,
   -diz·able
ox·tail
ox·tongue
ox·y·gen
ox·y·gen·ate
   -at·ed, -at·ing
ox·y·mo·ron
oys·ter
oys·ter bed
ozone
ozone lay·er

pace
  paced, pac·ing
pace·mak·er
pac·er
pace·set·ter
pachy·derm
pach·y·san·dra
Pa·cif·ic
pac·i·fi·er
pac·i·fist
pac·i·fy
  -fied, -fy·ing
pack·age
  -aged, -ag·ing
pack·age deal
pack·er
pack·et
pack·horse
pack·ing
pact
pad
  pad·ded, pad·ding
pad·dle
  -dled, -dling
pad·dock
pad·lock
pa·dre
pa·gan
pa·gan·ism

pa·gan·ize
  -ized, -iz·ing
pag·eant
pag·eant·ry
pag·i·nate
  -nat·ed, -nat·ing
pag·i·na·tion
page-file
paid
pail (bucket; cf.
  pale)
pain (hurt; cf. *pane*)
  pain·less
pain·ful
pain·kill·er
pains·tak·ing
paint·brush
paint·er
pair (two; cf. *pare,
  pear*)
pa·ja·mas
Pa·ki·stan
pal·ace
pal·at·able
pal·ate (roof of the
  mouth; cf. *palette,
  pallet*)
pa·la·tial

pale (white; cf. *pail*)
  pal·er, pal·est,
  pal·ing
pa·le·on·tol·o·gy
Pal·es·tine
Pal·es·tin·ian
pal·ette (for paint;
  cf. *palate, pallet*)
pal·i·mony
pal·i·sade
pall·bear·er
pal·let (couch; cf.
  palate, palette)
pal·lid
pal·lor
palm
pal·met·to
palm·ist
palm·ist·ry
palm·top
pal·o·mi·no
pal·pa·ble
pal·pate (examine
  by touch; cf.
  palpitate)
pal·pi·tate (throb;
  cf. *palpate*)
pal·sy
  -sied, -sy·ing

pal·try (trivial; cf.
   poultry)
  -tri·er, -tri·est
pam·per
  -pered, -per·ing
pam·phlet
pan
  panned, pan·ning
pan·a·cea
pa·nache
Pan·a·ma
Pan-Amer·i·can
pan·cake
pan·chro·mat·ic
pan·cre·as
pan·dem·ic
pan·de·mo·ni·um
pane (of glass; cf.
  pain)
pan·el
  -eled, -el·ing
pan·el·ist
pan·han·dle
pan·ic
  -icked, -ick·ing
pan·ic-strick·en
pan·ora·ma
pan·sy
  -sies
pan·the·on
pan·ther
pan·to·mime
  -mimed, -mim·ing

pan·try
pa·pa·cy
  -cies
pa·pal
pa·pa·raz·zi (pl)
  -raz·zo (sing)
pa·pa·ya
pa·per
pa·per·less
pa·per·net
pa·per·weight
pa·per·work
pa·pier-mâ·ché
pa·poose
pa·pri·ka
pa·py·rus
par·a·ble
pa·rab·o·la
para·chute
  -chut·ed, -chut·ing
pa·rade
par·a·digm
par·a·dise
par·a·dox·i·cal
par·af·fin
par·a·gon
para·graph
Par·a·guay
par·a·keet
para·lan·guage
para·le·gal
par·al·lel
par·al·lel bars

par·al·lel·ism
par·al·lel·o·gram
par·al·lel port
pa·ral·y·sis
  -ses (pl)
par·a·lyt·ic
par·a·lyze
  -lyzed, -lyz·ing
para·med·ic
pa·ram·e·ter
par·a·mount
para·noia
para·noid
par·a·pet
par·a·pher·na·lia
para·phrase
  -phrased,
  -phras·ing
para·ple·gia
para·pro·fes·sion·al
par·a·site
para·sol
para·troop·er
par·boil
par·cel (bundle; cf.
  partial)
  -celed, -cel·ing
parch·ment
par·don
  -doned, -don·ing
par·don·able
par·don·er

pare (peel; cf. *pair, pear*)
  pared, par·ing
par·ent
  pa·ren·tal
par·ent·age
pa·ren·the·sis
  -the·ses (pl),
  -thet·ic,
  -thet·i·cal·ly
par·ent·hood
par·fait
pa·ri·etal
pari-mu·tu·el
par·ish (church; cf. *perish*)
pa·rish·io·ner
par·i·ty
  -ties
park·way
par·lay (gamble)
par·lia·ment
par·lia·men·tar·i·an
par·lia·men·ta·ry
par·lor
Par·me·san
pa·ro·chi·al
par·o·dy
  -dies
pa·role
  -roled, -rol·ing
par·ox·ysm
par·rot

parse
  -pars·ing, pars·er
par·si·mo·ni·ous
par·si·mo·ny
pars·ley
pars·nip
par·son
par·son·age
par·take
part·ed
par·tial (part; cf. *parcel*)
par·tial·i·ty
par·tic·i·pant
par·tic·i·pate
  -pat·ed, -pat·ing
par·tic·i·pa·tion
par·ti·ci·ple
par·ti·cle
par·tic·u·lar
par·tic·u·lar·i·ty
par·tic·u·lar·ize
  -ized, -iz·ing
par·tic·u·lar·ly
par·ti·san
par·ti·tion
part·ly
part·ner
part·ner·ship
par·tridge
part-time
par·tu·ri·tion

par·ty
  -ties, -tied, -ty·ing
par value
Pas·cal (philosopher)
PAS·CAL (computer language)
pass
pass·able
pas·sage
pas·sage·way
pass·book
pas·sé
passed (of movement; cf. *past*)
pas·sen·ger
pass·er·by
  pass·ers·by (pl)
pass-fail
pas·si·ble
pass·ing
pas·sion
pas·sion·ate
pas·sive
pas·sive-ma·trix
pass·key
Pass·over
pass·port
pass·word
past (of time; cf. *passed*)
paste
  past·ed, past·ing

pas·tel
pas·tern
pas·teur·iza·tion
pas·teur·ize
  -ized, -iz·ing
pas·time
pas·tor
pas·to·ral
pas·to·ral·ism
pas·tor·ate
pas·tra·mi
past·ry
  -ries
pas·ture
  -tured, -tur·ing
pas·ty
  -ties
patch·work
pâ·té
pa·tent (adj)
pat·ent (n, v)
pa·ter·nal
pa·ter·nal·ism
pa·ter·ni·ty
pa·thet·ic
path·find·er
path·name
pa·thog·ra·phy
patho·log·i·cal
pa·thol·o·gy
  -gies
pa·thos
path·way

pa·tience
pa·tient
pa·tio
pa·tri·arch
pa·tri·ar·chy
  -chies
pa·tri·cian
pat·ri·mo·ny
pa·tri·ot
pa·tri·ot·ic
pa·tri·o·tism
pa·trol
  -trolled, -trol·ling
pa·tron
pa·tron·age
pa·tron·ize
  -ized, -iz·ing
pat·ter
pat·tern
pat·ty
  -ties
pau·ci·ty
paunch
pau·per
pause
pave
pa·vil·ion
paw
pawn·bro·ker
pay
  paid, pay·ing
pay·able
pay·back

pay·check
pay·day
pay·ee
pay·load
pay·ment
pay off (v)
pay·off (n)
pay-per-view
pay·roll
pay-TV
PC card
peace (calm; cf. *piece*)
peace·able
peace·ful
peace·keep·ing
peace·mak·er
peace·time
peach
pea·cock
peak (top; cf. *peek, pique*)
peal (loud ringing; cf. *peel*)
pea·nut
pear (fruit; cf. *pair, pare*)
pearl
pear-shaped
peas·ant
peb·ble
pec·to·ral

pe·cu·liar
  -liar·ly
pe·cu·liar·i·ty
  -ties
pe·cu·ni·ary
ped·a·gog·ic
ped·a·gogue
ped·a·go·gy
ped·al (of a bicycle;
  cf. *peddle*)
  -aled, -al·ing
pe·dan·tic
ped·dle (sell; cf.
  pedal)
  -dled, -dling
ped·dler
ped·es·tal
pe·des·tri·an
pe·di·a·tri·cian
pe·di·at·rics
ped·i·cure
ped·i·gree
ped·i·ment
pe·dom·e·ter
peek (look; cf. *peak,
  pique*)
peel (pare; cf. *peal*)
peer (look; cf. *pier*)
peer·less
peeve
peg
  pegged, peg·ging
Peg·a·sus

pel·i·can
pel·let
pell-mell
pel·lu·cid
pelt
pel·vis
pen
  penned, pen·ning
pe·nal
pe·nal·ize
  -ized, -iz·ing
pen·al·ty
  -ties
pen·ance
pen-based
pen·chant
pen·cil
  -ciled, -cil·ing
pen·dant
pen·dent
pend·ing
pen·du·lous
pen·du·lum
pen·e·tra·ble
  -bil·i·ty
pen·e·trate
  -trat·ed, -trat·ing
pen·e·tra·tion
pen·guin
pen·i·cil·lin
pen·in·su·la
pen·i·tence
pen·i·tent

pen·i·ten·tial
pen·i·ten·tia·ry
pen·knife
pen·man·ship
pen·nant
pen·ni·less
pen·ny
  -nies
pen·ny ante (n)
pen·ny-ante (adj)
pen·ny·weight
pe·nol·o·gy
pen·sion
  -sioned, -sion·ing
pen·sive
  -sive·ly,
  -sive·ness
pen·ta·gon
  -tag·o·nal
pen·tath·lon
Pen·te·cost
pent·house
Pen·ti·um
pe·nult
pen·ul·ti·mate
pen·u·ry
pe·on
pe·o·ny
  -nies
peo·ple
  -pled, -pling
pep·per
  -pered, -per·ing

pep·per-and-salt
pep·per·corn
pep·per·mint
pep·pery
pep·sin
pep talk
per
per an·num
per·cale
per cap·i·ta
per·ceive
 -ceived, -ceiv·ing,
 -ceiv·able
per·cent
per·cent·age
per·cen·tile
per·cept
per·cep·ti·ble
per·cep·tion
per·cep·tive
per·cep·tu·al
Per·che·ron
per·co·late
 -lat·ed, -lat·ing
per·co·la·tor
per·cus·sion
per di·em
Per·e·grine fal·con
pe·remp·to·ry
pe·ren·ni·al
per·e·stroi·ka
per·fect
per·fect·ible

per·fec·tion
per·fo·rate
 -rat·ed, -rat·ing
per·fo·ra·tion
per·form
 -form·er
per·for·mance
per·fume
 -fumed, -fum·ing
per·fum·er
per·func·to·ry
 -to·ri·ly
per·haps
per·il·ous
 -ous·ness
pe·rim·e·ter
per·i·na·tal
pe·ri·od
pe·ri·od·ic
pe·ri·od·i·cal
 -cal·ly
pe·riph·er·al
pe·riph·ery
 -er·ies
peri·scope
per·ish (die; cf.
 parish)
per·ish·able
 -abil·i·ty
peri·to·ni·tis
per·i·win·kle
per·jure
 -jured, -jur·ing

per·jur·er
per·ju·ry
per·ma·nence
per·ma·nen·cy
per·ma·nent
per·me·abil·i·ty
per·me·able
per·me·ate
 -at·ed, -at·ing
per·me·ation
per·mis·si·ble
per·mis·sion
per·mis·sive
 -sive·ness
per·mit
 -mit·ted, -mit·ting
per·mu·ta·tion
per·ni·cious
 -cious·ness
per·ox·ide
per·pen·dic·u·lar
per·pe·trate
 -trat·ed, -trat·ing,
 -tra·tion
per·pet·u·al
 -al·ly
per·pet·u·ate
 -at·ed, -at·ing,
 -a·tion
per·pe·tu·ity
 -ities
per·plex

per·plex·i·ty
  -ties
per·qui·site
per se
per·se·cute (harass;
    cf. *prosecute*)
  -cut·ed, -cut·ing
per·se·cu·tion
per·se·ver·ance
per·se·vere
  -vered, -ver·ing,
  -ver·ing·ly
Per·sian
per·sim·mon
per·sist
per·sis·tence
per·sis·tent
per·son
per·son·able
per·son·age
per·son·al (not pub-
    lic; cf. *personnel*)
per·son·al dig·i·tal
  as·sis·tant
per·son·al·i·ty
  -ties
per·son·al·ize
per·son·al·ly
per·son·i·fi·ca·tion
per·son·i·fy
per·son·nel
    (employees; cf.
    personal)

per·spec·tive
    (appearance to
    the eye; cf.
    prospective)
per·spi·ra·tion
per·spire
  -spired, -spir·ing
per·suade
  -suad·ed,
  -suad·ing
per·sua·sion
per·sua·sive
  -sive·ness
per·tain
per·ti·na·cious
per·ti·nent
per·turb
Pe·ru
pe·ruse
  -rused, -rus·ing,
  -rus·al
per·vade
  -vad·ed, -vad·ing
per·va·sive
  -sive·ness
per·verse
  -verse·ness,
  -ver·si·ty
per·ver·sion
per·ver·sive
per·vert
peso

pes·si·mism
  -mist
pes·si·mis·tic
pes·ti·cide
pes·ti·lence
pes·ti·lent
pet
  pet·ted, pet·ting
peta·bit
peta·byte
pet·al
pe·tite (small)
pe·ti·tion
  -tioned, -tion·ing,
  -tion·er
pet·ri·fy
  -fied, -fy·ing
pe·tro·leum
pe·trol·o·gy
pet sit·ting
pet·ti·coat
pet·ty
  -ti·er, -ti·est,
  -ti·ness
pet·u·lant
pe·tu·nia
pew·ter
pha·lanx
  -lanx·es (pl)
phan·tom
pha·raoh
phar·i·see
phar·ma·ceu·ti·cal

phar·ma·cist
phar·ma·cy
-cies
phar·ynx
phase
phased, phas·ing
phase out (v)
phase·out (n)
pheas·ant
phe·nom·e·nal
phe·nom·e·non
-na (pl)
phi·lan·der
-dered, -der·ing,
-der·er
phil·an·throp·ic
-i·cal·ly
phi·lan·thro·py
-pies
phi·lat·e·list
phi·lat·e·ly
phil·a·tel·ic
Phil·har·mon·ic
Phil·ip·pines
phi·lol·o·gy
phi·los·o·pher
philo·soph·i·cal
-cal·ly
phi·los·o·phy
-phies
phil·ter (drug; cf.
filter)
phlegm

phleg·mat·ic
pho·bia
phoe·nix
Phoe·nix
phone tag
pho·net·ic
-net·i·cal
pho·nics
pho·no·graph
pho·ny
phos·phate
phos·pho·resce
-resced, -resc·ing
phos·pho·res·cence
phos·pho·res·cent
phos·pho·ric
phos·pho·rous (adj)
phos·pho·rus (n)
pho·to·con·duc·
tiv·i·ty
pho·to·copy
-cop·ier
pho·to·elec·tric
pho·to·en·grav·ing
pho·to·gen·ic
-ni·cal·ly
pho·to·graph
-tog·ra·pher
pho·to·graph·ic
-i·cal·ly
pho·tog·ra·phy
pho·to·jour·nal·ism
pho·to·re·al·ism

pho·to·sen·sor
pho·to·syn·the·sis
phrase
phrased,
phras·ing
phrase·ol·o·gy
phreak
phre·nol·o·gy
-gist
phy·log·e·ny
phys·ic (medicine;
cf. *physique,
psychic*)
phys·i·cal (of the
body; cf. *fiscal*)
-cal·ly, -cal·ness
phy·si·cian
phys·i·cist
phys·ics
phys·i·ol·o·gy
-gist
phy·sique (of the
body; cf. *physic,
psychic*)
pi·a·nis·si·mo
pi·a·nist
pi·ano (n)
pi·anos
pi·ca
pic·a·dor
pic·a·yune
-yun·ish

pic·co·lo
  -los
pick·er·el
pick·et
pick·le
  -led, -ling
pick·lock
pick·pock·et
pick up (v)
pick·up (n)
pic·nic
  -nicked, -nick·ing,
  -nick·er
pi·co·sec·ond
pic·to·graph
pic·to·ri·al
  -al·ly
pic·ture
  -tured, -tur·ing
pic·tur·esque
  -esque·ly,
  -esque·ness
pid·gin (language;
  cf. *pigeon*)
piece (part; cf.
  peace)
  pieced, piec·ing
piece·meal
pie chart
pie·crust
pie·plant
pier (dock; cf. *peer*)

pierce
  pierced, pierc·ing
Pierre
pi·e·ty
  -eties
pi·geon (bird; cf.
  pidgin)
pi·geon-toed
pig·gy·back
pig·ment
pig·men·ta·tion
pig·skin
pik·er
pi·laf
pi·las·ter
pile
  piled, pil·ing
pil·fer
  -fered, -fer·ing,
  -fer·age
pil·grim
pil·grim·age
  -aged, -ag·ing
pil·ing
pil·lage
  -laged, -lag·ing,
  -lag·er
pil·lar
pil·low
pil·low·case
pi·lot
pi·lot·house
pi·lot light

pi·men·to
  -tos
pim·ple
pin·afore
pin·cush·ion
pine
  pined, pin·ing
pine·ap·ple
pin·feath·er
pin·hole
pin·ion
pink·eye
pin·na·cle (highest
  point; cf.
  pinochle)
  -cled, -cling
pi·noch·le (card
  game; cf.
  pinnacle)
pin·point
pin·stripe
pin·up
pi·o·neer
pi·ous
pipe dream
pipe·line
pip·er
pi·pette
pipe wrench
pi·quant
pique (provoke; cf.
  peak, peek)
  piqued, piqu·ing

208

pi·ra·cy
  -cies
pi·ra·nha
pi·rate
  -rated, -rat·ing
pir·ou·ette
pis·ta·chio
pis·til (of plant; cf.
  pistol, pistole)
pis·tol (weapon; cf.
  pistil, pistole)
pis·tole (old coin; cf.
  pistil, pistol)
pis·ton
pitch
pitch-dark
pitch·er
pitch·fork
pit·e·ous
pit·fall
pithy
  pith·i·ly
piti·able
piti·ful
  -ful·ly, -ful·ness
piti·less
pit·tance
pi·tu·itary
pity
  pit·ied, pity·ing
piv·ot
piv·ot·al
pix·el

piz·za
piz·zazz
piz·ze·ria
pla·ca·ble
plac·ard
pla·cate
  -cated, -cat·ing,
  -ca·tion
pla·ce·bo
  -bos
place·kick
place mat
place·ment
plac·id
pla·gia·rism
  -rist
pla·gia·rize
  -rized, -riz·ing
plague
  plagued,
  plagu·ing
plain (simple; cf.
  plane)
plain·clothes·man
plain·spo·ken
plain·text
plain·tiff (com-
  plainant; cf.
  plaintive)
plain·tive (mourn-
  ful; cf. *plaintiff*)
  -tive·ly, -tive·ness

plait (fold; cf. *plat,
  plate, pleat*)
plan
  planned,
  plan·ning
plane (airplane; cf.
  plain)
plan·et
plan·e·tar·i·um
plan·e·tary
plank
plank·ton
plan·tain
plan·tar (of the sole;
  cf. *planter*)
plan·ta·tion
plant·er (farmer; cf.
  plantar)
plaque
plas·ma
plas·ter
  -tered, -ter·ing,
  -ter·er
plas·ter·board
plas·tic
plas·tic·i·ty
plat (map; cf. *plait,
  plate, pleat*)
plate (dish; cf. *plait,
  plat, pleat*)
pla·teau
plat·en
plat·form

209

plat·i·num
plat·i·tude
plat·i·tu·di·nous
pla·ton·ic
pla·toon
plat·ter
plau·dit
plau·si·bil·i·ty
  -ties
plau·si·ble
  -ble·ness, -bly
play back (v)
play·back (n)
play·er
play·ful
play·ground
play off (v)
play-off (n)
play·pen
play·suit
play·thing
play·wright
pla·za
plea
plead
  plead·ed,
  plead·ing,
  plead·able
pleas·ant
pleas·ant·ry
  -ries
please
  pleased, pleas·ing

plea·sur·able
plea·sure
pleat (arrange in
  pleats; cf. *plait,
  plat, plate*)
pleb·i·scite
pledge
  pledged,
  pledg·ing
plen·i·tude
plen·te·ous
plen·ti·ful
plen·ty
ple·num
ple·si·o·chron·ous
pleth·o·ra
pleu·ri·sy
Plex·i·glas
pli·able
  -abil·i·ty
pli·ant
pli·ers
plod
  plod·ded,
  plod·ding,
  plod·der
plot
  plot·ted, plot·ting,
  plot·ter
plug
  plugged,
  plug·ging
Plug and Play

plum (fruit; cf.
  plumb, plume)
plum·age
plumb (weight; cf.
  plum, plume)
plumb·er
plumb·ing
plumb line
plume (feather; cf.
  plum, plumb)
plum·met
plump·ness
plun·der
plunge
  plunged,
  plung·ing
plung·er
plu·ral
plu·ral·ism
  -is·tic
plu·ral·i·ty
  -ties
plu·ral·ize
  -ized, -iz·ing
plu·toc·ra·cy
  -cies
plu·to·ni·um
ply·wood
pneu·mat·ic
pneu·mo·nia
pneu·mon·ic
poach·er

pock·et
  -et·ful
pock·et·knife
pock·et-sized
po·di·a·try
  -trist
po·di·um
po·em
po·esy
  -esies
po·et
po·et·ic
po·et·ry
poi·gnan·cy
poi·gnant
poin·set·tia
point
point-and-click
point-blank
point·ed
point·er
point·less
point-of-sale
  ter·mi·nal
poise
poi·son
  -soned, -son·ing
poi·son·ous
poi·son-pen (adj)
pok·er
Po·land
po·lar

po·lar·i·ty
  -ties
po·lar·iza·tion
po·lar·ize
  -ized, -iz·ing
Po·lar·oid
pole (rod; cf. *poll*)
  poled, pol·ing
po·lem·ic
po·lem·i·cal
pole vault (n)
pole-vault (v)
po·lice·man
po·lice·wom·an
pol·i·cy
  -cies
pol·i·cy·hold·er
pol·ish
Pol·ish
po·lit·bu·ro
po·lite
  -lit·er, -lit·est,
  -lite·ness
pol·i·tic
po·lit·i·cal
  -cal·ly
pol·i·ti·cian
pol·i·tics
pol·ka
poll (vote; cf. *pole*)
pol·len
pol·li·nate
  -nat·ed, -nat·ing

poll tax
pol·lute
  -lut·ed, -lut·ing,
  -lut·er
pol·lu·tion
pol·ter·geist
poly·chlo·rin·at·ed·
  biphenyl (PCB)
poly·chro·mat·ic
poly·chrome
poly·es·ter
poly·eth·yl·ene
po·lyg·a·mous
po·lyg·a·my
  -mist
poly·gon
poly·graph
poly·mor·phism
Poly·ne·sia
poly·no·mi·al
pol·yp
poly·syl·lab·ic
poly·syl·la·ble
poly·tech·nic
poly·un·sat·u·rat·ed
pome·gran·ate
pom·mel
  -meled, -mel·ing
pom·pa·dour
pom·pos·i·ty
  -ties
pomp·ous
  -ous·ness

pon·cho
pon·der
  -dered, -der·ing
pon·der·a·ble
pon·der·ous
pon·tiff
pon·tif·i·cal
pon·tif·i·cate
pon·toon
po·ny
  -nies
poo·dle
pool·room
poor·ly
pop
  popped, pop·ping
pop·corn
pop·gun
pop·lar (tree; cf.
  popular)
pop·lin
pop·over
pop·py
  -pies
pop·u·lace (people;
  cf. *populous*)
pop·u·lar (widely
  liked; cf. *poplar*)
pop·u·lar·i·ty
pop·u·lar·ize
  -ized, -iz·ing,
  -iza·tion

pop·u·late
  -lat·ed, -lat·ing
pop·u·la·tion
pop·u·lous (thickly
  populated; cf.
  populace)
pop-up
por·ce·lain
por·cu·pine
pore (study; cf.
  pour)
  pored, por·ing
por·nog·ra·phy
  -no·graph·ic
  -no·graph·i·cal·ly
por·poise
por·ridge
por·ta·ble
  -bly, -bil·i·ty
por·tage
  -taged, -tag·ing
por·tal
por·tend
por·tent
por·ten·tous
por·ter
por·ter·house
port·fo·lio
port·hole
por·ti·co
por·tion
  -tioned, -tion·ing

port·ly
  -li·er, -li·ness
por·trait
por·tray
por·tray·al
Por·tu·gal
Por·tu·guese
po·si·tion
  -tioned, -tion·ing
pos·i·tive
  -tive·ly, -tive·ness
pos·i·tron
pos·se
pos·sess
  -sess·or
pos·sessed
pos·ses·sion
pos·ses·sive
pos·si·bil·i·ty
  -ties
pos·si·ble
  -bly
post·age
post·al
post·box
post·card
post·date
post·doc·tor·al
post·er
pos·te·ri·or
pos·ter·i·ty
pos·tern
post·grad·u·ate

post·haste
post·hole
post·hu·mous
post·hyp·not·ic
post·lude
post·mark
post·mas·ter
post·mis·tress
post·mor·tem
post of·fice (n)
post·op·er·a·tive
post·paid
post·par·tum
post·pone
  -poned, -pon·ing,
  -pone·ment
post·script
post·sec·ond·ary
post·test
pos·tu·lant
pos·tu·late
  -lat·ed, -lat·ing
pos·ture
  -tured, -tur·ing
po·ta·ble
pot·ash
po·tas·si·um
po·ta·to
  -toes
pot·bel·ly
po·ten·cy
  -cies
po·tent

po·ten·tate
po·ten·tial
po·ten·ti·al·i·ty
pot·hole
po·tion
pot·luck
Po·to·si
pot·pie
pot·pour·ri
pot·shot
pot·tage
pot·ter
pot·tery
  -ter·ies
pouch
poul·tice
  -ticed, -tic·ing
poul·try (fowl; cf.
  paltry)
pound·age
pour (rain; cf. *pore*)
  pour·able
pov·er·ty
pow·der
  -dered, -der·ing
pow·er·ful
pow·er·less
pow·er pack
pow·er play
pow·wow
prac·ti·ca·ble (feasi-
  ble; cf. *practical*)
  -bly, -bil·i·ty

prac·ti·cal (useful;
  cf. *practicable*)
  -cal·i·ty, -cal·ness
prac·ti·cal·ly
prac·tice
prac·ti·cum
prac·ti·tio·ner
prag·mat·ic
prag·ma·tism
  -tist
prai·rie
praise
  praised, prais·ing
praise·wor·thy
pra·line
prank·ish
prat·tle
  -tled, -tling
pray (beseech; cf.
  prey)
prayer (address or
  petition)
pray·er (one who
  prays)
preach
  preach·er
pre·am·ble
pre·ap·prove
pre·can·cel
  -cel·la·tion
pre·car·i·ous
  -ous·ness

pre·cau·tion
-tion·ary
pre·cede (go before;
   cf. *proceed*)
   -ced·ed, -ced·ing
pre·ce·dence (prior-
   ity)
pre·ce·dent
pre·ced·ing
pre·cept
pre·cep·tive
pre·cep·tor
pre·ces·sion
   -sion·al
pre·cinct
pre·cious
prec·i·pice
pre·cip·i·tate
   -tat·ed, -tat·ing,
   -tate·ly
pre·cip·i·ta·tion
pre·cip·i·tous
pre·cise
pre·ci·sion
pre·clude
   -clud·ed, -clud·ing
pre·co·cious
   -cious·ness
pre·con·ceive
pre·con·cep·tion
pre·cook
pre·cur·sor
   -so·ry

pre·date
pred·a·tor
pred·a·to·ry
pre·de·cease
pre·de·ces·sor
pre·des·ti·na·tion
pre·des·tine
pre·de·ter·mine
pre·dic·a·ment
pred·i·cate
   -cat·ed, -cat·ing
pred·i·ca·tion
pre·dict
   -dict·able,
   -dict·abil·i·ty,
   -dic·tive
pre·dic·tion
pre·dis·pose
   -po·si·tion
pred·ni·sone
pre·dom·i·nance
pre·dom·i·nant
pre·dom·i·nate
pre·em·i·nence
pre·em·i·nent
pre·empt
pre·emp·tive
pre·ex·ist
pre·fab·ri·cate
pref·ace
   -aced, -ac·ing
pref·a·to·ry
pre·fect

pre·fer
   -ferred, -fer·ring
pref·er·a·ble
pref·er·ence
pref·er·en·tial
pre·fix
pre·flight
preg·nan·cy
   -cies
preg·nant
pre·heat
pre·his·tor·ic
pre·judge
prej·u·dice
   -diced, -dic·ing
prej·u·di·cial
   -cial·ly, -cial·ness
prel·ate
pre·lim·i·nary
pre·lude
pre·ma·ture
   -ture·ly,
   -ture·ness,
   -tu·ri·ty
pre·med·i·tate
pre·med·i·ta·tion
pre·mier
prem·ise
pre·mi·um
pre·mo·ni·tion
pre·mon·i·to·ry
pre·na·tal
pre·oc·cu·pan·cy

pre·oc·cu·pa·tion
pre·oc·cu·pied
pre·oc·cu·py
pre·or·dain
  -dain·ment,
  -di·na·tion
pre·pack·age
prep·a·ra·tion
pre·par·a·tive
pre·pa·ra·to·ry
pre·pare
  -par·ing
prepared
pre·pared·ness
pre·pay
pre·pon·der·ance
pre·pon·der·ant
prep·o·si·tion
  -tion·al
pre·pos·sess
pre·pos·sess·ing
pre·pos·ses·sion
pre·pos·ter·ous
pre·re·cord
pre·reg·is·ter
pre·re·lease
pre·req·ui·site
pre·rog·a·tive
pres·age (n)
pre·sage (v)
Pres·by·te·ri·an
pre·school

pre·scribe (order as
  a remedy; cf.
  proscribe)
  -scribed,
  -scrib·ing
pre·scrip·tion
pre·scrip·tive
pres·ence (of mind;
  cf. *presents*)
pre·sent (v)
pres·ent (adj, n)
pre·sent·able
  -able·ness, -ably,
  -abil·i·ty
pre·sen·ta·tion
pres·ent-day
pre·sen·tee
pre·sen·ti·ment
  (foreboding; cf.
  presentment)
pres·ent·ly
pre·sent·ment
  (from grand jury;
  cf. *presentiment*)
pres·ents (gifts; cf.
  presence)
pre·serve
  pre·served,
  pre·serv·ing,
  pres·er·va·tion
pre·side
  -sid·ed, -sid·ing
pres·i·den·cy

pres·i·dent
  -den·tial,
  -den·tial·ly
press
press box
press·ing
press·mark
press·room
press·run
pres·sure
pres·sur·ize
  -ized, -iz·ing,
  -iza·tion
pres·ti·dig·i·ta·tion
pres·tige
pres·ti·gious
pre·sum·able
pre·sume
  -sumed, -sum·ing
pre·sump·tion
pre·sump·tu·ous
pre·sup·pose
pre·tax
pre·tend
pre·tend·ed
pre·tense
pre·ten·sion
pre·ten·tious
pre·test
pre·text
pre·treat
pret·ty
  -ti·er, -ti·est, -ti·ly

215

pret·zel
pre·vail
pre·vail·ing
prev·a·lence
prev·a·lent
pre·var·i·cate
pre·vent
  -vent·able,
  -vent·abil·i·ty
pre·ven·tion
  pre·ven·tive or
  pre·ven·ta·tive
pre·view
pre·vi·ous
  -ous·ly,
  -ous·ness
pre·vi·sion
  (foresight; cf.
  provision)
prey (victim; cf.
  pray)
price
  priced, pric·ing
price-cut·ter
price-fix·ing
price in·dex
price·less
price tag
prick·le
prick·ly
  -li·er, -li·est
pride
  prid·ed, prid·ing

priest
priest·hood
priest·ly
pri·ma·cy
pri·ma don·na
pri·ma fa·cie
pri·mar·i·ly
pri·ma·ry
  -ries
pri·mate
prim·er
prime time
pri·me·val
prim·i·tive
pri·mo·gen·i·ture
pri·mor·di·al
prim·rose
prince·ly
prin·cess
prin·ci·pal (chief;
  cf. *principle*)
  -pal·ly
prin·ci·pal·i·ty
prin·ci·ple (rule; cf.
  principal)
print·able
print·er
print·ing
print out (v)
print·out (n)
pri·or
pri·or·i·ty
  -ties

prism
pris·mat·ic
pris·on
pris·on·er
pris·tine
pri·va·cy
pri·vate
  -vate·ly, -vate·ness
pri·va·tion
priv·et
priv·i·lege
  -leged, -leg·ing
privy
prize
  prized, priz·ing
prob·a·bil·i·ty
prob·a·ble
prob·a·bly
pro·bate
  -bat·ed, -bat·ing
pro·ba·tion
  -tion·ary
pro·ba·tion·er
probe
  probed, prob·ing
prob·lem
prob·lem·at·ic
pro·bos·cis
  -cis·es (pl)
pro·ce·dur·al
pro·ce·dure
pro·ceed (move for-
  ward; cf. *precede*)

pro·ceed·ing
pro·cess
pro·ces·sion
pro·ces·sion·al
pro·ces·sor
pro·claim
proc·la·ma·tion
pro·cliv·i·ty
pro·cras·ti·nate
  -nat·ed, -nat·ing,
  -na·tion
pro·cre·ate
  -at·ed, -at·ing,
  -ation
proc·tor
proc·u·ra·tor
pro·cure
  -cured, -cur·ing,
  -cur·ance
pro·cure·ment
prod·i·gal
pro·di·gious
prod·i·gy
  -gies
pro·duce
  -duced, -duc·ing,
  -duc·ible
pro·duc·er
prod·uct
pro·duc·tion
pro·duc·tive
pro·duc·tiv·i·ty
pro·fane

pro·fan·i·ty
  -ties
pro·fess
pro·fes·sion
pro·fes·sion·al
  -al·ly
pro·fes·sion·al·ism
pro·fes·sor
  -so·ri·al
pro·fes·sor·ship
prof·fer
  -fered, -fer·ing
pro·fi·cien·cy
pro·fi·cient
pro·file
  -filed, -fil·ing
prof·it (gain; cf.
  prophet)
prof·it·able
prof·i·teer
prof·li·gate
pro for·ma
pro·found
pro·fun·di·ty
pro·fuse
  -fuse·ly
  -fuse·ness
pro·fu·sion
prog·e·ny
  -nies
prog·no·sis
  -ses (pl)
prog·nos·tic

prog·nos·ti·cate
prog·nos·ti·ca·tion
pro·gram
  -grammed,
  -gram·ming,
  -gram·ma·ble
pro·gram·mat·ic
pro·gram·mer
prog·ress (n)
pro·gress (v)
pro·gres·sion
pro·gres·sive
pro·hib·it
pro·hi·bi·tion·ist
pro·hib·i·tive
proj·ect (n)
pro·ject (v)
pro·jec·tile
pro·jec·tion·ist
pro·jec·tor
pro·le·tar·i·an
pro·le·tar·i·at
pro·lif·er·ate
  -at·ed, -at·ing
pro·lif·er·a·tion
pro·lif·ic
pro·logue
pro·long
prom·e·nade
  -nad·ed, -nad·ing
prom·i·nence
prom·i·nent
pro·mis·cu·ity

pro·mis·cu·ous
prom·ise
  -ised, -is·ing
prom·is·so·ry
prom·is·so·ry note
pro·mote
  -mot·ed, -mot·ing
pro·mot·er
pro·mo·tion
prompt
pro·mul·gate
  -gat·ed, -gat·ing,
  -ga·tion
pro·noun
pro·nounce
  -nounced,
  -nounc·ing,
  -nounce·able
pro·nounce·ment
pro·nun·ci·a·tion
proof·read·er
pro·pa·gan·da
pro·pa·gan·dize
  -dized, -diz·ing
prop·a·gate
  -gat·ed, -gat·ing
prop·a·ga·tion
pro·pane
pro·pel
  -pelled, -pel·ling
pro·pel·lant
pro·pel·ler
pro·pen·si·ty

pro·per
prop·er·tied
prop·er·ty
  -ties
proph·e·cy (n)
  (prediction; cf.
  prophesy)
  -cies
proph·e·sy (v) (pre-
  dict; cf. *prophecy*)
  -sied, -sy·ing
proph·et (predicts
  future; cf. *profit*)
pro·phet·ic
pro·phy·lac·tic
pro·pi·ti·ate
  -at·ed, -at·ing
pro·pi·tious
pro·po·nent
pro·por·tion
pro·por·tion·al
pro·por·tion·ate
pro·pos·al
pro·pose (state; cf.
  purpose)
  -pos·ing
pro·posed
prop·o·si·tion
  -tion·al
pro·pri·etary
pro·pri·etor
pro·pri·ety
  -eties

pro·pul·sion
pro·rate
  -rat·ed, -rat·ing
pro·sa·ic
pro·scribe (outlaw;
  cf. *prescribe*)
prose
pros·e·cute (legal
  trial; cf. *persecute*)
  -cut·ed, -cut·ing
pros·e·cu·tion
pros·e·cu·tor
pros·e·lyte
pros·pect
pro·spec·tive
  (expected; cf.
  perspective)
pro·spec·tus
pros·per
  -pered, -per·ing
pros·per·i·ty
pros·per·ous
pros·tate
pros·the·sis
pros·thet·ic
prosth·odon·tics
pros·ti·tute
  -tut·ed, -tut·ing
pros·trate
pro·tag·o·nist
pro·tect
  -tec·tive,
  -tec·tive·ly

pro·tec·tion
pro·tec·tion·ist
  -tion·ism
pro·tec·tor
pro·tec·tor·ate
pro·té·gé
pro·tein
pro tem
pro tem·po·re
pro·test
prot·es·tant
pro·tes·ta·tion
pro·to·col
pro·to·plasm
pro·to·type
pro·tract
pro·trac·tion
pro·trac·tor
pro·trude
pro·tru·sion
pro·tru·sive
proud
prove
  proved, prov·ing,
  prov·able
prov·erb
pro·ver·bi·al
pro·vide
  -vid·ed, -vid·ing
prov·i·dence
Prov·i·dence
prov·i·dent
prov·i·den·tial

pro·vid·er
prov·ince
pro·vin·cial
pro·vin·cial·ism
pro·vi·sion (act of
  providing; cf.
  prevision)
pro·vi·sion·al
pro·vi·so
prov·o·ca·tion
pro·voc·a·tive
pro·voke
  -voked, -vok·ing
pro·vost
prow·ess
prox·i·mal
prox·im·i·ty
prox·i·mo
proxy
  prox·ies
Pro·zac
prude
pru·dence
pru·dent
pru·den·tial
prune
  pruned, prun·ing
pry
  pried, pry·ing
psalm
psalm·book
psalm·ist
pseu·do

pseu·do·code
pseud·onym
pso·ri·a·sis
psy·che·del·ic
psy·chi·a·try
  -chi·at·ric,
  -chi·a·trist
psy·chic (of the
  mind; cf. *physic,*
  physique)
psy·cho·anal·y·sis
  -an·a·lyst
psy·cho·an·a·lyze
psy·cho·graph
psy·cho·log·i·cal
psy·chol·o·gy
  -gies, -gist
psy·cho·path
psy·cho·sis
  -ses (pl)
psy·cho·so·mat·ic
psy·cho·ther·a·py
psy·chot·ic
pu·ber·ty
pub·lic
pub·lic ad·dress
  sys·tem
pub·lic as·sis·tance
pub·li·ca·tion
pub·lic do·main
pub·li·cist
pub·lic·i·ty

pub·li·cize
  -cized, -ciz·ing
pub·lic·ly
pub·lish
  -lish·able
pub·lish·er
pud·ding
pud·dle
  -dled, -dling
pudgy
  pudg·i·er,
  pudg·i·ness
pueb·lo
  -los
Pueb·lo
Puer·to Rico
puff
  puff·i·ness, puffy
pu·gi·lism
pug·na·cious
  -na·cious·ness,
  -nac·i·ty
Pu·lit·zer
pull·back
pull down (v)
pull-down menu
pul·ley
pull over (v)
pull·over (n, adj)
pul·mo·nary
pulp
pul·pit
pulp·wood

pul·sar
pul·sate
  -sat·ed, -sat·ing
pul·sa·tion
pulse
pul·ver·ize
  -ized, -iz·ing, -iz·er
pum·ice
pum·mel
  -meled, -mel·ing
pum·per·nick·el
pump·kin
punch
punch line
punc·tu·al
  -al·ly, -al·i·ty
punc·tu·ate
punc·tu·a·tion
punc·ture
  -tured, -tur·ing
pun·dit
pun·gen·cy
pun·gent
pun·ish
  -ish·able, -ish·er
pun·ish·ment
pu·ni·tive
pun·ster
punt·er
pu·ny
  -ni·er, -ni·est
pu·pil
pup·pet

pup·pet·ry
  -ries
pup·py
  -pies
pup tent
pur·chase
  -chased, -chas·ing,
  -chas·able
pu·ree
  -reed, -ree·ing
pure·ly
pur·ga·to·ry
  -ries
purge
  purged, purg·ing
pu·ri·fi·ca·tion
pu·ri·fy
  -fied, -fy·ing, -fi·er
pur·ist
pu·ri·tan
pu·ri·ty
pur·loin
pur·ple
pur·port
pur·port·ed·ly
pur·pose (inten-
  tion; cf. *propose*)
pur·pose·ly
purr
purse
purs·er
pur·su·ance
pur·su·ant

pur·sue
  -sued, -su·ing,
  -su·er
pur·suit
pur·vey·ance
pur·vey·or
pur·view
push
push but·ton (n)
push-but·ton (adj)
push·cart
push·ing
push·over (n)
push-pull (adj)
push-up (n)
pushy
  push·i·er,
  push·i·est,
  push·i·ness
pus·tu·lant
pus·tule
put
  put, put·ting
put down (v)
put-down (n)
put off
put-on (adj, n)
pu·tre·fy
  -fied, -fy·ing
pu·trid
putt
put·ter

put·ty
  -ties
put up (v)
put-up (adj)
puz·zle
  -zled, -zling, -zler
puz·zle·ment
pyg·my
  -mies
Pyong·yang
py·or·rhea
pyr·a·mid
pyre
Pyr·e·nees
py·ro·ma·nia
  -ni·ac
py·ro·tech·nics
py·rox·y·lin
py·thon

Qa·tar
quack·ery
quad·bit
quad·ran·gle
  qua·dran·gu·lar
quad·rant
qua·drat·ic
qua·dren·ni·al
qua·dren·ni·um
quad·ri·ceps
quad·ri·lat·er·al
quad·ri·ple·gic
qua·dru·ple
  -pled, -pling
qua·dru·plet
qua·dru·pli·cate
  -cat·ed, -cat·ing
quag·mire
quail
Quak·er
qual·i·fi·ca·tion
qual·i·fied
qual·i·fy
  -fied, -fy·ing
qual·i·ta·tive
qual·i·ty
  -ties
qualm

quan·da·ry
  -ries
quan·ti·fy
  -fied, -fy·ing
quan·ti·ta·tive
  -tive·ly, -tive·ness
quan·ti·ty
  -ties
quan·tum
  quan·ta (pl)
quar·an·tine
quar·rel
  -reled, -rel·ing
quar·rel·some
quar·ry
  -ries, -ried, -ry·ing
quar·ter
quar·ter·back
quar·ter·fi·nal
quar·ter·ly
quar·ter·mas·ter
quar·tet
quar·tile
quar·to
quarts (measures;
  cf. *quartz*)
quartz (mineral; cf.
  quarts)

qua·sar
qua·si
qua·si-ju·di·cial
qua·si-pub·lic
quay (wharf; cf. *key*)
quea·sy
  -si·er, -si·est,
  -si·ness
Que·bec
queen-size
queer
quer·u·lous
que·ry
  -ries, -ried,
  -ry·ing
ques·tion
ques·tion·able
  -ably
ques·tion·naire
queue (waiting line;
  cf. *cue*)
  queued, queu·ing
quib·ble
  -bled, -bling
quick·en
  -ened, -en·ing

quick-freeze (v)
  -froze, -fro·zen,
  -freez·ing
quick·ie
quick·sand
quick·sil·ver
quick-tem·pered
qui·et (silent; cf.
  quit, quite)
  -et·ness
qui·etude
qui·nine
quin·tes·sence
  quint·es·sen·tial
quin·tet
quin·tu·plet
quip
  quipped,
  quip·ping
quire (24 sheets; cf.
  choir)
quirk
  quirky,
  quirk·i·ness
quit (leave; cf. *quiet,*
  quite)
quit·claim
quite (completely;
  cf. *quiet, quit*)
quit·ter
quiv·er
  -ered, -er·ing
quix·ot·ic

quiz
  quizzed, quiz·zing
quiz·zi·cal
quo·rum
quo·ta
quot·able
quo·ta·tion
quote
  quot·ed, quot·ing
quo·tid·i·an
quo·tient
QWER·TY

rab·bi
rab·bit
rab·ble
 -bled, -bling
rab·ble-rous·er
ra·bid
ra·bies
 -bies (pl)
rac·coon
race·horse
rac·er
race·track
ra·cial
rac·ing
rac·ism
 -ist
rack·et
rack·e·teer
ra·con·teur
ra·dar
ra·dar·scope
ra·di·al
ra·di·ance
ra·di·ant
ra·di·ate
 -at·ed, -at·ing
ra·di·a·tion
ra·di·a·tor
rad·i·cal

rad·i·cal·ism
ra·dio
ra·dio·ac·tive
ra·dio·iso·tope
ra·di·ol·o·gy
ra·di·om·e·ter
 -e·try
ra·dio·ther·a·py
rad·ish
ra·di·um
ra·di·us
 ra·dii (pl)
ra·don
raf·fle
 -fled, -fling
raf·ter
rag·a·muf·fin
rag·ged (adj)
rag·ing
rag·lan
rag·time
rag·weed
rail·ing
rail·road
rail·way
rai·ment
rain (water; cf.
 reign, rein)
rain·bow

rain check
rain·coat
rain·drop
rain·fall
rain gauge
rain·mak·ing
rain·proof
rain·spout
rain·squall
rain·storm
rain·wa·ter
rain·wear
rainy
 rain·i·er, rain·i·est
raise (lift; cf. *rays,*
 raze)
 raised, rais·ing
rai·sin
rai·son d'être
rake
 raked, rak·ing
Ra·leigh
ral·ly
 -lied, -ly·ing
ram·ble
 -bled, -bling
ram·bler
ram·bunc·tious
ram·i·fi·ca·tion

224

ram·i·fy
  -fied, -fy·ing
ram·pant
ram·part
ram·rod
ram·shack·le
ranch·er
ran·cid
ran·cor
ran·cor·ous
ran·dom
ran·dom-ac·cess
  mem·o·ry (RAM)
rangy
  rang·i·er,
  rang·i·est
ran·kle
  -kled, -kling
ran·sack
ran·som
rap (strike; cf. *wrap*)
  rapped (struck; cf.
    rapt, wrapped),
  rap·ping
rape
  raped, rap·ing,
  rap·ist
rap·id
  -id·ness
rap·id-fire
ra·pid·i·ty
ra·pi·er

rap·pel (to descend;
  cf. *repel*)
rap·port
rap·proche·ment
rapt (engrossed; cf.
  rapped, wrapped)
  rapt·ly, rapt·ness
rap·ture
  -tur·ous
rare·bit
rar·efac·tion
rar·efied
rar·efy
  -efied, -efy·ing
rare·ly
rar·i·ty
  -ties
ras·cal
rash
  rash·ness
rasp·ber·ry
ras·ter
ratch·et
rate
  rat·ed, rat·ing
rath·er
raths·kel·ler
rat·i·fy
  -fied, -fy·ing,
  -fi·ca·tion
ra·tio
ra·tion
  -tioned, -tion·ing

ra·tio·nal (reason-
  able; cf. *rationale*)
ra·tio·nale (basis; cf.
  rational)
ra·tio·nal·ize
  -ized, -iz·ing,
  -iza·tion
rat·tan
rat·tle
  -tled, -tling
rat·tle·snake
rat·trap
rau·cous
  -cous·ness
rav·age
  -aged, -ag·ing
rav·el
  -eled, -el·ing
ra·ven
rav·en·ous
ra·vine
rav·i·o·li
raw·hide
rayon
rays (light beams;
  cf. *raise, raze*)
raze (tear down; cf.
  raise, rays)
  razed, raz·ing
ra·zor
ra·zor·back
re·act
re·ac·tion

re·ac·tion·ary
  -ar·ies
re·ac·tor
read·able
  -ably, -abil·i·ty
read·er·ship
readi·ly
read-on·ly
  mem·o·ry (ROM)
ready
  readi·er, readi·est
ready-made
ready-to-wear
re·al (true; cf. *reel*)
re·al es·tate
re·al·ism
  -ist, -is·tic,
  -is·ti·cal·ly
re·al·i·ty (real event;
  cf. *realty*)
  -ties
re·al·iza·tion
re·al·ize
  -ized, -iz·ing,
  -iz·able
re·al·ly
realm
real time (n)
real-time (adj)
Re·al·tor
re·al·ty (property; cf.
  reality)

re·arm
  -ar·ma·ment
re·ar·range
rea·son
  -soned, -son·ing
rea·son·able
  -ably
re·as·sess·ment
re·as·sur·ance
re·as·sure
re·bate
  -bat·ed, -bat·ing
reb·el (n)
re·bel (v)
  -belled, -bel·ling
re·bel·lion
re·bel·lious
re·birth
re·buff
re·buke
  -buked, -buk·ing
re·but
  -but·ted, -but·ting
re·but·tal
re·cal·ci·trant
re·call
  -call·able
re·cant
  -can·ta·tion
re·ca·pit·u·late
  -lat·ed, -lat·ing
re·ca·pit·u·la·tion
re·cap·ture

re·cede
  -ced·ed, -ced·ing
re·ceipt
re·ceiv·able
re·ceive
  -ceived, -ceiv·ing
re·ceiv·er·ship
re·cent
re·cep·ta·cle
re·cep·tion
re·cep·tion·ist
re·cep·tive
  -tiv·i·ty
re·cess
re·ces·sion
re·ces·sion·al
re·ces·sive
rec·i·pe
re·cip·i·ent
re·cip·ro·cal
  -cal·ly
re·cip·ro·cate
  -cat·ed, -cat·ing
re·cip·ro·ca·tion
rec·i·proc·i·ty
  -ties
re·cit·al
rec·i·ta·tion
re·cite
  -cit·ed, -cit·ing,
  -cit·er
reck·less

reck·on
-oned, -on·ing

rec·claim

rec·la·ma·tion

re·cline
-clined, -clin·ing

re·cluse
-clu·sive

rec·og·ni·tion

re·cog·ni·zance

rec·og·nize
-nized, -niz·ing,
-niz·able

re·coil

re·col·lect (collect
again; cf. *recollect*)

rec·ol·lect (recall; cf.
re-collect)

rec·om·mend
-mended,
-mend·ing,
-mend·able

rec·om·men·da·tion

re·com·mit
-mit·ment

rec·om·pense
-pensed,
-pens·ing

rec·on·cile
-ciled, -cil·ing,
-cile·ment

rec·on·cil·i·a·tion
-cil·ia·to·ry

re·con·di·tion

re·con·firm
-fir·ma·tion

re·con·nais·sance

re·con·noi·ter
-noi·tered,
-noi·ter·ing

re·con·sid·er

re·con·struc·tion

rec·ord (v)

rec·ord (n)

re·coup
-coup·able,
-coup·ment

re·course

re·cov·er (cover
again; cf. *recover*)

re·cov·er (regain; cf.
re-cover)
-ered, -er·ing

re·cov·er·y
-er·ies

rec·re·ation

re·crim·i·nate
-nat·ed, -nat·ing,
-na·tion

re·cruit

rect·an·gle

rect·an·gu·lar

rec·ti·fi·er

rec·ti·fy
-fied, -fy·ing,
-fi·ca·tion

rec·to·ry
-ries

rec·tum

re·cu·per·ate
-at·ed, -at·ing,
-a·tion

re·cur
-curred, -cur·ring,
-cur·rence

re·cur·sion

re·cy·cle

red·bird

red-blood·ed

red-car·pet (adj)

Red Cross

re·dec·o·rate

re·deem
-deem·able

re·deem·er

re·demp·tion

re·de·vel·op·ment

red-hand·ed (adj,
adv)

red·head

re·dis·trib·ute

re·dis·trict

re·dou·ble

re·dress

re·duce
-duced, -duc·ing,
-duc·ible

re·duc·tion

re·dun·dan·cy
-cies

re·dun·dant

red·wood

re·ed·u·cate

reek (smell; cf. *wreck*)

reel (spool; cf. *real*)

re·elect

re·em·ploy

re·en·act

re·en·trance

re·en·trant

re·en·try

re·fer

-fer·ring

ref·er·ee

-eed, -ee·ing

ref·er·ence

-enced, -enc·ing

ref·er·en·dum

re·fer·ral

re·ferred

re·fine

-fined, -fin·ing

re·fine·ment

re·fin·ery

-er·ies

re·flag

re·flect

re·flec·tion

re·flec·tive

-tive·ly, -tive·ness

re·flec·tor

re·flex

re·for·es·ta·tion

re·form

ref·or·ma·tion

re·for·ma·to·ry

-ries

re·formed

re·frac·tion

re·frac·to·ry

-ries

re·frain

re·fresh

re·fresh·ment

re·frig·er·ate

-at·ed, -at·ing,

-a·tion

re·frig·er·a·tor

ref·uge

ref·uges,

ref·ug·ing

ref·u·gee

re·fund

-fund·able

re·fur·bish

re·fus·al

re·fuse (v)(reject)

-fused, -fus·ing

ref·use (n)(garbage)

re·fute

-fut·ed, -fut·ing,

-fut·able

re·gain

re·gal

re·gale

-galed, -gal·ing

re·gard

re·gard·less

re·gat·ta

re·gen·cy

-cies

re·gen·er·ate

re·gen·er·a·tive

re·gent

reg·gae

re·gime

reg·i·men

re·gion

re·gion·al

reg·is·ter (enroll; cf.

registrar)

-tered, -ter·ing

reg·is·trar (record

keeper; cf.

register)

reg·is·tra·tion

reg·is·try

-tries

re·gress

re·gres·sion

re·gres·sive

re·gret

-gret·ted,

-gret·ting,

-gret·ful

re·gret·ta·ble

reg·u·lar

reg·u·lar·i·ty

-ties

reg·u·late
-lat·ed, -lat·ing,
-la·to·ry
reg·u·la·tion
re·gur·gi·tate
-tat·ed, -tat·ing
re·ha·bil·i·tate
-tat·ed, -tat·ing
re·hears·al
re·hearse
-hearsed,
-hears·ing
Reich·stag
reign (sovereignty;
cf. *rain, rein*)
re·im·burse
-bursed, -burs·ing,
-burs·able
re·im·burse·ment
rein (of a horse; cf.
rain, reign)
re·in·car·na·tion
rein·deer
re·in·force
re·in·force·ment
re·in·state
-stat·ed, -stat·ing,
-state·ment
re·in·sure
re·in·vest
re·is·sue
re·it·er·ate
-at·ed, -at·ing,
-a·tion

re·ject
re·jec·tion
re·joice
-joiced, -joic·ing,
-joic·ing·ly
re·join
re·ju·ve·nate
-nat·ed, -nat·ing,
-na·tion
re·lapse
-lapsed, -laps·ing
re·late
-lat·ed, -lat·ing
re·la·tion·al
re·la·tion·ship
rel·a·tive
rel·a·tiv·i·ty
-ties
re·lax
re·lax·ation
re·laxed
re·lay
-layed, -lay·ing
re·lease
-leased, -leas·ing
rel·e·gate
-gat·ed, -gat·ing,
-ga·tion
re·lent
re·lent·less
rel·e·vance
rel·e·vant
re·li·able

re·li·ance
re·li·ant
rel·ic
re·lief
re·lieve
-lieved, -liev·ing,
-liev·er
re·li·gion
re·li·gious
re·lin·quish
rel·ish
re·lo·cate
-ca·tion
re·luc·tance
re·luc·tant
re·ly
-lied, -ly·ing
re·main
re·main·der
-dered, -der·ing
re·mark
re·mark·able
re·me·di·al
rem·e·dy
-dies, -died,
-dy·ing
re·mem·ber
-bered, -ber·ing,
-ber·able
re·mem·brance
re·mind
-mind·er
rem·i·nisce
-nisced, -nisc·ing

rem·i·nis·cence
rem·i·nis·cent
re·mis·sion
re·mit·tance
rem·nant
re·mod·el
re·morse
re·mote
  -mote·ly,
  -mote·ness
re·mov·al
re·move
  -moved, -mov·ing
re·mu·ner·ate
  -at·ed, -at·ing,
  -a·tor
re·mu·ner·a·tion
re·mu·ner·a·tive
re·nais·sance
ren·der
  -dered, -der·ing,
  -der·able
ren·dez·vous
  ren·dez·vous (pl)
ren·di·tion
ren·e·gade
re·nege
  -neged, -neg·ing,
  -neg·er
re·ne·go·tia·ble
re·ne·go·ti·ate
re·new
re·new·able

re·new·al
re·nounce
  -nounced,
  -nounc·ing,
  -nounce·ment
ren·o·vate
  -vat·ed, -vat·ing,
  -va·tion
re·nown
rent·al
re·nun·ci·a·tion
re·open
re·or·der
re·or·ga·ni·za·tion
re·pair
rep·a·ra·tion
re·pa·tri·ate
  -at·ed, -at·ing,
  -a·tion
re·pay
  -paid, -pay·ing,
  -pay·able
re·peal
re·peat
re·pel (drive back;
  cf. *rappel*)
  -pelled, -pel·ling
re·pel·lent
re·pent
re·pen·tance
re·pen·tant
re·per·cus·sion
rep·er·toire

rep·er·to·ry
  -ries
rep·e·ti·tion
rep·e·ti·tious
re·pet·i·tive
  -tive·ly, -tive·ness
re·pet·i·tive strain
  in·jury (RSI)
re·place
  -place·able,
  -plac·er
re·place·ment
re·plen·ish
  -ish·able,
  -ish·ment
re·plete
rep·li·ca
rep·li·cate
  -cat·ed, -cat·ing
re·ply
  -plies, -plied,
  -ply·ing
re·port
re·port·er
re·pose
  -posed, -pos·ing
re·pos·i·to·ry
  -ries
re·pos·sess
  -sess·or
rep·re·hen·si·ble
rep·re·sent
  -sent·able, -sent·er

rep·re·sen·ta·tion
rep·re·sen·ta·tive
re·press
  -pres·sive
re·prieve
rep·ri·mand
re·print
re·pri·sal
re·proach
  -proach·ful,
  -proach·ful·ly,
  -proach·able
re·pro·duce
re·pro·duc·tion
re·pro·duc·tive
re·prog·ra·pher
re·pro·graph·ics
re·proof
re·prove
  -proved, -prov·ing,
  -prov·ing·ly
rep·tile
rep·til·ian
re·pub·lic
re·pub·li·can
re·pu·di·ate
  -at·ed, -at·ing
re·pu·di·a·tion
re·pug·nance
re·pug·nant
re·pulse
  -pulsed, -puls·ing
re·pul·sion

re·pul·sive
rep·u·ta·ble
rep·u·ta·tion
re·pute
  -put·ed, -put·ing
re·quest
re·qui·em
re·quire
  -quired, -quir·ing
re·quire·ment
req·ui·site
req·ui·si·tion
re·run
  -ran, -run·ning
re·sal·able
re·scind
res·cue
  -cued, -cu·ing,
  -cu·er
re·search
re·sem·blance
re·sem·ble
  -bled, -bling
re·sent
re·sent·ful
re·sent·ment
res·er·va·tion
  -tion·ist
re·serve
res·er·voir
re·shuf·fle
re·side
  -sid·ed, -sid·ing

res·i·dence (home;
  cf. *residents*)
res·i·den·cy
  -cies
res·i·den·tial
res·i·dents (those
  who reside; cf.
  residence)
re·sid·u·al
res·i·due
re·sign
res·ig·na·tion
re·sil·ience
re·sil·ient
res·in
re·sist
re·sis·tance
re·sis·tant
re·sis·tor
res·o·lu·tion
re·solve
  -solved, -solv·ing,
  -solv·able
res·o·nance
res·o·nant
re·sort
re·sound
re·source
re·source·ful
re·spect
re·spect·able
  -able·ness, -ably,
  -abil·i·ty

re·spect·ful
-ful·ly (with
deference; cf.
respectively)
re·spec·tive
re·spec·tive·ly (in
that order; cf.
respectfully)
res·pi·ra·tion
-ra·to·ry
res·pi·ra·tor
re·spite
re·splen·dent
re·spond
re·spon·dent
re·sponse
re·spon·si·bil·i·ty
-ties
re·spon·si·ble
re·spon·sive
rest (repose; cf.
wrest)
res·tau·rant
res·tau·ra·teur
rest home
res·ti·tu·tion
rest·less
res·to·ra·tion
re·store
-stored, -stor·ing
re·strain
re·straint
re·strict

re·stric·tion
re·stric·tive
re·sult
re·sume (v)(begin
again; cf. *résumé*)
-sumed, -sum·ing
ré·su·mé (n)
(summary; cf.
resume)
re·sump·tion
re·sur·gence
res·ur·rect
res·ur·rec·tion
re·sus·ci·tate
-tat·ed, -tat·ing,
-ta·tion
re·tail
re·tail·er
re·tain
re·tain·er
re·tal·i·ate
-at·ed, -at·ing,
-a·tion
re·tal·i·a·to·ry
re·tar·da·tion
re·ten·tion
re·ten·tive
ret·i·cence
ret·i·cent
ret·i·na
re·tire
-tired, -tir·ing
re·tire·ment

re·tool
re·touch
re·trace
re·tract
-tract·able
re·trac·tion
re·treat
re·trench
ret·ri·bu·tion
re·trieve
-trieved,
-triev·ing,
-triev·abil·i·ty
re·triev·er
ret·ro·ac·tive
ret·ro·nym
ret·ro·spect
ret·ro·spec·tive
-tive·ly
re·turn
re·turn·able
re·union
re·unite
re·us·able
re·use
re·veal (make
known; cf. *revel*)
rev·eil·le
rev·el (celebrate; cf.
reveal)
rev·e·la·tion
re·venge
-venged,
-veng·ing

rev·e·nue

re·verb

re·ver·ber·ate
  -at·ed, -at·ing

re·ver·ber·a·tion

re·vere
  -vered, -ver·ing

rev·er·ence

rev·er·end

rev·er·ent

re·ver·sal

re·verse
  -versed, -vers·ing

re·vers·ible

re·vert

re·view (restudy; cf.
  revue)

re·view·er

re·vile
  -viled, -vil·ing

re·vise
  -vised, -vis·ing

re·vi·sion

re·vi·tal·ize
  -iz·ed, -iz·ing

re·viv·al

re·vive
  -vived, -viv·ing

re·vo·ca·ble

re·vo·ca·tion

re·voke
  -voked, -vok·ing

re·volt

rev·o·lu·tion

rev·o·lu·tion·ary
  -ar·ies

rev·o·lu·tion·ist

rev·o·lu·tion·ize
  -ized, -iz·ing

re·volve

re·volv·er

re·vue (theatrical
  performance; cf.
  review)

re·vul·sion

re·ward

re·wind
  -wound, -wind·ing

re·word

re·work

re·write
  -wrote, -writ·ten,
  -writ·ing

rhap·so·dy
  -dies

rheo·stat

rhet·o·ric

rhe·tor·i·cal

rheum (watery dis-
  charge; cf. *room*)

rheu·mat·ic

rheu·ma·tism

rhine·stone

rhi·ni·tis

rhi·noc·er·os
  -os·es (pl)

Rho·de·sia

rho·do·den·dron

rhu·barb

rhyme
  rhymed, rhym·ing

rhythm

rhyth·mic

rib·bon

ric·er

Rich·mond

rick·ets

rick·ety

ric·o·chet
  -cheted, -chet·ing

rid·dle
  -dled, -dling

rid·i·cule
  -culed, -cul·ing

ri·dic·u·lous

rif·fle (shuffle; cf.
  rifle)
  -fled, -fling

ri·fle (gun; cf. *riffle*)
  -fled, -fling

right (correct; cf.
  rite, write)

right-click

righ·teous
  -teous·ness

right·ful

right hand (n)

right-hand (adj)

right-of-way
   rights-of-way (pl)
right-to-die
right-to-life
right-to-work
right·size
rig·id
ri·gid·i·ty
   -ties
rig·or
rig·or·ous
ring (a bell; cf.
   wring)
ring·mas·ter
ring·side
ring·worm
rinse
Rio de Ja·nei·ro
ri·ot·ous
rip·en
   -ened, -en·ing
rip off (v)
rip-off (n)
rip·ple
   -pled, -pling
rise
   rose, ris·en,
   ris·ing
risk
ris·qué
rite (ceremony; cf.
   right, write)
rit·u·al

ri·val
   -valed, -val·ing
ri·val·ry
   -ries
riv·er·bed
riv·et
Riv·i·era
road (highway; cf.
   rode, rowed)
road·block
road·way
road·work
rob
   robbed, rob·bing
rob·bery
   -ber·ies
rob·in
ro·bot
ro·bot·ics
ro·bust
rock bot·tom
rock·et
rode (did ride; cf.
   road, rowed)
ro·dent
ro·deo
   -de·os
rogue (scoundrel; cf.
   rouge)
role (part; cf. *roll*)
roll (turn over; cf.
   role)
roll·back

roll call
Roll·er·blade
roll·er coast·er
ro·maine
ro·mance
   -manced,
   -manc·ing
Ro·ma·nia
ro·man·tic
ro·man·ti·cism
rood (crucifix; cf.
   rude)
roof·top
rook·ery
   -er·ies
rook·ie
room (of a house; cf.
   rheum)
room·er (lodger; cf.
   rumor)
room·ful
room·mate
roost·er
root (of a tree; cf.
   rout, route)
root beer
ro·sa·ry
   -ries
ro·sette
rose·wood
ros·in
ros·ter
ros·trum

ro·ta·ry
  -ries
ro·tate
  -tat·ed, -tat·ing
ro·ta·tion
rote (memory; cf.
  wrote)
Roth IRA
ro·tis·ser·ie
ro·tor
ro·to·scop·ing
ro·tund
ro·tun·da
rouge (red coloring;
  cf. *rogue*)
  rouged, roug·ing
rough (rude; cf. *ruff*)
  rough·er,
  rough·est
rough·age
rough·en
  -ened, -en·ing
rough·neck
rou·lette
round-the-clock
round-trip
rout (disperse; cf.
  root, route)
route (highway; cf.
  root, rout)
  rout·ed, rout·ing
rou·ter
rou·tine

rou·tin·ize
  -ized, -iz·ing
row
row·boat
row·dy
  -di·er, -di·est,
  -di·ness
rowed (did row; cf.
  road, rode)
roy·al
roy·al·ist
roy·al·ty
  -ties
rub
  rubbed, rub·bing
rub·ber
rub·ber band
rub·ber·ize
  -ized, -iz·ing
rub·ber stamp (n)
rub·ber-stamp (v, adj)
rub·bish
rub·ble
rub·down
ru·bel·la
ru·bric
ruck·us
rud·der
rud·dy
rude (rough; cf. *rood*)
  rud·er, rud·est
ru·di·ment
ru·di·men·ta·ry

rue·ful
ruff (collar; cf.
  rough)
ruf·fi·an
ruf·fle
  -fled, -fling
rug·ged
  -ged·ness
ru·in·ous
rul·er
rum·ble
  -bled, -bling
ru·mi·nant
rum·mage
  -maged, -mag·ing
ru·mor (gossip; cf.
  roomer)
  -mored, -mor·ing
rum·ple
  -pled, -pling
rum·pus
run away (v)
run·away (adj, n)
run down (v)
run-down (adj)
run·down (n)
rung (a bell; cf.
  wrung)
run in (v)
run-in (n)
run·ner
run·ner-up
  run·ners-up (pl)

235

run off (v)
run·off (n)
run on (v)
run-on (adj, n)
run over (v)
run-over (adj)
run·over (n)
run through (v)
run-through (n)
run·time
rup·ture
   -tured, -tur·ing
ru·ral
rush hour
rus·set
Rus·sia
rus·tic
rus·tle
   -tled, -tling
rust·proof (adj)
ru·ta·ba·ga
ruth·less
   -less·ness
Rwan·da
Rwan·dan
rye (grain; *cf. wry*)

S

Sab·bath
sab·bat·i·cal
sa·ber
sa·ber·met·rics
sa·ble
sab·o·tage
   -taged, -tag·ing
sab·o·teur
sac (pouch in animal; cf. *sack*)
sac·cha·rin (n)
sac·cha·rine (adj)
sack (bag; cf. *sac*)
sac·ra·ment
sac·ra·men·tal
Sac·ra·men·to
sa·cred
sac·ri·fice
   -ficed, -fic·ing
sac·ri·fi·cial
sac·ri·lege
   -le·gious
sac·ro·sanct
sad·den
   -dened, -den·ing
sad·dle
   -dled, -dling
sa·dism
   -dist, -dis·tic

sa·do·mas·och·ism
   -och·ist
   -och·is·tic
safe-de·pos·it box
safe·guard
safe·keep·ing
safe·ty
   -ties
saf·fron
sa·ga
sa·ga·cious
sa·gac·i·ty
sail (of a ship; cf. *sale*)
   sail·able
sail·boat
sail·cloth
sail·fish
sail·or
Saint Lu·cia
saint·ly
sal·able
   -abil·i·ty
sal·ad
sal·a·man·der
sa·la·mi
sal·a·ry
   -ries, -ried
sale (selling; cf. *sail*)

Sa·lem
sales
sales·clerk
sales·per·son
sales·room
sales slip
sales tax
sa·lient
sa·line
sa·li·va
sal·i·vary
salm·on
sa·lon (shop; cf. *saloon*)
sa·loon (tavern; cf. *salon*)
sal·tine
Salt Lake City
salt·shak·er
salt·wa·ter (adj)
salty
   salt·i·er, salt·i·est
sal·u·tary
   -tari·ly, -tari·ness
sal·u·ta·tion
sa·lu·ta·to·ri·an
sa·lute
   -lut·ed, -lut·ing

sal·vage
  -vaged, -vag·ing,
  -vage·able
sal·va·tion
salve
Sa·mar·i·tan (n)
sa·mar·i·tan (adj)
same·ness
sam·pan
sam·ple
  -pled, -pling
sam·pler
sam·pling
san·a·to·ri·um
  -riums
sanc·ti·fi·ca·tion
sanc·ti·fy
  -fied, -fy·ing
sanc·ti·mo·nious
  -nious·ness
sanc·tion
  -tioned, -tion·ing
sanc·ti·ty
  -ties
sanc·tu·ary
  -ar·ies
sanc·tum
san·dal
san·dal·wood
sand·bag
sand·bank
sand·bar
sand·blast
sand·box

sand·lot
sand·pa·per
sand·pip·er
sand·stone
sand·storm
sand·wich
san·guine
  -guine·ly,
  -guine·ness,
  -guin·i·ty
san·i·tary
  -tari·ly
san·i·ta·tion
san·i·ty
San Jo·se
San Juan
San Sal·va·dor
sans
sans ser·if
San·ta Fe
San·ti·a·go
San·to Do·min·go
sap·ling
sap·phire
sap·suck·er
sap·wood
Sa·ra·je·vo
sar·casm
sar·cas·tic
  -ti·cal·ly
sar·co·ma
  -mas
sar·dine
sar·don·ic

sar·gas·so
sa·rong
sar·sa·pa·ril·la
sar·to·ri·al
Sas·katch·e·wan
sas·sa·fras
sa·tan·ic
satch·el
sat·el·lite
sa·tia·ble
sa·tiate (adj)
sa·ti·ate (v)
  -at·ed, -at·ing
sat·in
sat·in·wood
sat·ire
sa·tir·ic
  -i·cal·ly
sat·is·fac·tion
sat·is·fac·to·ri·ly
sat·is·fac·to·ry
sat·is·fy
  -fied, -fy·ing
sat·u·rate
  -rat·ed, -rat·ing
sat·u·ra·tion
Sat·ur·day
sauce
sau·cer
Sau·di Ara·bia
sau·er·bra·ten
sau·er·kraut
sau·na
saun·ter

238

sau·sage
sau·té
  -téed, -té·ing
sav·age
  -aged, -ag·ing,
  -age·ly
sa·van·na
sa·vant
sav·ior
sa·vory
sav·vy
saw·dust
saw·horse
saw·mill
sax·o·phone
say
  says, said, say·ing
say-so
scab·bard
scaf·fold
scal·able
scald
scale
  scaled, scal·ing
scal·lion
scal·lop
scal·pel
scan
  scanned,
  scan·ning
scan·dal
scan·dal·ize
  -ized, -iz·ing

scan·dal·ous
Scan·di·na·vian
scan·ner
scanty
  scant·i·er,
  scant·i·est
scape·goat
scarce·ly
scar·ci·ty
  -ties
scare
  scared, scar·ing
scarf
  scarves or scarfs
  (pl)
scar·i·fy
  -fied, -fy·ing
scar·let
scath·ing
scat·ter
scav·en·ger
sce·nar·io
scene (locale; cf.
  seen)
scen·ery
  -er·ies
sce·nic
scent (odor; cf. *cent,*
  sent)
scep·ter
sched·ule
  -uled, -ul·ing
sche·ma

sche·mat·ic
scheme
  schemed,
  schem·ing
schism
schizo·phre·nia
schmaltz
schol·ar
schol·ar·ly
schol·ar·ship
scho·las·tic
school-age
school·bag
school board
school bus
school·child
school dis·trict
school·room
school·teach·er
school·work
schoo·ner
sci·at·i·ca
sci·ence
sci·en·tif·ic
  -i·cal·ly
sci·en·tist
scin·til·la
scin·til·late
  -lat·ed, -lat·ing
sci·on
scis·sors
scle·ro·sis
score·board

score·card
score·keep·er
scorn·ful
scor·pi·on
scot-free
scoun·drel
scour
scourge
  scourged,
  scourg·ing
scout·mas·ter
scram·ble
  -bled, -bling
scrap·book
scratch
scrawl
screech
screen
  screen·able
screen·play
screw·ball
scrib·ble
  -bled, -bling
scrim·mage
  -maged, -mag·ing
scrim·shaw
script
  -script·ed,
  script·ing
scrip·tur·al
scrip·ture
scroll
scroll bar

scrooge
scrounge
  scrounged,
  scroung·ing
scrub
  scrubbed,
  scrub·bing
scrump·tious
scru·ple
  -pled, -pling
scru·pu·lous
scru·ti·nize
  -nized, -niz·ing
scru·ti·ny
  -nies
scuf·fle
  -fled, -fling
scull (boat; cf. *skull*)
sculp·tor
sculp·tur·al
sculp·ture
  -tured, -tur·ing
scur·vy
scut·tle
  -tled, -tling
scythe (blade; cf. *sigh*)
sea (ocean; cf. *see*)
sea·coast
sea·far·er
sea·food
sea gull
seal

seal·ing (making secure; cf. *ceiling*)
seal·ant
seam (sewn; cf. *seem*)
  seam·less
sé·ance
sea·plane
sea·port
sear (burn; cf. *seer*)
search
  search·able,
  search·er,
  search·ing·ly
search·light
sea·shell
sea·shore
sea·sick
sea·son
  -soned, -son·ing
sea·son·able
sea·son·al
  -al·ly
sea·son·al
  af·fec·tive
  dis·or·der (SAD)
seat belt
seat·ing
sea·wall
sea·ward
sea·wa·ter
sea·weed
sea·wor·thy
  -thi·ness

se·cant
se·cede
  -ced·ed, -ced·ing
se·ces·sion
se·clude
  -clud·ed, -clud·ing
se·clu·sion
seco·bar·bi·tal
sec·ond
sec·ond·ary
  -ari·ly
sec·ond class (n)
sec·ond-class (adj)
sec·ond-hand (adj)
sec·ond-rate (adj)
se·cre·cy
  -cies
se·cret
sec·re·tary
  -tar·ies, -tari·al
se·crete
  -cret·ed, -cret·ing
se·cre·tion
se·cre·tive
  -tive·ly, -tive·ness
sec·tar·i·an
sec·tion
sec·tion·al
sec·tor
  -tored, -tor·ing
sec·u·lar
sec·u·lar·ism

se·cure
  -cur·er, -cur·est,
  -cur·ing
se·cu·ri·ty
  -ties
se·dan
se·date
  -dat·ed, -dat·ing
se·da·tion
sed·a·tive
sed·en·tary
sed·i·ment
sed·i·men·ta·ry
se·di·tion
se·duce
  -duced, -duc·ing
se·duc·tion
se·duc·tive
  -tive·ness
see (perceive; cf.
  sea)
  saw, seen, see·ing,
  see·able
seed (of a plant; cf.
  cede)
seed·ling
seem (appear; cf.
  seam)
seem·ly
  -li·er, -li·est,
  -li·ness
seen (form of verb
  see; cf. *scene*)

seep·age
seer (prophet; cf.
  sear)
see·saw
see-through (adj)
seg·ment
seg·re·gate
seg·re·gat·ed
seg·re·ga·tion
seg·re·ga·tion·ist
se·gue
  -gued, -gue·ing
seis·mic
seis·mo·graph
seis·mom·e·ter
seize
  seized, seiz·ing
sei·zure
sel·dom
se·lect
se·lec·tion
se·lec·tive
self
  selves (pl)
self-ad·dressed
self-as·sured
self-cen·tered
self-com·posed
self-con·fi·dence
self-con·tained
self-con·trol
self-de·fense
self-de·struc·tion

self-de·ter·mi·na·tion
self-dis·ci·pline
self-ed·u·cat·ed
self-em·ployed
self-es·teem
self-ev·i·dent
self-ex·e·cut·ing
self-ex·plan·a·to·ry
self-ex·pres·sion
self-gov·ern·ment
self-help
self-im·age
self-in·crim·i·na·tion
self-in·dul·gence
self-in·sured
self-in·ter·est
self·ish
self-made
self-paced
self-pity
self-pos·sessed
self-pos·ses·sion
self-pres·er·va·tion
self-pro·claimed
self-pro·mo·ter
self-re·gard
self-re·li·ance
self-re·spect
self-sac·ri·fice
self·same
self-sat·is·fac·tion
self-start·er
self-suf·fi·cien·cy

self-suf·fi·cient
self-sup·port
self-taught
self-willed
self-wind·ing
sell·er (one who
    sells; cf. *cellar*)
sell out (v)
sell·out (n)
selt·zer
sel·vage
se·man·tic
sem·a·phore
sem·blance
se·mes·ter
semi·an·nu·al
semi·au·to·mat·ic
semi·au·ton·o·mous
semi·cir·cle
semi·civ·i·lized
semi·clas·si·cal
semi·co·lon
semi·con·duc·tor
semi·con·scious
semi·dark·ness
semi·fi·nal
semi·month·ly
sem·i·nar
sem·i·nary
    -nar·ies
semi·per·ma·nent
semi·pre·cious
semi·pri·vate

semi·pro·fes·sion·al
semi·re·tire·ment
semi·skilled
semi·sweet
semi·trans·lu·cent
semi·trans·par·ent
semi·week·ly
semi·year·ly
sen·ate
sen·a·tor
sen·a·to·ri·al
send-off (n)
Sen·e·gal
se·nile
se·nil·i·ty
se·nior
se·nior·i·ty
sen·sa·tion
sen·sa·tion·al
sense·less
sens·es (sensations;
    cf. *census*)
sen·si·bil·i·ty
    -ties
sen·si·ble
sen·si·tive
sen·si·tiv·i·ty
sen·si·tize
sen·sor (sensing
    device; cf. *censer,
    censor*)
sen·so·ry
sen·su·al

sen·su·ous

sent (dispatched; cf. *cent, scent*)

sen·tence
-tenced, -tenc·ing

sen·ti·ment

sen·ti·men·tal
-tal·ly

sen·ti·men·tal·ism

sen·ti·men·tal·i·ty

sen·ti·nel
-neled, -nel·ing

sen·try
-tries

Seoul

sep·a·ra·ble
-ble·ness, -bil·i·ty

sep·a·rate

sep·a·ra·tion

sep·a·rat·ist

Sep·tem·ber

sep·tic

sep·tu·a·ge·nar·i·an

se·quel

se·quel·izer

se·quence
-quenced, -quenc·ing

se·quenc·er

se·quen·tial
-tial·ly

se·ques·ter
-tered, -ter·ing

se·quin

se·quoia

Ser·bia

ser·e·nade
-nad·ed, -nad·ing, -nad·er

ser·en·dip·i·ty

se·rene

se·ren·i·ty

serf (peasant; cf. *surf*)

serge (cloth; cf. *surge*)

ser·geant

se·ri·al (series; cf. *cereal*)

se·ri·al port

se·ri·al·ize
-ized, -iz·ing, -iza·tion

se·ries (related group; cf. *serious, serous*)

ser·if

se·ri·ous (grave; cf. *series, serous*)

se·ri·ous-mind·ed

ser·mon

se·rous (like serum; cf. *cirrus, series, serious*)

ser·pent

ser·ra·tion

se·rum

ser·vant

serve
served, serv·ing

serv·er

ser·vice
-viced, -vic·ing

ser·vice·able

ser·vile

ser·vi·tude

ses·a·me

ses·qui·cen·ten·ni·al

ses·sion (meeting; cf. *cession*)

set·back (n)

set·screw

set·tee

set·tle·ment

set·tling

set up (v)

set·up (n)

sev·en·teen
-teenth

sev·enth
-enths

sev·en·ty
-ties, ti·eth

sev·er
-ered, -er·ing

sev·er·al

sev·er·ance

se·vere
-vere·ly
-vere·ness,
-ver·i·ty
sew (stitch; cf. *so,
sow*)
sewed, sewn,
sew·ing
sew·age
sew·er
sew·er·age
sex·a·ge·nar·i·an
sex·ism
-ist
sex·tet
sex·ton
sex·u·al·i·ty
Sey·chelles
shab·by
-bi·er, -bi·est,
-bi·ness
shack·le
shade
shad·ed, shad·ing
shad·ow
shad·owy
Shang·hai
shake up (v)
shake-up (n)
shall
shal·lot
shal·low
sham

sham·ble
-bled, -bling
shame
shamed,
sham·ing
shame·faced
shame·ful
shame·less
sham·poo
sham·rock
shang·hai
-haied, -hai·ing
shan·ty
-ties
shape·less
shape·ly
-li·er, -li·est,
-li·ness
share
shared, shar·ing
shared log·ic
sys·tem
shared re·source
sys·tem
share·hold·er
share·ware
shark·skin
sharp·en
-ened, -en·ing,
-en·er
sharp·er
sharp-eyed
sharp·shoot·er

sharp-sight·ed
sharp-tongued
sharp-wit·ted
shat·ter·proof
shawl
sheaf
shear (cut; cf. *sheer*)
sheared, shorn,
shear·ing
sheath (n)
sheaths
sheathe (v)
sheathed,
sheath·ing
sheep·dog
sheep·herd·er
sheep·ish
sheep·skin
sheer (thin; cf.
shear)
sheet met·al
shel·lac
-lacked, -lack·ing
shell·fish
shell game
shell·proof
shell shock (n)
shell-shocked (adj)
shel·ter
-tered, -ter·ing
shelve
sher·bet
sher·iff

shield
shift·less
Shi·loh
shim·mer
  -mered, -mer·ing
shim·my
  -mies, -mied,
  -my·ing
shine
shin·gle
  -gled, -gling
ship
  shipped,
  ship·ping
ship·mas·ter
ship·mate
ship·ment
ship·per
ship·wreck
ship·yard
shirr·ing
shirt·tail
shirt·waist
shish ke·bab
shiv·er
  -ered, -er·ing
shock·proof
shod
shoe
shoe·horn
shoe·lace
shoe·string

shone (gave light;
  cf. *shown*)
shook-up
shoot (fire; cf. *chute*)
shop
  shopped,
  shop·ping
shop·lift·er
shop·per
shop·talk
shop·worn
shore·line
short·age
short·bread
short·cake
short·change
short cir·cuit (n)
short-cir·cuit (v)
short·com·ing
short·cut
short·en·ing
short·fall
short·hand·ed
short·horn
short-lived
short-range (adj)
short·sight·ed
short-spo·ken
short·stop
short-tem·pered
short-term
short-wind·ed
should

shoul·der
  -dered, -der·ing
shov·el
  -eled, -el·ing
shov·el·ware
show
  showed, shown,
  show·ing
show·er
shown (displayed;
  cf. *shone*)
show off (v)
show-off (n)
show·place
show·room
showy
  showi·er,
  show·i·est,
  show·i·ness
shrap·nel
shred
  shred·der,
  shred·ding
shrewd
  shrewd·ness
shriek
shrimp
shrink·age
shriv·el
  -eled, -el·ing
shrub·bery
  -ber·ies
shud·der
  -dered, -der·ing

shuf·fle
  -fled, -fling
shut down (v)
shut·down (n)
shut in (v)
shut-in (adj, n)
shut off (v)
shut·off (n)
shut out (v)
shut·out (n)
shut·ter
shut·tle
  -tled, -tling
shy
  shi·er, shi·est,
  shy·ness
Si·am
Si·be·ria
sib·ling
Si·cil·ian
Sic·i·ly
sick·en·ing
sick·le
sick leave
sick·ness
sick·room
side
  sid·ed, sid·ing
side·burns
side·line
side·show
side step (n)
side·step (v)

side·swipe
side·track
side·walk
side·wall
side·ways
si·dle
  -dled, -dling
siege
Si·er·ra Le·one
Si·er·ra Ma·dre
Si·er·ra Ne·va·da
si·es·ta
sieve
  sieved, siev·ing
sigh (sound; cf.
  scythe)
sight (vision; cf. *cite,
  site*)
sight·less
sight·ly
  sight·li·ness
sight-read (v)
sight-see·ing
sign
  sign·ee, sign·er
signed
sig·nal
  -naled, -nal·ing
sig·na·to·ry
sig·na·ture
sig·net
sig·nif·i·cance
sig·nif·i·cant

sig·ni·fy
  -fied, -fy·ing
si·lage
si·lence
  -lenced,
  -lenc·ing
si·lenc·er
si·lent
sil·hou·ette
  -ett·ed, -ett·ing
sil·i·cate
sil·i·con (element;
  cf. *silicone*)
sil·i·cone (com-
  pound; cf. *silicon*)
silk·worm
silky
sil·ly
  -li·er, -li·est
si·lo
sil·ver
sil·ver·ware
sil·very
sim·i·an
sim·i·lar
sim·i·lar·i·ty
sim·mer
  -mered, -mer·ing

sim·ple
  -pler, -plest
sim·plex
sim·plic·i·ty

sim·pli·fy
  -fied, -fy·ing,
  -fi·ca·tion
sim·plism
  -plis·tic
sim·ply
sim·u·lar
sim·u·late
  -lat·ed, -lat·ing
sim·u·la·tion
si·mul·ta·neous
sin
  sinned, sin·ning
since
sin·cere
  -cer·er, -cer·est,
  -cere·ly
sin·cer·i·ty
sin·ew
sin·ewy
sin·ful
  -ful·ly, -ful·ness
Sin·ga·pore
singe
  singed, singe·ing
sin·gle
sin·gle-hand·ed
  -ed·ness

sin·gle-mind·ed
  -ed·ness
sin·gle-space (v)
sin·gu·lar

sin·gu·lar·i·ty
sin·is·ter
sin·u·ous
si·nus
si·phon
  -phoned,
  -phon·ing
si·ren
sir·loin
sis·ter-in-law
  sis·ters-in-law (pl)
sit·com
sit-down (n)
site (place; cf. *cite,
  sight*)
  sit·ed, sit·ing
site li·cense
sit-in (n)
sit·u·ate
  -at·ed, -at·ing
sit·u·a·tion
sit up (v)
sit-up (n)
six·teen
  -teenth
sixth
  sixths
six·ty
  -ties, -ti·eth
siz·able
size
  sized, siz·ing
siz·zle
  -zled, -zling

skate·board
skat·er
skein
skel·e·tal
skel·e·ton
skep·tic
skep·ti·cal
skep·ti·cism
sketch
sketch·book
sketchy
  sketch·i·er,
  sketch·i·est
skew·er
ski (blade for snow;
  cf. *sky*)
  skis (pl. of *ski*; cf.
  skies), skied,
  ski·ing, ski·er
skid
  skid·ded,
  skid·ding
skilled
skill·ful
skim
  skimmed,
  skim·ming
skimpy
skin
  skinned,
  skin·ning
skin·tight

S   skip/slow motion

skip
   skipped,
      skip·ping
skir·mish
skull (bone of head;
   cf. *scull*)
skunk
sky (atmosphere; cf.
   ski)
   skies (pl. of *sky*;
      cf. *skis*)
sky blue (n)
sky·box
sky·cap
sky·div·ing
sky·jack
sky·light
sky·line
sky·rock·et
sky·scrap·er
sky·surf·ing
sky·ward
sky·way
slack·en
   -ened, -en·ing
sla·lom
slam
   slammed,
      slam·ming
slan·der
   -dered, -der·ing,
   -der·ous·ly
slap
   slapped, slap·ping

slap·stick
slaugh·ter
slav·ery
slav·ish
slay (kill; cf. *sleigh*)
slea·zy
   -zi·er, -zi·est,
   -zi·ness
sledge
sledge·ham·mer
sleep·er
sleep·less
sleep·walk·er
sleep·wear
sleepy
   sleep·i·er,
   sleep·i·est,
   sleep·i·ness
sleeve
sleigh (winter vehi-
   cle; cf. *slay*)
slen·der
sleuth
slide
   slid·ing
slight
slim
   slim·mer,
   slim·mest
slime
sling·shot
slip
   slipped, slip·ping
slip·case

slip·cov·er
slip·knot
slip-on (n)
slip-over (n)
slip·per
slip·pery
   -peri·er, -peri·est,
   -peri·ness
slip sheet (n)
slip-sheet (v)
slip·shod
slip up (v)
slip-up (n)
slith·er
sliv·er
sloe (fruit; cf. *slow*)
slo·gan
sloop
slope
   sloped, slop·ing
slop·py
   -pi·er, -pi·est,
   -pi·ness
sloth·ful
slouch
slouchy
   slouch·i·ness
Slo·va·kia
Slo·ve·nia
slov·en·ly
slow (not fast; cf.
   sloe)
slow·down (n)
slow mo·tion (n)

slow-mo·tion (adj)
slow-wit·ted
sludge
slug
  slugged, slug·ging
slug·gish
slum
slum·ber
slush
small·pox
smart
  smart·ness
smart·card
smash·up (n)
smat·ter·ing
smil·ey
  -eys
smith·er·eens
smoke·house
smoke·less
smok·er
smok·ing room (n)
smok·ing-room
  (adj)
smoky
smol·der
  -dered, -der·ing
smooth
smor·gas·bord
smoth·er
  -ered, -er·ing
smudge
  smudged,
  smudg·ing

smug·gle
  -gled, -gling
sna·fu
snag
  snagged,
  snag·ging
snail·mail
snail-paced
snake·skin
snap
  snapped,
  snap·ping
snap·drag·on
snap·shot
snare drum
sneak·er
sneak·er·net
sneer
sneeze
  sneezed,
  sneez·ing
sneeze·guard
snick·er
snide
  snide·ly,
  snide·ness
snip
  snipped,
  snip·ping
snip·py
  -pi·er, -pi·est
snob
snob·bery

  -ber·ies
snob·bish
  -bish·ness
snooze
snor·kel
snow·ball
snow·bank
snow·blow·er
snow·bound
snow·capped
snow·drift
snow·drop
snow·fall
snow·flake
snow·man
snow·mo·bile
snow·plow
snow·shoe
snow·storm
snow·suit
snowy
snub
  snubbed,
  snub·bing
snub-nosed
so (thus; cf. *sew, sow*)
soap·box
soap·suds
soapy
  soap·i·er,
  soap·i·ness

soar (rise aloft; cf. *sore*)

so·ber
  -bered, -ber·ing

so·bri·ety

so-called

soc·cer

so·cia·bil·i·ty
  -ties

so·cia·ble
  -ble·ness, -bly

so·cial

so·cial·ism

so·cial·ist

so·cial·ite

so·cial·ize
  -ized, -iz·ing

so·cial·ly

so·cial-mind·ed

so·ci·etal

so·ci·ety
  -et·ies

so·cio·eco·nom·ic

so·cio·log·i·cal

so·ci·ol·o·gy
  -gist

sock·et

so·da

sod·den

so·di·um

soft
  soft·ish, soft·ly,
  soft·ness

soft·ball

soft-boiled

soft copy

soft·en
  -ened, -en·ing

soft·heart·ed

soft soap (n)

soft-soap (v)

soft-spo·ken

soft·ware

soft·wood

sog·gy
  -gi·er, -gi·est,
  -gi·ness

soil

so·journ

so·lace

so·lar

sol·der

sol·dier

sold-out

sole (only; cf. *soul*)

so·le·cism

sole·ly

sol·emn

so·lem·ni·ty
  -ties

so·le·noid

so·lic·it

so·lic·i·ta·tion

so·lic·i·tor

so·lic·i·tous

so·lic·i·tude

sol·id

sol·i·dar·i·ty

so·lid·i·fy
  -fied, -fy·ing,
  -fi·ca·tion

so·lid·i·ty
  -ties

sol·id-state

sol·il·o·quy
  -quies

sol·i·taire

sol·i·tary

sol·i·tude

so·lo

sol·stice

sol·u·bil·i·ty

sol·u·ble

so·lu·tion

solv·able
  -abil·i·ty

solve
  solved, solv·ing

sol·ven·cy

sol·vent

So·ma·lia

som·ber

som·bre·ro

some (part; cf. *sum*)

some·body (pron)

some·day (adv)

some·how

some·one (pron)

some·place (adv)

som·er·sault
some·thing
some·time (adv)
some·what
some·where
som·nam·bu·lism
son (child; cf. *sun*)
so·na·ta
song·bird
song·book
song·fest
song·writ·er
son-in-law
   sons-in-law (pl)
son·net
soothe
sooth·say·er
so·phis·ti·cate
so·phis·ti·cat·ed
so·phis·ti·ca·tion
soph·ist·ry
soph·o·more
so·pra·no
sor·cer·er
sor·cery
sor·did
sore (painful; cf.
   soar)
   sor·er, sor·est
sor·ghum
so·ror·i·ty
   -ties
sor·rel

sor·row
sor·row·ful
sor·ry
souf·flé
sought
sou·kous
soul (spirit; cf. *sole*)
soul-search·ing
sound bite
sound·board
sound·proof (adj, v)
sound·scape
soup du jour
source
sour·dough
South Af·ri·ca
South Amer·i·ca
south·bound
south·east
south·er·ly
south·ern
South·ern·er
South Ko·rea
south·land
south·paw
south pole
south·west
sou·ve·nir
sov·er·eign
sov·er·eign·ty
   -ties
so·vi·et
sow (n)(pig)

sow (v)(plant; cf.
   sew, so)
   sowed, sown,
   sow·ing
soy
soy·bean
space
   spaced, spac·ing
space-age
space·craft
space·flight
space shut·tle
space suit
spa·cious
   -cious·ness
spa·ghet·ti
spam
   -spam·med,
   spam·ming
span·gle
span·iel
spare
   spared, spar·ing
spare·ribs
spar·kle
   -kled, -kling
spar·row
spas·mod·ic
spas·tic
spa·tial
spat·ter
spat·u·la
speak·er

spear
spear·mint
spe·cial
  -cial·ly, -cial·ness
spe·cial·ist
spe·cial·iza·tion
spe·cial·ize
  -ized, -iz·ing
spe·cial·ty
  -ties
spe·cie (coin; cf.
  species)
spe·cies (variety; cf.
  specie)
spe·cif·ic
  -i·cal·ly
spec·i·fi·ca·tion
spec·i·fy
  -fy·ing
spec·i·fied
spec·i·men
spec·ta·cle
spec·tac·u·lar
spec·ta·tor
spec·ter
spec·trum
  -tra (pl)
spec·u·late
  -u·la·tor
spec·u·la·tion
spec·u·la·tive
spec·u·lum
speech

speech·less
speed·boat
speed·i·ly
speed lim·it
speed·om·e·ter
speed·up (n)
speed·way
spell
  spelled, spell·ing
spell·bound
spell-check
spell check·er
spe·lunk·er
spent
sphag·num
sphere
sphinx
  sphinx·es (pl)
spice
  spiced, spic·ing
spicy
spi·der
spiel
spig·ot
spike
  spiked, spik·ing
spin·ach
spi·nal

spin·dle
  -dled, -dling
spine·less
spin·et

spin off (v)
spin-off (n)
spin·ster
spi·ral
  -raled, -ral·ing
spi·rea
spir·it
spir·it·ed
spir·i·tu·al
  -al·ly, -al·ness
spir·i·tu·al·ism
  -al·ist
spir·i·tu·al·i·ty
  -ties
spite·ful
splash·board
splash·down
splash guard
splen·did
  -did·ness
splen·dor
splice
  spliced, splic·ing
splin·ter
split
  split·ting
split off
split screen
split shift
splurge
spoil·age
spo·ken
spokes·per·son

spo·li·a·tion
sponge
  sponged,
    spong·ing
spongy
spon·sor
  -sored, -sor·ing
spon·ta·ne·ity
spon·ta·ne·ous
  -ous·ness
spoof
  -ing
spool
  -ing
spoon-feed (v)
  spoon-fed,
    spoon-feed·ing
spoon·ful
  -fuls (pl)
spo·rad·ic
sports·cast
sports·man
sports·wear
sports·wom·an
sports·writ·er
sport-util·i·ty
  ve·hi·cle (SUV)
spot
  spot·ted, spot·ting
spot-check (v)
spot·less
spot·light (n, v)
  -light·ed,
    -light·ing

sprawl
spread ea·gle (n)
spread-ea·gle (adj, v)
spread·sheet
spree
spright·ly
  -li·ness
spring·board
Spring·fiel
spring·time
sprin·kle
  -kler
sprin·kling
sprint
sprock·et
sprout
spruce
spu·mo·ni or
  spu·mo·ne
spur
  spurred,
    spur·ring
spu·ri·ous
spurn
spur-of-the-
  mo·ment
spurt
sput·nik
sput·ter
spy
  spied, spy·ing
squab
squab·ble
  -bled, -bling

squad·ron
squal·id
  -id·ness
squall
squa·lor
squan·der
  -dered, -der·ing
square
  squared,
    squar·ing
square root
squash
squat
  squat·ted,
    squat·ting
squawk
squeak
squea·mish
squee·gee
squeeze
  squeez·able,
    squeez·abil·i·ty
squir·rel
  -reled, -rel·ing
squirt
Sri Lan·ka
sta·bil·i·ty
  -ties
sta·bi·lize
  -lized, -liz·ing,
    -li·za·tion
sta·bi·liz·er

sta·ble
stac·ca·to
sta·di·um
  -dia (pl)
staff
stage fright
stage·hand
stag·ger
  -gered, -ger·ing
stag·nant
stag·nate
  -nat·ed, -nat·ing,
  -na·tion
staid (sedate; cf.
  stayed)
stain·less
stair (steps; cf. *stare*)
stair·case
stair·way
stair·well
stake (marker; cf.
  steak)
stake·hold·er
stake out (v)
stake·out (n)
sta·lac·tite (hangs
  down)
sta·lag·mite (stands
  up)
stale
stale·mate
stal·lion
stal·wart

sta·men
stam·i·na
stam·mer
  -mered, -mer·ing
stam·pede
stance
stanch
stand-alone
stan·dard
stan·dard-bear·er (n)
stan·dard·bred
stan·dard·ize
  -ized, -iz·ing,
  -iza·tion
stand by (v)
stand·by (n, adj, adv)
stand in (v)
stand-in (n)
stand off (v)
stand·off (adj, n)
stand out (v)
stand·out (n)
stand·point
stand·still
stand up (v)
stand-up (adj)
stan·za
sta·ple
star
  starred, star·ring
star·board
starchy
star·dom

star·dust
stare (look; cf. *stair*)
star·fish
star·gaz·er
star·let
star·light
star·ling
star·ry-eyed
star-span·gled
star·tle
  -tled, -tling
start·up
star·va·tion
starve
  starved, starv·ing
state·hood
state·house
state·less
state·ly
  -li·ness
state·ment
states·man
state·wide
stat·ic
sta·tion
  -tioned, -tion·ing
sta·tion·ary (fixed;
  cf. *stationery*)
sta·tio·nery (paper;
  cf. *stationary*)
sta·tis·ti·cal
  -cal·ly
stat·is·ti·cian

sta·tis·tics
stat·u·ary
  -ar·ies
stat·ue (sculpture;
  cf. *stature,*
  statute)
stat·u·esque
stat·u·ette
stat·ure (height; cf.
  statue, statute)
sta·tus
sta·tus quo
stat·ute (law; cf.
  statue, stature)
stat·u·to·ry
stay
stayed (past tense of
  stay; cf. *staid*)
  stay·ing
stead·fast
steady
  steadi·er,
  steadi·est,
  steadi·ly
steak (meat; cf.
  stake)
steal (rob; cf. *steel*)
stealth
steam·boat
steam·er
steam heat·ing
steam·ship
steel (metal; cf.
  steal)

steel·work
steel·yard
stee·ple
stee·ple·chase
stee·ple·jack
stega·nog·ra·phy
steer
stein
stem
  stemmed,
  stem·ming
stem·ware
sten·cil
  -ciled, -cil·ing
ste·nog·ra·pher
ste·nog·ra·phy
  steno·graph·ic
step (walk; cf.
  steppe)
step·child
step down (v)
step-down (n)
step·fa·ther
step in (v)
step-in (n)
step·lad·der
step·moth·er
step·par·ent
steppe (plain; cf.
  step)
step stool
step up (v)
step-up (adj, n)

ste·reo
ste·reo·scope
ste·reo·type
ste·rile
ste·ril·ize
  -ized, -iz·ing,
  -iza·tion
ster·ling
ster·num
stetho·scope
stew·ard
stick·ler
stick-to-it·ive·ness
stick up (v)
stick·up (n)
sticky
  stick·i·er,
  stick·i·est,
  stick·i·ness
stiff·en
sti·fle
  -fled, -fling
stig·ma (sing)
  stig·ma·ta (pl)
stig·ma·tize
  -tized, -tiz·ing
stile (fence; cf. *style*)
sti·let·to
  -tos
still·born
still life
stilt·ed
stim·u·lant

stim·u·late
  -lat·ed, -lat·ing,
  -la·tion
stim·u·lus (sing)
  -li (pl)
stin·gy
  -gi·er, -gi·est,
  -gi·ness
stink·weed
sti·pend
stip·u·late
  -lat·ed, -lat·ing
stip·u·la·tion
stir
  stirred, stir·ring
stir-fry (v)
stir·rup
stock·ade
stock·bro·ker
stock car
stock·hold·er
stock·ing
stock-in-trade (n)
stock·man
stock·pile (n, v)
stock·room
stock·yard
stodgy
  stodg·i·er,
  stodg·i·est,
  stodg·i·ness
sto·ic
stom·ach

stom·ach·ache
stone·cut·ter
stone-deaf
stone·ma·son
stone·ware
stone·work
stop
  stopped,
  stop·ping
stop-and-go
stop·light
stop·watch
stor·age
store
  stored, stor·ing,
  stor·able
store·house
store·keep·er
store·room
store·wide
stormy
  storm·i·er,
  storm·i·est,
  storm·i·ness
sto·ry
  -ries
sto·ry·board
sto·ry·tell·er
stout·heart·ed
  -ed·ness
stow·age
stow away (v)
stow·away (n)

St. Paul
strad·dle
  -dled, -dling, -dler
strag·gle
  -gled, -gling, -gler
straight (direct; cf.
  strait)
straight·edge
straight·en
  -ened, -en·ing
straight·for·ward
strain
strait (narrow; cf.
  straight)
strait·laced or
  straight·laced
strange
  strang·er,
  strang·est,
  strange·ly
stran·gle
  -gled, -gling, -gler
stran·gle·hold
stran·gu·late
  -lated, -lat·ing
strap
  strapped,
  strap·ping
stra·te·gic
  -gi·cal, -gi·cal·ly
strat·e·gist
strat·e·gy
  -gies

strat·i·fy
  -fied, -fy·ing
strato·sphere
stra·tum
straw·ber·ry
stream
stream·lined
street·light
street-smart
strength
strength·en
  -ened, -en·ing
stren·u·ous
  -ous·ness
strep·to·coc·cus
  -coc·ci (pl)
stress·ful
  -ful·ly
stretch
strict
stric·ture
stri·dent
strike out (v)
strike·out (n)
strike·over (n)
strin·gent
strip
  stripped,
  strip·ping,
  strip·pa·ble
strong·hold
struc·tur·al
  -al·ly
struc·ture
  -tured, -tur·ing

strug·gle
  -gled, -gling
strych·nine
stub
  stubbed,
  stub·bing
stub·born
  -born·ness
stuc·co
stu·dent
studies
stu·dio
stu·di·ous
  -ous·ness
study
  stud·ied,
  study·ing
stuff
stuffy
  stuff·i·er,
  stuff·i·est,
  stuff·i·ness
stum·ble
stu·pen·dous
stu·pid
  -pid·ness
stu·pid·i·ty
  -ties
stu·por
stur·dy
  -di·er, -di·est,
  -di·ness
stur·geon
stut·ter

-ter·er
Stutt·gart
style (fashion; cf.
  stile)
  styled, styl·ing
style·book
style sheet
styl·ist
styl·ize
  -ized, -iz·ing,
  -iza·tion
sty·lus
  -li (pl)
sty·mie
  -mied, -mie·ing
sua·sion
suave
sub·as·sem·bly
sub·av·er·age
sub·base·ment
sub·class
sub·com·mit·tee
sub·con·scious
  -scious·ness
sub·con·tract
sub·con·trac·tor
sub·cu·ta·ne·ous
sub·di·vide
  -vid·er, -vi·sion
sub·due
  -dued, -du·ing
sub·head
sub·ject

sub·jec·tive
  -tive·ly, -tive·ness,
  -tiv·i·ty
sub·ju·gate
  -gat·ed, -gat·ing
sub·junc·tive
sub·lease
sub·let
  -let·ting
sub·lime
sub·lim·i·nal
sub·ma·rine
sub·merge
  -merged,
  -merg·ing,
  -mer·gence
sub·merse
  -mersed,
  -mers·ing,
  -mer·sion
sub·mers·ible
sub·mis·sion
sub·mis·sive
sub·mit
  -mit·ting, -mit·tal
sub·mit·ted
sub·nor·mal
  -mal·i·ty, -mal·ly
sub·note·book
sub·or·di·nate
  -nat·ed, -nat·ing,
  -na·tion
sub·plot

sub·poe·na
  -naed, -na·ing
sub·ro·ga·tion
sub·rou·tine
sub·scribe
  -scribed,
  -scrib·ing,
  -scrib·er
sub·script
sub·scrip·tion
sub·se·quent
sub·ser·vi·ent
sub·side
  -sid·ed, -sid·ing,
  -si·dence
sub·sid·iary
  -iar·ies
sub·si·dize
sub·si·dy
  -dies
sub·sist
sub·sis·tence
sub·stance
sub·stan·dard
sub·stan·tial
  -tial·ly
sub·stan·ti·ate
  -at·ed, -at·ing,
  -a·tion
sub·sti·tute
sub·sur·face
sub·ter·fuge
sub·ter·ra·nean

sub·ti·tle
sub·tle
sub·tle·ty
sub·tly
sub·to·tal
sub·tract
sub·trac·tion
sub·tra·hend
sub·trop·i·cal
sub·urb
  -ur·ban,
  -ur·ban·ite
sub·ur·bia
sub·ver·sion
  -ver·sion·ary,
  -ver·sive
sub·way
suc·ceed
suc·cess
suc·cess·ful
suc·ces·sion
suc·ces·sive
suc·ces·sor
suc·cinct
suc·cor (help; cf.
  sucker)
suc·co·tash
suc·cu·lent
suc·cumb
suck·er (fish; cf.
  succor)
suc·tion
Su·dan

sud·den

sue
  sued, su·ing

suede

su·et

suf·fer
  -fered, -fer·ing

suf·fice

suf·fi·cien·cy

suf·fi·cient

suf·fix

suf·fo·cate
  -cat·ed, -cat·ing,
  -ca·tion

suf·frage

sug·ar

sug·ar·cane

sug·ar·coat

sug·ar·plum

sug·gest

sug·ges·tion

sui·cid·al

sui·cide

suit (garment; cf.
  suite, sweet)

suit·able
  -able·ness, -ably,
  -abil·i·ty

suit·case

suite (group; cf. *suit,*
  sweet)

sul·fate

sul·fur

sulky
  sulk·i·ly,
  sulk·i·ness

sul·len

sul·tan

sul·try
  -tri·er, -tri·est,
  -tri·ness

sum (total; cf. *some*)
  summed,
  sum·ming

sum·ma cum lau·de

sum·ma·rize

sum·ma·ry (brief
  account; cf.
  summery)

sum·ma·tion

sum·mer·time

sum·mery (like
  summer; cf.
  summary)

sum·mit

sum·mon
  -moned, -mon·ing

sump·tu·ous

sun (in the sky; cf.
  son)

sun·bath (n)

sun·bathe (v)

sun·beam

sun·burn

sun·dae (ice cream;
  cf. *Sunday*)

Sun·day (day of the
  week; cf. *sundae*)

sun·di·al

sun·down

sun·dries (n)

sun·dry (adj)

sun·flow·er

sun·glass·es

sunk·en

sun·lamp

sun·light

sun·lit

sun·ny
  -ni·er, -ni·est,
  -ni·ly

sun·rise

sun·roof

sun·screen

sun·set

sun·shade

sun·shine

sun·spot

sun·stroke

sun·tan

sun·up

su·per·abun·dant

su·perb

su·per·com·pu·ter

su·per·con·duc·
  tiv·i·ty

su·per·con·duc·tor

su·per·ego

su·per·fi·cial

su·per·fi·ci·al·i·ty
su·per·flu·ous
su·per·high·way
su·per·hu·man
su·per·im·pose
su·per·in·tend
su·per·in·ten·dent
su·pe·ri·or
su·pe·ri·or·i·ty
  -ties
su·per·la·tive
su·per·ma·jor·i·ty
su·per·man
su·per·mar·ket
su·per·nat·u·ral
su·per·pow·er
su·per·script
su·per·sede
  -sed·ed, -sed·ing
su·per·size
su·per·son·ic
su·per·sti·tion
su·per·sti·tious
su·per·struc·ture
su·per·vise
  -vised, -vis·ing
su·per·vi·sion
su·per·vi·sor
  -so·ry
su·per·wom·an
sup·per
sup·plant
sup·ple

sup·ple·ment
sup·ple·men·tal
sup·ple·men·ta·ry
sup·pli·cate
  -cat·ed, -cat·ing,
  -ca·tion
sup·ply
  -plies, -plied,
  -ply·ing, -pli·er
sup·port
sup·port·er
sup·pose
  -posed, -pos·ing
sup·po·si·tion
sup·press
  -ible
sup·pres·sion
su·prem·a·cist
su·prem·a·cy
  -cies
su·preme
sur·charge
sure·fire
sure·foot·ed
sure·ly (certainly; cf.
  surly)
sure·ty
surf (waves; cf. *serf*)
sur·face
  -faced, -fac·ing
surf·board
surf·ing
surge (wave; cf.

  serge)
sur·geon
sur·gery
  -ger·ies
sur·gi·cal
Su·ri·na·me
sur·ly (sullen; cf.
  surely)
  -li·er, -li·est,
  -li·ness
sur·mise
  -mised, -mis·ing
sur·mount
  -mount·able
sur·name
sur·pass
sur·plice (garment;
  cf. *surplus*)
sur·plus (excess; cf.
  surplice)
sur·prise
  -prised, -pris·ing
sur·re·al·ism
sur·ren·der
  -dered, -der·ing
sur·rep·ti·tious
sur·ro·gate
sur·round
sur·tax
sur·veil·lance
sur·vey
  -veyed, -vey·ing
sur·vey·or

sur·viv·al
sur·viv·al·ist
sur·vive
  -vived, -viv·ing,
  -vi·vor
sus·cep·ti·bil·i·ty
sus·cep·ti·ble
su·shi
sus·pect
sus·pend
sus·pense
sus·pen·sion
sus·pi·cion
sus·pi·cious
sus·tain
sus·te·nance
su·ture
  -tured, -tur·ing
svelte
swab
  swabbed,
  swab·bing
swal·low
swamp
swap
  -swapped,
  swap·ping
swap·tions
sward (grass; cf.
  sword)
swas·ti·ka
swatch
Swa·zi·land

sweat·band
sweat·er
sweat·pants
sweat·shirt
sweaty
  sweat·i·er,
  sweat·i·est,
  sweat·i·ness
Swe·den
sweep·stakes
sweet (not sour; cf.
  suit, suite)
sweet·en
  -ened, -en·ing,
  -en·er
sweet·heart
sweet tooth
swel·ter
  -tered, -ter·ing
swerve
  swerved,
  swerv·ing
swim
  swim·ming,
  swim·mer
swim·ming·ly
swim·suit
swin·dle
  -dled, -dling,
  -dler
swing shift
switch·blade
switch·board

Swit·zer·land
swiv·el
  -eled, -el·ing
swoon
swoop
sword (weapon; cf.
  sward)
sword·fish
syc·a·more
Syd·ney
syl·lab·ic
syl·lab·i·cate
  -cat·ed, -cat·ing
syl·la·ble
syl·la·bus
  -bi (pl)
syl·lo·gism
sym·bi·o·sis
  -bi·ot·ic
sym·bol (emblem;
  cf. *cymbal*)
sym·bol·ic
  -bol·i·cal·ly
sym·bol·ism
sym·bol·ize
  -ized, -iz·ing,
  -iz·er
sym·met·ri·cal
sym·me·try
  -tries
sym·pa·thet·ic
sym·pa·thize
  -thized, -thiz·ing,
  -thiz·er

sym·pa·thy
  -thies
sym·phon·ic
sym·pho·ny
  -nies
sym·po·sium
symp·tom
syn·a·gogue
syn·chro·nic·i·ty
syn·chro·nism
syn·chro·ni·za·tion
syn·chro·nize
  -nized, -niz·ing
syn·chro·nous
syn·co·pate
  -pat·ed, -pat·ing
syn·di·cate
  -cat·ed, -cat·ing,
  -ca·tion
syn·drome
syn·er·gism
syn·er·gy
syn·od
syn·onym
syn·on·y·mous
syn·op·sis
  -op·ses (pl)
syn·tax
syn·the·sis
  -the·ses (pl)
syn·the·size
  -sized, -siz·ing
syn·thet·ic

Syr·a·cuse
Syr·ia
sy·ringe
syr·up
sys·op
sys·tem
sys·tem·at·ic
  -at·i·cal·ly
sys·tem·atize
  -atized,
  -atiz·ing,
  -ati·za·tion
sys·tem soft·ware
sys·tems anal·y·sis
sys·tems an·a·lyst
sys·tems
  in·te·gra·tor

tab
  tabbed,
  tab·bing
Ta·bas·co
tab·er·na·cle
ta·ble
  -bled, -bling
tab·leau
  -leaux (pl)
ta·ble·spoon
tab·let
ta·ble·ware
tab·loid
ta·boo
tab·u·lar
tab·u·late
  -lat·ed, -lat·ing,
  -la·tion
tab·u·la·tor
ta·chis·to·scope
ta·chom·e·ter
tac·it
  -it·ness
tac·i·turn
tack·le
  -led, -ling
tac·o·nite
tact·ful
tac·tic

tac·ti·cal
tad·pole
taf·fe·ta
tag
  tagged, tag·ging
tag·board
tag·gant
Ta·hi·ti
tail (end; cf. *tale*)
tail·coat
tail·gate (n, v)
  -gat·ed, -gat·ing
tail·light
tai·lor
tail·piece
tail·spin
tail wind
taint
Tai·pei
Tai·wan
Ta·jik·i·stan
take-no-pris·on·ers
take off (v)
take·off (n)
take-out (adj)
take·out (n)
take over (v)
take·over (n)
talc

tale (story; cf. *tail*)
tal·ent
  -ent·ed, -ent·less
talk·ative
  -ative·ness
Tal·la·has·see
tal·low
tal·ly
  -lies
tal·on
ta·ma·le
tam·a·rack
tam·bou·rine
tam·per
  -pered, -per·ing,
  -per·proof
tam·pon
tan·a·ger
tan·dem
tan·gent
tan·ger·ine
tan·gi·ble
  -ble·ness, -bly,
  -bil·i·ty
Tan·gier
tan·gle
  -gled, -gling
tangy

263

tank
  tank·ful
tan·ta·lize
  -lized, -liz·ing
tan·ta·mount
Tan·za·nia
tap
  tapped, tap·ping
tape
  taped, tap·ing
ta·per (diminish; cf.
  tapir)
tape-re·cord (v)
tap·es·try
tape·worm
tap·i·o·ca
ta·pir (animal; cf.
  taper)
tap·root
tar·an·tel·la
ta·ran·tu·la
tar·dy
  -di·er, -di·est,
  -di·ness
tare (weight; cf.
  tear)
tar·get
tar·iff
tar·la·tan
tar·nish
tar·pau·lin
tar·pon
tar·ra·gon

tar·tan
tar·tar
task
task·bar
task force
Tas·ma·nia
tas·sel
  -seled, -sel·ing
taste·ful
  -ful·ly, -ful·ness
tasty
  tast·i·ly, tast·i·ness
tat·ting
tat·too
taught (instructed;
  cf. *taut*)
taunt
taut (tight; cf.
  taught)
tav·ern
taw·dry
tax
  tax·able
tax·a·tion
tax-ex·empt
taxi
  tax·ied, taxi·ing
taxi·cab
taxi·der·my
tax·pay·er
tea (a drink; cf. *tee*)
teach·able
teach·er

tea·cup
tea·ket·tle
teak·wood
team (in sports; cf.
  teem)
team·mate
team·ster
team·work
tear (rip; cf. *tare*)
tear (weep; cf. *tier*)
tear·drop
tear sheet
tea·spoon
tea·time
tech·ie
tech·ni·cal
  -cal·ly
tech·ni·cal·i·ty
tech·ni·cian
tech·nique
tech·noc·ra·cy
tech·no·log·i·cal
  -cal·ly
tech·nol·o·gy
  -gies
tech·no·pho·bia
tech·no·struc·ture
tech·no·thrill·er
te·dious
  -dious·ness
tee (in golf; cf. *tea*)
teem (abound with;
  cf. *team*)

teen·age
teens
tee·to·tal·er
Te·he·ran
Te·ja·no
tele·cast
  -cast·ed, -cast·ing,
  -cast·er
tele·com·mu·ni·ca·tion
tele·com·mute
tele·com·mut·er
tel·e·com·put·ing
tele·con·fer·ence
  -enc·ing
tele·fac·sim·i·le
tele·gram
  -grammed,
  -gram·ming
tele·graph
tele·mar·ket·ing
te·lep·a·thy
tele·phone
te·le·pho·ny
tele·pho·to
tele·print·er
tele·pro·cess·ing
Tele·Promp·Ter
tele·scope
  -scoped, -scop·ing
tele·scop·ic
tele·shop·ping
tele·text
tele·thon

Tele·type
tel·evan·ge·list
tele·vise
  -vised, -vis·ing
tele·vi·sion
tele·work
tell
  tell·ing
Tel·net
te·mer·i·ty
  -ties
tem·per
  -pered, -per·ing,
  -per·able
tem·per·a·ment
tem·per·ance
tem·per·ate
tem·per·a·ture
tem·pest
tem·pes·tu·ous
tem·plate
tem·ple
tem·po
  -pi (pl)
tem·po·ral
  -ral·ly
tem·po·rari·ly
tem·po·rary
  -rar·ies
tempt
temp·ta·tion
ten·a·ble
te·na·cious

te·nac·i·ty
ten·an·cy
ten·ant
  -ant·able
ten·den·cy
  -cies
ten·der
  -der·ness
ten·der·heart·ed
ten·der·ize
  -ized, -iz·ing,
  -iza·tion
ten·der·loin
ten·don
ten·dril
ten·e·ment
ten·nis
ten·or
ten·pin
ten·sile
ten·sion
  -sioned, -sion·ing
ten-speed
ten·ta·cle
ten·ta·tive
  -tive·ly, -tive·ness
tenth
  tenths
ten·u·ous
ten·ure
tep·id
te·qui·la
tera·bit

tera·byte
ter·mi·na·ble
ter·mi·nal
ter·mi·nate
  -nat·ed, -nat·ing
ter·mi·na·tion
ter·mi·nol·o·gy
ter·mite
tern (bird; cf. *turn*)
ter·race
  -raced, -rac·ing
ter·ra fir·ma
ter·rain
ter·ra·pin
ter·rar·i·um
  -ia (pl)
ter·raz·zo
ter·res·tri·al
  -al·ly
ter·ri·ble
  -ble·ness, -bly
ter·ri·er
ter·rif·ic
  -i·cal·ly
ter·ri·fy
  -fied, -fy·ing
ter·ri·to·ri·al
ter·ri·to·ry
  -ries
ter·ror
ter·ror·ism
  -ist

ter·ror·ize
  -ized, -iz·ing
terse
  terse·ly, terse·ness
ter·tia·ry
  -ries
tes·ta·ment
test-drive
tes·ti·fy
  -fied, -fy·ing
tes·ti·mo·ni·al
tes·ti·mo·ny
  -nies
test tube (n)
test-tube (adj)
tet·a·nus
tête-à-tête
text
text·book
text ed·it·ing
tex·tile
tex·tu·al
tex·ture
  -tured, -tur·ing
Thai
Thai·land
than
thank
thank·ful
  -ful·ly, -ful·ness
thanks·giv·ing
the·ater

the·at·ri·cal
  -cal·ly
theft
their (possessive;
  cf. *there, they're*)
the·ism
theme
them·selves
then
thence·forth
theo·lo·gian
theo·log·i·cal
the·ol·o·gy
  -gies
the·o·rem
the·o·ret·i·cal
the·o·rize
  -rized, -riz·ing
the·o·ry
  -ries
ther·a·peu·tic
ther·a·pist
ther·a·py
  -pies
there (that place; cf.
  their, they're)
there·by
there·fore (conse-
  quently)
there·on
ther·mal
  -mal·ly
ther·mal print·er

ther·mo·dy·nam·ic
ther·mom·e·ter
ther·mo·stat
the·sau·rus
 -sau·ri (pl)
these
the·sis
 -ses (pl)
thes·pi·an
they're (they are; cf.
 their, there)
thi·a·mine
thick·et
thick-skinned
thief
 thieves (pl)
thiev·ish
thim·ble
thin
 thin·ner,
 thin·nest,
 thin·nish
third class (n)
third-class (adj)
third world
thirst·i·ly
thirsty
 thirst·i·er,
 thirst·i·est,
 thirst·i·ness
thir·teen
 -teenth

thir·ty
 -ties, -ti·eth
thith·er
tho·rac·ic
tho·rax
 -rax·es (pl)
thorn
 thorn·less,
 thorn·like
thorny
 thorn·i·er,
 thorn·i·est,
 thorn·i·ness
thor·ough (com-
 plete; cf. *threw,
 through*)
 -ough·ness
thor·ough·bred
thor·ough·fare
though
thought
thought·ful
 -ful·ness
thought-out
thou·sand
 -sandth
thread·bare
threat·en
 -ened, -en·ing,
 -en·er
three·fold
three·score
three·some

thresh·old
threw (past tense of
 throw; cf. *thor-
 ough, through*)
thrifty
 thrift·i·er,
 thrift·i·est,
 thrift·i·ness
thrive
 thrived, thriv·ing
throat
throe (effort; cf.
 throw)
throm·bo·sis
 -ses (pl)
throne (royal chair;
 cf. *thrown*)
throng
throt·tle
through (by means
 of; cf. *thorough,
 threw*)
through·out
through·put
throw (hurl; cf.
 throe)
 threw, thrown
 (hurled; cf.
 throne)
throw away (v)
throw·away (adj, n)
throw back (v)
throw·back (n)

thru·way

thumb·nail

thumb·print

thumb·screw

thumb·tack

thun·der·bolt

thun·der·head

thun·der·ous

thun·der·show·er

thun·der·storm

Thurs·day

thwart

thyme (spice; cf.
time)

thy·mus

thy·roid

Ti·bet

tib·ia

tic (twitching; cf.
tick)

tick (of a clock; cf.
tic)

tick·et

tick·le

-led, -ling

tick·ler

tid·al

tide (ocean; cf. *tied*)

tide·mark

tide·wa·ter

ti·dy

-di·er, -di·est,
-di·ly

tie

tied (past tense of
tie; cf. *tide*), ty·ing

tie·break·er

tie in (v)

tie-in (n)

tie·pin

tier (row; cf. *tear*)

ti·ger

tight·fist·ed

tight-lipped

tight-mouthed

tight·rope

tim·ber (wood; cf.
timbre)

-bered, -ber·ing

tim·ber·land

tim·ber·line

tim·bre (of the
voice; cf. *timber*)

time (duration; cf.
thyme)

timed, tim·ing

time-hon·ored

time·keep·er

time-lapse

time·less

time·ly

-li·er, -li·est,
-li·ness

time·piece

time·sav·ing

time-shar·ing

time sheet

time·ta·ble

time zone

tim·id

tim·id·ly,
ti·mid·i·ty

tinc·ture

-tured, -tur·ing

tinge

tinged, tinge·ing

tin·gle

-gled, -gling

tin·sel

-seled, -sel·ing

ti·ny

-ni·er, -ni·est,
-ni·ness

tip

tipped, tip·ping

tip·ster

tip·toe

-toed, -toe·ing

ti·rade

tire·some

-some·ly,
-some·ness

tis·sue

ti·tan

ti·tan·ic

tithe

tithed, tith·ing

tit·il·late

-lat·ed, -lat·ing

ti·tle
  -tled, -tling
ti·tle·hold·er
tit·mouse
tit·u·lar
to (preposition; cf.
  too, two)
toad·stool
toast
to·bac·co
to·bog·gan
To·ba·go
to·day
toe (of foot; cf. *tow*)
  toed, toe·ing
toe·nail
tof·fee
to·ga
to·geth·er
tog·gle
  -gled, -gling
To·go
toi·let
to·ken
To·kyo
tol·er·a·ble
  -bly, -bil·i·ty
tol·er·ance
tol·er·ant
tol·er·ate
  -at·ed, -at·ing
tol·er·a·tion
toll·booth

toll bridge
toll call
toll·gate
toll road
tom·a·hawk
to·ma·to
  -toes
to·mor·row
ton·al
tone
  toned, ton·ing
ton·er
Ton·ga
tongue
tongue-tied
ton·ic
to·night
ton·sil
ton·sil·lec·to·my
ton·sil·li·tis
too (also; cf. *to, two*)
tool·bar
tool·box
tool·house
tool·mak·er
tool·room
tooth·ache
tooth·brush
tooth·paste
tooth·pick
top
  topped,
  top·ping

to·paz
top·coat
To·pe·ka
top·ic
top·i·cal
to·pog·ra·phy
to·pol·o·gy
top se·cret
top·side
top·soil
torch·bear·er
torch·light
to·re·ador
tor·ment
tor·men·tor
tor·na·do
  -does
tor·pe·do
  -does, -doed,
  -do·ing
torque
tor·rent
tor·ren·tial
  -tial·ly
tor·rid
tor·so
tor·ti·lla
tor·toise·shell
tor·tu·ous (winding;
  cf. *torturous*)
tor·ture
  -tured, -tur·ing,
  -tur·er

tor·tur·ous (painful;
   cf. *tortuous*)
Tory
   Tories (pl)
to·tal
   -taled, -tal·ing
to·tal·i·tar·i·an
to·tal·i·ty
   -ties
to·tal·ly
to·tem
touch down (v)
touch·down (n)
tou·ché
touch·pad
touch·tone
touch up (v)
touch-up (n)
touchy
tough
   tough·ness
tou·pee
tour·ism
tour·ist
tour·na·ment
tour·ney
   -neys, -neyed,
   -ney·ing
tour·ni·quet
tow (pull; cf. *toe*)
to·ward
tow·boat

tow·el
   -eled, -el·ing
tow·er
town·ship
towns·peo·ple
tow·rope
tox·emia
tox·ic
   -ic·i·ty
tox·i·col·o·gy
trace
   traced, trac·ing,
   trace·able
tra·chea
   -che·ae (pl)
track (path; cf. *tract*)
   track·less
track·ball
track·ing
tract (treatise; area;
   cf. *track*)
trac·tion
trac·tor
trade-in (n)
trade·mark
trade name
trade-off (n)
tra·di·tion
   -tion·al, -tion·al·ly,
   -tion·less
traf·fic
   -ficked, -fick·ing

trag·e·dy
   -dies
trag·ic
   -i·cal, -i·cal·ly
trail·blaz·er
trail·er
   -er·ing
train·able
train·ee
train·er
trait
trai·tor
tra·jec·to·ry
   -ries
tram·ple
   -pled, -pling, -pler
tram·po·line
tran·quil
   -quil·ly
tran·quil·iz·er
tran·quil·li·ty
trans·act
trans·ac·tion
trans·at·lan·tic
trans·ceiv·er
tran·scend
tran·scen·dent
tran·scen·den·tal
tran·scen·den·tal·ism
trans·con·ti·nen·tal
tran·scribe
   -scribed,
   -scrib·ing

tran·script
tran·scrip·tion
trans·du·cer
trans·fer
  -ferred, -fer·ring,
  -fer·able
trans·fer·ence
trans·fig·ure
trans·fix
  -fix·ion
trans·form
trans·for·ma·tion
trans·form·er
trans·fuse
  -fused, -fus·ing
trans·gen·der
trans·gress
trans·gres·sion
tran·sient
tran·sis·tor
tran·sit
tran·si·tion
tran·si·tive
tran·si·to·ry
trans·late
  -lat·ed, -lat·ing,
  -la·tor
trans·la·tion
trans·lit·er·ate
trans·lu·cent
trans·mis·sion
trans·mit
  -mit·ted, -mit·ting,
  -mit·tal

trans·oce·an·ic
tran·som
trans·par·en·cy
  -cies
trans·par·ent
tran·spire
  -spired, -spir·ing
trans·plant
  -plant·able,
  -plan·ta·tion
tran·spon·der
trans·port
trans·por·ta·tion
trans·pose
  -posed, -pos·ing,
  -pos·able
trans·po·si·tion
trans·verse
Tran·syl·va·nia
trap
  trapped, trap·ping
tra·peze
trau·ma
  -mas(pl)
  -mata (pl)
tra·vail (toil; cf.
  travel)
trav·el (journey; cf.
  travail)
  -eled, -el·ing
trav·el agent
trav·el·er
tra·verse
  -versed, -vers·ing,

  -vers·able
trav·es·ty
  -ties
treach·er·ous
treach·ery
  -er·ies
trea·dle
tread·mill
trea·son
trea·sure
trea·sur·er
trea·sury
treat
trea·tise
treat·ment
trea·ty
  -ties
tre·ble
tree·top
tree·ware
tre·foil
trel·lis
trem·ble
tre·men·dous
  -dous·ness
trem·or
trem·u·lous
trench
tren·chant
Tren·ton
trep·i·da·tion
tres·pass
tres·tle
tri·ad

tri·al
tri·an·gle
tri·an·gu·lar
tri·ath·lete
tri·ath·lon
trib·al
  -al·ly
tribe
tri·bu·nal
tri·bune
trib·u·tary
  -tar·ies
trib·ute
trick·ery
trick·le
trick·ster
tri·col·or
tri·cy·cle
tri·dent
tri·en·ni·al
tri·fle
  -fled, -fling
tri·fo·cal
trig·ger
  -gered, -ger·ing
trig·o·nom·e·try
tril·lion
tril·li·um
tril·o·gy
  -gies
Trin·i·dad
trin·ket

trip
  tripped, trip·ping
tri·ple
  -pled, -pling
trip·li·cate
  -cat·ed, -cat·ing,
  -ca·tion
tri·pod
tri·umph
  -um·phal
tri·um·phant
triv·et
triv·ia
triv·i·al
trol·ley
  -leys
trom·bone
  -bon·ist
troop (of soldiers; cf.
  troupe)
troop·ship
tro·phy
  -phies
trop·ic
trot
  trot·ted,
  trot·ting
trou·ba·dour
trou·ble
  -bled, -bling
trou·ble·shoot·er

trou·ble·some
  -some·ly,
  -some·ness
troupe (of actors; cf.
  troop)
trou·ser
trous·seau
  -seaux (pl)
trow·el
tru·an·cy
tru·ant
truck·load
truf·fle
tru·ism
  -is·tic
tru·ly
trum·pet
trum·pet·er
trun·cate
  -cat·ed, -cat·ing
trust·ee
  trust·eed,
  trust·ee·ing
trust·ee·ship
trust·ful
trust fund
trust·wor·thy
  -thi·ness
truth
  truths
truth·ful
try out (v)
try·out (n)

tryst
tset·se fly
T-shirt
tu·ba
tu·ber
tu·ber·cu·lar
tu·ber·cu·lin
tu·ber·cu·lo·sis
tu·bu·lar
Tues·day
tug
   tugged,
   tug·ging
tu·ition
tu·lip
tu·lip·wood
tulle
tum·ble
   -bled, -bling
tum·bler
tum·ble·weed
tu·mor
   -mor·like
tu·mult
tu·mul·tu·ous
tu·na
tune
   tuned, tun·ing
tune·ful
tune-up
tung·sten
tu·nic
Tu·ni·sia

tun·nel
   -neled, -nel·ing
tur·ban (headdress;
   cf. *turbine*)
tur·bine (engine; cf.
   turban)
tur·bo·jet
tur·bu·lence
tur·bu·lent
tu·reen
tur·key
   -keys
Tur·key
Turk·men·i·stan
tur·mer·ic
tur·moil
turn (rotate; cf. *tern*)
turn·about
turn around (v)
turn·around (n)
turn·around time
turn down (v)
turn·down (adj, n)
turn in (v)
turn-in (n)
tur·nip
turn·key
   -keys
turn off (v)
turn·off (n)
turn over (v)
turn·over (adj, n)
turn·pike

turn·stile
turn·ta·ble
tur·pen·tine
tur·quoise
tur·ret
tur·tle·dove
tur·tle·neck
tus·sle
   -sled, -sling
tu·te·lage
tu·tor
tu·to·ri·al
Tu·va·lu
TV-M
TV-Y
twelve
   twelfth
twen·ty
   -ties, -ti·eth
twen·ty-twen·ty
twice
twi·light
twin·ax·i·al cab·le
two-way
twist
twitch
two (one and one; cf.
   to, too)
two-piece (adj, n)
two-ply
ty·coon
ty·ing

type
  typed, typ·ing
type·cast
type·face
type·over
type·script
type·set·ter
type·write
  -wrote,
  -writ·ten
type·writ·er
ty·phoid
ty·phoon
ty·phus
typ·i·cal
typ·i·fy
  -fied, -fy·ing
typ·ist
ty·po
ty·pog·ra·pher
ty·po·graph·i·cal
ty·ran·ni·cal
tyr·an·nize
  -nized, -niz·ing
tyr·an·ny
  -nies
ty·rant
ty·ro

ubiq·ui·tous
ubiq·ui·ty
ug·li·ness
ug·ly
  -li·er, -li·est
Ukraine
uku·le·le
ul·cer
ul·cer·ation
ul·cer·ous
ul·te·ri·or
ul·ti·mate
ul·ti·ma·tum
ul·tra·mod·ern
ul·tra·na·tion·al·is·m
ul·tra·son·ic
ul·tra·vi·o·let
um·bil·i·cal
um·brage
um·brel·la
um·pire
un·abat·ed
un·able
un·abridged
un·ac·cept·able
un·ac·com·pa·nied
un·ac·count·able
un·ac·cus·tomed

un·adul·ter·at·ed
un·af·fect·ed
un·al·ter·able
un·am·big·u·ous
un-Amer·i·can
unan·i·mous
un·as·sum·ing
un·au·tho·rized
un·avail·able
un·avoid·able
un·aware
un·bal·anced
un·be·com·ing
un·be·liev·able
un·bend
un·bi·ased
un·but·ton
un·cer·tain
un·cer·tain·ty
un·char·i·ta·ble
un·civ·i·lized
un·cle
un·clean
un·com·fort·able
un·com·mit·ted
un·com·mu·ni·ca·tive
un·com·pli·men·ta·ry

un·com·pressed
  -press·ing
un·com·pro·mis·ing
un·con·cerned
un·con·di·tion·al
un·con·quer·able
un·con·scio·na·ble
un·con·scious
un·con·trol·la·ble
un·con·ven·tion·al
un·con·vinc·ing
  -ing·ly
un·cor·rect·ed
unc·tion
un·de·ni·able
un·der·age
un·der·arm
un·der·brush
un·der·class·man
un·der·clothes
un·der·cov·er
un·der·cur·rent
un·der·de·vel·oped
un·der·dog
un·der·em·ploy·ment
un·der·go

275

un·der·grad·u·ate
un·der·ground
un·der·line
un·der·ly·ing
un·der·mine
un·der·neath
un·der·pass
un·der·priv·i·leged
un·der·rate
un·der·score
un·der·sell
un·der·shirt
un·der·side
un·der·signed
un·der·stand
un·der·stood
un·der·study
un·der·tak·er
un·der·tone
un·der·tow
un·der·val·ue
un·der·wa·ter
un·der way (adv)
un·der·way (adj)
un·der·wear
un·der·weight
un·der·went
un·der·world
un·der·write
un·de·sir·able
un·do (unfasten; cf.
    undue)

un·doubt·ed·ly
un·due (excessive;
    cf. *undo*)
un·du·la·tion
un·du·ly
un·earned
un·earth·ly
un·eas·y
    -eas·i·ness
un·ed·it·ed
un·em·ployed
un·en·cum·bered
un·equal
un·equiv·o·cal
un·err·ing
un·even
un·ex·pect·ed
un·fa·mil·iar
    -iar·i·ty
un·fa·vor·able
un·fore·seen
un·for·get·ta·ble
un·for·tu·nate
    -nate·ly
un·furl
un·gain·ly
uni·cast
uni·code
uni·fi·ca·tion
uni·form
uni·for·mi·ty
    -ties

Uni·form
    Re·source
    Lo·ca·tor (URL)
uni·fy
    -fied, -fy·ing
uni·lat·er·al
un·im·peach·able
un·im·proved
un·in·hib·it·ed
un·in·sured
un·in·tel·li·gi·ble
union
union·ize
    -ized, -iz·ing
unique
    unique·ly,
    unique·ness
uni·sex
uni·son
unit
unite
Unit·ed Arab
    Emir·ates
Unit·ed King·dom
Unit·ed States
uni·ty
    -ties
uni·ver·sal
Uni·ver·sal
    Prod·uct Code
    (UPC)
uni·verse
uni·ver·si·ty
un·kind·ly

un·know·ing
un·known
un·law·ful
un·leash
un·less
un·like·ly
un·lim·it·ed
un·manned
un·mind·ful
un·mit·i·gat·ed
un·named
un·nat·u·ral
un·nec·es·sary
un·nerve
 -nerv·ing·ly
un·ob·tru·sive
un·oc·cu·pied
un·or·tho·dox
un·paid
un·par·al·leled
un·pleas·ant
un·prec·e·dent·ed
un·prof·it·able
un·qual·i·fied
un·ques·tion·able
un·rav·el
un·re·al
un·rea·son·able
un·ruly
 -rul·i·ness
un·sat·is·fac·to·ry
 -ri·ly
un·sa·vory

un·scathed
un·scru·pu·lous
un·so·cia·ble
 -bil·i·ty
un·so·phis·ti·cat·ed
un·speak·able
un·think·able
un·ti·dy
 -di·ly, -di·ness
un·tie
un·til
un·time·ly
un·told
un·touch·able
un·truth·ful
un·used
un·usu·al
 -al·ly
un·want·ed
 (undesired; cf.
 unwonted)
un·war·rant·ed
un·wary
un·wieldy
 -wield·i·ly,
 -wield·i·ness
un·wont·ed (unac-
 customed; cf.
 unwanted)
un·wor·thy
 -thi·ly, -thi·ness
un·writ·ten

un·zip
 -zipped, zip·ping
up·bring·ing
up·com·ing
up·date
up·grade
up·heav·al
up·hill (adj, adv, n)
up·hold
 -held, hold·ing
up·hol·ster
up·hol·stery
up·keep
up·land
up·lift
up·link
up·load
up·on
up·per
up·per·case
up·per class (n)
up·per-class (adj)
up·per-class·man
up·per·cut
up·per·most
up·right
up·ris·ing
up·roar·i·ous
up·root
up·set
 -set·ting
up·shot
up·stage

277

up·stairs
up·start
up·state (adj, adv, n)
up·stream
up·swing
up·talk
up·tight
up-to-date
up·turn
up·ward
ura·ni·um
ur·ban (of city; cf. *urbane*)
ur·bane (suave; cf. *urban*)
ur·ban·iza·tion
ur·chin
urge
   urged, urg·ing
ur·gen·cy
   -cies
ur·gent
ur·gi·cen·ter
uri·nary
urn (vase; cf. *earn*)
Uru·guay
us·able
us·age
use
   used
use·ful
use·ful·ness
use·less

Use·net
us·er-friend·ly
user·name
User·net
ush·er
   -ered, -er·ing
us·ing
usu·al
   -al·ly
usu·rer
usu·ri·ous
usurp
usu·ry
   -ries
uten·sil
uter·ine
util·i·tar·i·an
util·i·ty
   -ties
uti·li·za·tion
uti·lize
   -liz·ing
uti·lized
ut·most
uto·pia
ut·ter
ut·ter·ance
Uz·bek·i·stan

va·can·cy
  -cies
va·cant
va·cate
  -cat·ed, -cat·ing
va·ca·tion
  -tioned,
  -tion·ing,
  -tion·er
vac·ci·nate
  -nat·ed, -nat·ing
vac·ci·na·tion
vac·cine
V-chip
vac·il·late
  -lat·ed, -lat·ing
vac·il·la·tion
vac·u·ous
vac·u·um
vag·a·bond
va·gi·na
va·gran·cy
  -cies
va·grant
vague
  vagu·er, vagu·est,
  vague·ly,
  vague·ness

vain (conceited; cf.
  vane, vein)
va·lance (drapery;
  cf. *valence*)
vale (valley; cf. *veil*)
vale·dic·to·ri·an
vale·dic·to·ry
  -ries
va·lence (combining
  power; cf. *valance*)
val·en·tine
va·let
val·iant
val·id
  va·lid·i·ty
val·i·date
  -dat·ed, -dat·ing
val·i·da·tion
va·lise
val·ley
  -leys
val·or
valu·able
val·u·a·tion
val·ue
val·ue-ad·ded
  re·sell·er
val·ue-ad·ded tax
valve

vam·pire
Van·cou·ver
van·dal·ism
vane (weather; cf.
  vain, vein)
van·guard
va·nil·la
van·ish
van·i·ty
  -ties
van·quish
van·tage
Va·nu·a·tu
va·por
  -pored, -por·ing
va·por·ize
  -ized, -iz·ing,
  -iza·tion
va·por·iz·er
va·por·ous
va·por·ware
vari·able
  -abil·i·ty
vari·ance
vari·ant
vari·a·tion
var·i·cose
var·ied

var·ie·gate
  -gat·ed, -gat·ing
var·ie·ga·tion
va·ri·e·ty
var·i·ous
var·nish
vary (diversify; cf.
  very)
  var·ied, vary·ing
vas·cu·lar
va·sec·to·my
  -mies
Vas·e·line
Vat·i·can
Vat·i·can City
vaude·ville
vault
vec·tor
vee·jay
veg·e·ta·ble
veg·e·tar·i·an
veg·e·tate
  -tat·ed, -tat·ing
veg·e·ta·tion
veg·e·ta·tive
ve·he·mence
ve·he·ment
ve·hi·cle
ve·hic·u·lar
veil (garment; cf.
  vale)
vein (blood vessel;
  cf. *vain, vane*)

ve·loc·i·ty
  -ties
ve·lour
ven·det·ta
ven·dor
ve·neer
ven·er·a·ble
ven·er·ate
  -at·ed, -at·ing
ven·er·a·tion
Ve·ne·tian
Ven·e·zu·e·la
ven·geance
venge·ful
  -ful·ly, -ful·ness
ven·i·son
ven·om·ous
ven·ti·late
  -lat·ed, -lat·ing
ven·ti·la·tion
ven·ti·la·tor
ven·tri·cle
ven·tril·o·quism
ven·tril·o·quist
ven·ture
  -tured, -tur·ing
ven·ture·some
  -some·ly,
  -some·ness
ven·ue
ve·ra·cious (truth-
  ful; cf. *voracious*)

ve·rac·i·ty
  -ties
Ve·ra·cruz
ve·ran·da
ver·bal
  -bal·ly
ver·bal·ism
ver·bal·ize
  -ized, -iz·ing,
  -iza·tion
ver·ba·tim
ver·biage
ver·bose
  -bose·ly,
  -bose·ness,
  -bos·i·ty
ver·dict
verge
  verged, verg·ing
ver·i·fi·ca·tion
ver·i·fy
  -fied, -fy·ing
ver·mil·ion or
  ver·mil·lion
ver·min
  -min (pl)
ver·nac·u·lar
ver·nal
Ve·ron·i·ca
ver·sa·tile
ver·sa·til·i·ty
ver·si·fi·ca·tion

ver·si·fy
 -fied, -fy·ing
ver·sion
ver·sus
ver·te·bra
 -brae (pl)
ver·te·brate
ver·tex
 ver·ti·ces (pl)
ver·ti·cal
 -cal·ly, -cal·ness
very (extremely; cf.
 vary)
ves·per
ves·sel
ves·tige
vest·ment
vet·er·an
vet·er·i·nary
 -nar·ies
ve·to
 -toes
ve·toed
vex·a·tion
via
vi·a·ble
 -bil·i·ty
via·duct
Vi·ag·ra
vi·al (bottle; cf. *vile,
 viol*)
vi·brant

vi·brate
 -brat·ed, -brat·ing
vi·bra·tion
vi·bra·to
vi·bra·tor
vic·ar
vi·car·i·ous
vice (sin; cf. *vise*)
vice-chan·cel·lor
vice pres·i·dent
vice ver·sa
vi·chys·soise
vi·cin·i·ty
 -ties
vi·cious
vic·tim
vic·tim·ize
 -ized, -iz·ing
vic·tor
vic·to·ri·ous
vic·to·ry
 -ries
vi·cu·ña
vid·eo
vid·eo·cas·sette
vid·eo·con·fer·ence
 -fer·enc·ing
vid·eo·disc or
 vid·eo·disk
vid·eo dis·play
 ter·mi·nal
vid·eo·phone
vid·eo·tape

vid·eo·tex
vie
 vied, vy·ing
Vi·en·na
Viet·nam
Viet·nam·ese
view·point
vig·il
vig·i·lance
vig·i·lant
vig·i·lan·te
vi·gnette
vig·or·ous
vile (odious; cf. *vial,
 viol*)
vil·i·fy
 -fied, -fy·ing,
 -fi·er
vil·lage
vil·lain
vil·lain·ous
vin·ai·grette
vin·di·cate
 -cat·ed, -cat·ing
vin·di·ca·tion
vin·dic·a·tive
 (justifying; cf.
 vindictive)
vin·dic·tive (venge-
 ful; cf. *vindicative*)
vin·e·gar
vine·yard
vin·tage

vi·ol (instrument; cf.
vial, vile)
vi·o·la
vi·o·late
-lat·ed, -lat·ing
vi·o·lence
vi·o·lent
vi·o·let
vi·o·lin
vi·per
vir·gin
Vir·gin Is·lands
vir·ile
vi·ril·i·ty
vir·tu·al
vir·tu·al·ly
vir·tu·al mem·o·ry
vir·tu·al re·al·i·ty
vir·tue
vir·tu·os·i·ty
-ties
vir·tu·o·so
vir·u·lent
vi·rus
vi·sa
vis·age
vis-à-vis
vis·count
vise (tool; cf. *vice*)
vis·i·bil·i·ty
vis·i·ble
-ble·ness, -bly

vi·sion
-sion·al, -sion·al·ly
vi·sion·ary
-ar·ies
vis·it
-it·ing
vis·i·ta·tion
vis·i·tor
vi·sor
vis·ta
vi·su·al
-al·ly
vi·su·al aid
Vis·u·al Ba·sic
vi·su·al·ize
-ized, -iz·ing
vi·ta
vi·tae (pl)
vi·tal
vi·tal·i·ty
-ties
vi·tal·ize
-ized, -iz·ing,
-iza·tion
vi·ta·min
vi·va
vi·va·cious
viv·id
-id·ness, -id·ly
vi·vip·a·rous
vivi·sec·tion
vix·en
vo·cab·u·lary
-lar·ies

vo·cal
-cal·ly
vo·cal·ist
vo·cal·ize
-ized, -iz·ing,
-iza·tion
vo·ca·tion (career;
cf. *avocation*)
vo·ca·tion·al
-al·ly
vo·cif·er·ous
-ous·ness
vod·ka
voice
voiced, voic·ing
voice·less
voice mail
voice·net
voice-over
voice rec·og·ni·tion
void·able
vol·a·tile
-tile·ness, -til·i·ty
vol·ca·nic
vol·ca·no
-noes
vo·li·tion
vol·ley
-leys, -leyed,
-ley·ing
vol·ley·ball
volt·age
vol·u·ble

vol·ume
-umed, -um·ing
vol·u·met·ric
vo·lu·mi·nous
vol·un·ta·rism
vol·un·tary
-tar·ies, -tari·ly,
-tari·ness
vol·un·teer
vol·un·teer·ism
vo·lup·tuous
vom·it
voo·doo
-doos
vo·ra·cious (greedy;
cf. *veracious*)
-cious·ness
vo·rac·i·ty
vor·tex
-ti·ces (pl)
vote
vot·ed, vot·ing
vo·tive
-tive·ly, -tive·ness
vouch
vouch·er
vow·el
voy·age
-aged, -ag·ing,
-ag·er
vox·el
vul·ca·ni·za·tion

vul·ca·nize
-nized, -niz·ing,
-niz·er
vul·gar
vul·gar·ism
vul·gar·i·ty
-ties
vul·gar·iza·tion
vul·ner·a·ble
-ble·ness, -bly,
-bil·i·ty
vul·ture

wad
    wad·ded,
    wad·ding
wad·dle
    -dled, -dling
wa·fer
waf·fle
    -fled, -fling
wag
    wagged, wag·ging
wage
    waged, wag·ing
wa·ger
    -gered, -ger·ing
wag·on
waif
waist (blouse; cf.
    waste)
waist·line
wait (delay; cf.
    weight)
wait·er
wait·ress
wait·ron
wait·staff
waive (abandon; cf.
    wave)
    waived, waiv·ing

waiv·er (abandon-
    ment; cf. *waver*)
wake
    waked, wak·ing
walk
walk·ie-talk·ie
walk-in (adj, n)
Walk·man
walk-on (n)
walk out (v)
walk·out (n)
walk-through
walk·over (n)
walk-up (n, adj)
wal·let
wall·eye
wal·low
wall·pa·per (n, v)
wal·nut
wal·rus
waltz
wan·der
    -dered, -der·ing
wan·der·lust
wan·na·be
want (desire; cf.
    wont, won't)
wan·ton

war
    warred, war·ring
war·bler
war·den
ward·robe
ware (goods; cf.
    wear, where)
ware·house
war·fare
war·fa·rin
war·head
war-horse
warm·heart·ed
war·mon·ger
warmth
warm up (v)
warm-up (n)
warn·ing
warp
war·rant
war·rant·able
war·ran·tee (person;
    cf. *warranty*)
war·ran·tor
war·ran·ty (guaran-
    tee; cf. *warrantee*)
    -ties
war·rior
War·saw

war·ship
war·time
wary
  wari·ly, wari·ness
wash·able
  -abil·i·ty
wash·cloth
wash out (v)
wash·out (n)
wasn't (was not)
waste (needless
  destruction; cf.
  waist)
  wast·ed, wast·ing
waste·bas·ket
waste·ful
  -ful·ly, -ful·ness
waste·land
waste·pa·per
watch
watch·dog
watch·ful
watch out (v)
watch·tow·er
watch·word
wa·ter
wa·ter·borne
wa·ter·col·or
wa·ter·cress
wa·ter·fall
wa·ter·fowl
wa·ter·front
wa·ter·line

wa·ter·logged
wa·ter·mark
wa·ter·mel·on
wa·ter pipe
wa·ter po·lo
wa·ter·proof
wa·ter·re·pel·lent
wa·ter·re·sis·tant
wa·ter·shed
wa·ter·spout
wa·ter·tight
wa·ter·way
wa·ter·works
wa·tery
  -ter·i·ness
watt·age
wave (beckon; cf.
  waive)
  waved, wav·ing
wave·length
wa·ver (hesitate; cf.
  waiver)
  -vered, -ver·ing
wavy
  wav·i·er, wav·i·est,
  wav·i·ness
waxy
way (direction; cf.
  weigh, whey)
way·lay
  -laid, -lay·ing
way·side
way·ward

weak (adj)(feeble; cf.
  week)
weak·en
  weak·ened,
  weak·en·ing
weak·heart·ed
weak·ling
weak-mind·ed
weak·ness
weal (state; welt; cf.
  *we'll, wheal,
  wheel*)
wealth
wealthy
  wealth·i·er,
  wealth·i·est,
  wealth·i·ness
weap·on
weap·on·ry
wear (clothes; cf.
  ware, where)
wear·able
  -abil·i·ty
wea·ri·less
wea·ri·some
wea·ry
  -ri·er, -ri·est, -ri·ly
wea·sel
  -seled, -sel·ing
weath·er (atmo-
  spheric condi-
  tions; cf. *whether*)

weath·er·ize
   -iza·tion
weath·er·proof
weav·er
web
   webbed, web·bing
Web brows·er
web·cam
Web·cast·er
Web·cast·ing
Web·i·sode
Web·mas·ter
Web page
Web site
wed
   wed·ded,
   wed·ding
we'd (we would)
wedge
   wedged, wedg·ing
Wedg·wood
Wednes·day
week (n)(7 days; cf.
   weak)
week·day
week·end
wee·vil
weigh (ponder; cf.
   way, whey)
weight (poundage;
   cf. *wait*)
weight·less
   -less·ness

weighty
weird
wel·come
   -comed, -com·ing
weld
wel·fare
wel·far·ism
well
we'll (we will; cf.
   *weal, wheal,
   wheel*)
well-be·ing
well-bred
well-con·di·tioned
well-de·fined
well-found·ed
well-groomed
well-ground·ed
well-han·dled
well·head
well-heeled
well-in·formed
well-known
well-mean·ing
well-off
well-read
well-round·ed
well-spo·ken
well-thought-of
well-timed
well-to-do
well-wish·er
well-worn

went
were
we're (we are)
weren't (were not)
were·wolf
west·bound
west·er·ly
west·ern
West·ern·er
West·ern Sa·moa
West In·dies
west·ward
wet (moist; cf. *whet*)
   wet·ted, wet·ting
wet blan·ket (n)
wet·land
we've (we have)
whale
   whaled, whal·ing
whale·bone
wharf
   wharves (pl)
wharf·age
what·ev·er
what-if
what·so·ev·er
wheal (welt; cf.
   weal, we'll, wheel)
wheel (turn; cf.
   weal, we'll, wheal)
wheel·bar·row
wheel·chair
whence

when·ev·er
when·so·ev·er
where (in what
   place; cf. *ware,
   wear*)
where·as
where·by
where·fore
where·in
where·so·ev·er
where·up·on
wher·ev·er
where·with·al
whet (sharpen; cf.
   wet)
   whet·ted,
   whet·ting
wheth·er (if; cf.
   weather)
whey (part of
   milk; cf. *way,
   weigh*)
which (pronoun; cf.
   witch)
which·ev·er
which·so·ev·er
while (during; cf.
   wile)
   whiled, whil·ing
whim·per
   -pered, -per·ing
whim·si·cal
   -cal·ly, -cal·ness

whine (cry; cf. *wine*)
   whined, whin·ing
whip
   whipped,
   whip·ping
whip·lash
whip·poor·will
whirl·pool
whirl·wind
whisk
whis·ker
whis·key
whis·per
   -pered, -per·ing
whis·tle
   -tled, -tling
whis·tle-blow·ing
whis·tler
white·cap
white-col·lar
white·fish
whit·en
   -ened, -en·ing
white·out
white·wash
whith·er (where; cf.
   wither)
whit·tle
   -tled, -tling, -tler
who·ev·er
whole (entire; cf.
   hole)
whole·heart·ed

whole·sale
whole·some
whol·ly (entirely; cf.
   holey, holly, holy)
whom·ev·er
who's (who is; cf.
   whose)
whose (possessive
   of *who;* cf. *who's*)
why
wick·ed·ness
wick·er·work
wick·et
wide-an·gle (adj)
wide-ar·ea
   net·work (WAN)
wide-awake (adj)
wid·en
wide·spread
wid·ow
wid·ow·er
width
wield
wie·ner
wife
   wives (pl)
wild·cat
wil·der·ness
wild·fire
wild·life
wile (trick; cf. *while*)
   wiled, wil·ing
will·ful

287

will·pow·er

win
  win·ning,
  win·less,
  win·na·ble

wind

wind·blown

wind·break

wind·burn

wind·fall

wind·jam·mer

wind·mill

win·dow

win·dow·pane

win·dow-shop (v)
  win·dow-shop·per
  (n)

win·dow·sill

wind·pipe

wind·proof

wind·shield

wind·storm

wind·swept

wind up (v)

wind·up (adj, n)

wind·ward

wine (drink; cf.
  whine)

wine·glass

wine·grow·er

wine·press

wine·shop

wing

wing·span

wing·spread

win·ner

win·some
  -some·ly,
  -some·ness

win·ter
  -tered, -ter·ing

win·ter·ize
  -ized, -iz·ing

win·ter-kill (v)

win·try or win·tery

win-win

wire·less

wire·tap

wir·ing

wis·dom

wise
  wise·ly, wise·ness

wish·bone

wish·ful

wist·ful
  -ful·ly, -ful·ness

witch (hag; cf.
  which)

witch·craft

with

with·draw

with·draw·al

with·er (shrivel; cf.
  whither)
  -ered, -er·ing

with·hold

with·in

with·out

with·stand
  -stood

wit·ness

wit·ti·cism

wit·ting·ly

wit·ty
  -ti·ly, -ti·ness

wiz·ard

woe·be·gone

wolf·hound

wol·ver·ine

wom·an
  wom·en (pl)

wom·an·ly
  -li·ness

womb

won (did win; cf.
  one)

won·der
  -dered, -der·ing

won·der·ful

won·der·land

won·der·ment

won·drous
  -drous·ness

wont (custom; cf.
  want, won't)

won't (will not; cf.
  want, wont)

wood (lumber; cf.
  would)

wood carv·ing (n)
  wood-car·ver
wood·chuck
wood·cut·ter
wood·ed
wood·en
wood·land
wood·lot
wood·peck·er
wood·pile
wood·wind
wood·work
wool·en
wool·ly or wool·ie
  -lies
word
word·book
wordy
  word·i·er,
  word·i·est,
  word·i·ly
word-of-mouth (adj)
word pro·cess·ing
word pro·ces·sor
word wrap
work
  worked, work·ing
work·able
work·a·hol·ic
work·bas·ket
work·bench
work·book
work·day

work force
work load
work·man
work·man·like
work·man·ship
work of art
work out (v)
work·out (n)
work·peo·ple
work·place
work·room
work·sheet
work·shop
work·sta·tion
work·ta·ble
work·week
work·wom·an
World Bank
world-class
world·ly
  -li·ness
world·wide
World Wide Web
worm·wood
worn-out
wor·ri·some
wor·ry
  -ries, -ried, -ry·ing
worse
wor·ship
  -shiped, ship·ing,
  -ship·er
worst

worth
worth·less
  -less·ness
worth·while (adj)
  -while·ness
wor·thy
  -thi·ly, -thi·ness
would (auxiliary
  verb; cf. *wood*)
wouldn't (would
  not)
wound
wran·gle
  -gled, -gling
wrap (envelope; cf.
  rap)
wrapped
  (enveloped; cf.
  rapped, rapt),
  wrap·ping
wrap·around
wrap·per
wrap up (v)
wrap-up (n)
wrath
wreath (n)
wreathe (v)
wreck (ruin; cf. *reek*)
wreck·age
wreck·er
wren
wrench

wrest (pull away; cf.
  rest)
wres·tle
  -tled, -tling
wretch·ed
  -ed·ness
wrig·gle
  -gled, -gling, -gly
wring (twist; cf.
  ring)
wrin·kle
  -kled, -kling
wrist
wrist·watch
writ
write (compose; cf.
  right, rite)
write in (v)
write-in (adj, n)
write off (v)
write-off (n)
write-once, read
  many (WORM)
write pro·tec·tion
write up (v)
write-up (n)
writhe
  writhed, writh·ing
writ·ing
writ·ten
wrong
  wronged,
  wrong·ing

wrong·do·er
wrong·do·ing
wrong·ful
  -ful·ly, -ful·ness
wrote (did write; cf.
  rote)
wrought
wrung (twisted; cf.
  rung)
wry (perverse; cf.
  rye)
WYSIWYG

Xan·a·du
xan·than gum
x-ax·is
Xe·non
xe·no·phobe
xe·no·pho·bia
Xeno
xe·rog·ra·phy
   xe·ro·graph·ic
xe·rox (v)
Xe·rox
X mo·dem
X-rated
X ray (n)
X-ray (adj, v)
X serv·er
Xter·mi·nal
xy·lem
xy·lo·phone

yacht
ya·da-ya·da-ya·da
Ya·gi
Ya·hoo
yak
yam
yank
Yan·kee
Ya·na
yard·age
yard line
yard·mas·ter
yard·stick
yar·mul·ke
yarn
yawl
yawn
y-ax·is
year·book
year-end (n, adj)
year·ling
year·long
year·ly
yearn
year-round
yeast
yel·low
    -low·ish
yelp

Yem·en
yen
    yenned,
    yen·ning
yeo·men
ye·shi·va or
    ye·shi·vah
yes-man
yes·ter·day
yes·ter·year
yet
yew (tree; cf. *ewe, you*)
Yid·dish
yield
yield·ing
yip
yipped, yip·ping
Ymo·dem
yo·del
    -deled, -del·ing
yo·ga
yo·gi
yo·gurt
yoke (harness; cf. *yolk*)
yo·kel
yolk (of egg; cf. *yoke*)

Yom Kip·pur
yon·der
yore (past time; cf. *your, you're*)
you (pronoun; cf. *ewe, yew*)
young
    youn·ger,
    youn·gest,
    young·ish,
    young·ness
young·ster
your (possessive of *you;* cf. *yore, you're*)
you're (you are; cf. *yore, your*)
your·self
    -selves (pl)
youth·ful
    -ful·ly, -ful·ness
yowl
yo-yo
yt·ter·bi·um
yt·tri·um
yuc·ca
Yu·go·sla·via
Yu·kon
yule

yule·tide
Yu·ma
yup·pie

Z

zag
  zagged, zag·ging
Za·greb
Zaire
Zam·be·zi
Zam·bia
za·ny
  -nies, -ni·ly,
  -ni·ness
Zan·zi·bar
zap
Za·ria
zeal
zeal·ot
zeal·ous
  -ous·ness
ze·bra
zeit·geist
ze·nith
zeph·yr
zep·pe·lin
ze·ro
  -ros
zest
zestful
  -ful·ly, -ful·ness
zig·zag
  -zagged, -zag·ging
zilch

Zim·ba·bwe
zinc
zinc ox·ide
zine
zin·nia
Zi·on·ism
  -ist
zip
  zipped, zip·ping
zip code
Zip drive
zip file
zip·per
zip·pered
zir·con
zir·co·ni·um
zith·er
zo·di·ac
Zoe·trope
Z mo·dem
zone
  zoned, zon·ing
zoo·log·i·cal
zo·ol·o·gy
zouk
zuc·chi·ni
Zu·lu
Zu·ni
Zu·rich

zwie·back

Appendix

Spelling Tips

Understanding the following common families of spelling patterns may help to avoid many spelling errors.

The Final Consonant
When is a final consonant doubled?

1. When a word of one syllable (*skin*) ends in a single consonant (ski*n*) preceded by a single vowel (sk*i*n), double the final consonant before a suffix that begins with a vowel (skinn*ing*) or before the suffix -*y* (skinn*y*).

beg	beggar	begged
star	starring	starry
swim	swimming	swimmer

Exception: When a one-syllable word ends in *y* preceded by a single vowel, do not double the *y* before a suffix beginning with a vowel.

pay	payee
joy	joyous
toy	toying

2. When a word of more than one syllable ends in a single consonant (prefe*r*) preceded by a single vowel (prefe*r*) and the accent falls on the last syllable of the root word (pre*fer*), double the final consonant before a suffix beginning with a vowel (preferr*ed*).

forbid	forbidden
occur	occurring
begin	beginning
allot	allotted

Spelling Tips

Exception: If the accent shifts to the first syllable of such a word when a suffix beginning with a vowel is added, do not double the final consonant.

> preferred *but* preferable
> transferred *but* transferee

When is a final consonant not doubled?

1. When a word of one syllable ends in a single consonant (sa*d*) preceded by a single vowel (s*a*d), do not double the final consonant before a suffix beginning with a consonant (sad*l*y).

glad	gladly
boy	boyhood
wit	witness

2. When a word of more than one syllable ends in a single consonant (cance*l*) preceded by a single vowel (canc*e*l) and the accent does not fall on the last syllable of the root word, do not double the final consonant before a suffix beginning with a vowel (cancel*ed*).

total	totaled	totaling
credit	credited	creditor
abandon	abandoned	abandoning
model	modeled	modeling

3. When a word of one or more syllables ends in a single consonant (stou*t*) preceded by more than one vowel (sto*u*t), do not double the final consonant before any suffix, whether it begins with a consonant (stout*l*y) or a vowel (stout*er*).

riot	riotous
equal	equaled
deceit	deceitful

4.   When a word of one or more syllables ends with more than one consonant (ha*nd*), do not double the final consonant before any suffix.

cold	colder
warm	warmly
bless	blessed
sleigh	sleighing

The Final Silent *e*

1.   Words ending in silent *e* usually drop the *e* before a suffix beginning with a vowel and before the suffix *y*.

accuse	accusing
able	ably
escalate	escalation
ease	easy
bandage	bandaging

2.   Words ending in *ce* or *ge* usually retain the *e* before a suffix beginning with *a* or *o*.

knowledge	knowledgeable
exchange	exchangeable
advantage	advantageous
courage	courageous

3.   Words ending in silent *e* usually retain the *e* before a suffix beginning with a consonant.

name	namely
sincere	sincerely
one	oneness

4.   Words ending in *ie* change the *ie* to *y* before adding *ing*.

die	dying
lie	lying

Spelling Tips

The Final *y*

1. Words ending in *y* preceded by a consonant change the *y* to *i* before any suffix except one beginning with *i*.

apply	applied *but* applying	
reply	replied *but* replying	
comply	complied	complies *but* complying
imply	implied	implies *but* implying

2. Words ending in *y* preceded by a vowel usually retain the *y* before any suffix.

pray	praying	prayed
lay	laying	
employ	employable	

Words with *ei* and *ie*

Put *i* before *e* except after *c* or when sounded like *a* as in *neighbor* or *weigh*.

believe	friend		(*i* before *e*)
receive	conceive		(except after *c*)
vein	eight	their	(sounded as *a*)

Words Ending in *-cede*, *-ceed*, and *-sede*

1. Only one word ends in *-sede*: supersede.

2. Only three words end in *-ceed*: exceed, proceed, succeed.

3. All other words ending with the syllable pronounced "seed" are spelled *-cede*: precede, accede, intercede.

---

*The Spelling Tips section is based on *The Gregg Reference Manual, Ninth Edition,* Sabin, William, pages 176-182.

Style for Writing Numbers

Number expression is an area of English style about which even the experts sometimes disagree. Basically, numbers may be expressed either as figures or as spelled words.

Decisions about the use of figures or words may depend on any of several factors. A number expressed in figures is readily recognized and quickly comprehended. A number expressed as spelled words, on the other hand, is less obvious. Figures are considered less formal than numbers as spelled words. The following guidelines explain the most-used ways of handling numbers in writing.

1. The Basic Number Rule

Most occurrences of numbers in written material can be covered by the following basic rule: the numbers one through ten are spelled, while numbers greater than ten are expressed in figures. Numbers used with units of measure should always be expressed in figures.

Within 20 days, six students will complete the program.

The speaker brought four handouts for each of the 66 people.

The room is 9 feet by 12 feet.

2. The First Word of a Sentence

A number used as the first word of a sentence should always be spelled.

Eighteen boxes of books arrived at the library.

Two horses were hitched to the carriage.

Hyphenation of Compound Adjectives

3. The Same Kind of Data

If one number in a list of related numbers is larger than ten, all numbers in that list should be expressed in figures.

Please send 4 pens, 9 markers, and 12 envelopes.

I bought two cups, five plates, and six glasses.

4. Two Numbers Together

Often when two numbers occur together in a sentence, one of the numbers is part of a compound expression modifying a noun. One of the numbers—usually the first one—should be spelled, and the other should be express-ed in figures. The first number should be spelled unless its spelling will make an awkwardly long expression.

I need wallpaper to cover one 8-foot panel.

Please order 500 eight-page booklets.

If two numbers appear together in a sentence and both are expressed in the same style, use a comma to separate them.

On December 13, 428 students will graduate.

When the clock struck nine, four knocks sounded at the door.

Hyphenation of Compound Adjectives

Sometimes two or more words express a single meaning in modifying a noun. That expression, called a compound adjective, is hyphenated.

We need to keep an up-to-date calendar.

Long after winter ended, I found my long-lost gloves.

Abbreviations and Acronyms

Abbreviations

An abbreviation is a shortened form of a word or phrase. In some kinds of writing the use of abbreviations is appropriate. These include reports, statistical data, in-house documents and communications of an informal nature. However, in more formal kinds of writing, the use of most abbreviations should be avoided.

If a writer is doubtful about whether use of abbreviations is appropriate in a given situation, he or she should spell out the complete word or phrase. The very common abbreviations of people's titles, educational degrees, or times of day are always acceptable.

Many abbreviations—but not all—end with a period. If a period occurs within an abbreviation, no space appears after the period. The following list shows some common abbreviations:

Mr., Mrs., Ms., Dr., Sen., Rep., Fr., the Rev., Ph.D., M.S., M.B.A., B.S.Ed., B.S., B.B.A., a.m., p.m., etc. (and so on), i.e (that is), vs. (versus), et al. (and others), cf. (compare), e.g. (for example).

Some abbreviations are pronounced in their abbreviated form, letter by letter. These very common abbreviations are represented by all-capital letters with no punctuation. The following list shows examples of some of these abbreviations:

IBM (International Business Machines), IRS (Internal Revenue Service), FBI (Federal Bureau of Investigation), SEC (Securities and Exchange Commission), UN (United Nations), TV (television), S & L (savings and loan), GOP

Abbreviations and Acronyms

(Grand Old Party), SS (social security), CD (certificate of deposit), FTC (Federal Trade Commission), IQ (Intelligence Quotient), ACLU (American Civil Liberties Union), CRT (cathode-ray tube), CPU (central processing unit), OCR (optical character reader).

Some abbreviations of this type have even replaced the names which they originally represented.

Acronyms

The abbreviations shown above are pronounced by individual alphabetic letter. An acronym, on the other hand, is a series of letters which is read as a word. It appears in all-capital letters with no spaces or punctuation, just as the above-listed abbreviations do, but an acronym is pronounceable. The following list shows some examples of acronyms:

SALT (Strategic Arms Limitation Talks), ZIP (Zone Improvement Program), HUD (Housing and Urban Development), IRA (Individual Retirement Act), CAD (computer-aided design), COBOL (Common Business-Oriented Language), ROM (read-only memory).

Acronyms sometimes use only the first letter of each word the acronym represents (SALT). At other times, the acronym may use more than one letter from one or more words (COBOL).

Troublesome Place Names

United States

Alabama
Anniston
Bessemer
Gadsden
Montgomery
Phenix City
Scottsboro
Talladega
Tallassee
Tuscaloosa

Alaska
Anchorage
Fairbanks
Juneau
Sitka
Valdez

Arizona
Flagstaff
Nogales
Phoenix
Scottsdale
Tempe
Tucson
Yuma

Arkansas
Arkadelphia
Blytheville
Little Rock

Paragould
Pine Bluff

California
Alameda
Anaheim
Berkeley
Cerritos
Chula Vista
El Cajon
Escondido
Fresno
Inglewood
Littlerock
Los Angeles
Monterey
Oxnard
Pasadena
Pittsburg
Redding
Sacramento
San Bernardino
San Diego
San Francisco
San Jose
Santa Cruz
Torrance
Van Nuys
Yucaipa

Colorado
Arvada
Denver

Durango
Englewood
Greeley
Northglenn
Pueblo
Salida

Connecticut
Bridgeport
Danbury
Greenwich
Hartford
Meriden
Naugatuck
Norwich
Southington
Stamford

Delaware
Bellfonte
Dover
Milford
Newark
Wilmington

Florida
Boca Raton
Daytona Beach
Fort Lauderdale
Gainesville
Hialeah
Kissimmee
Miami

303

Troublesome Place Names

Okeechobee
Orlando
Pensacola
Sarasota
Tallahassee

Georgia
Atlanta
Dahlonega
LaFayette
Macon
Savannah
Smyrna
Valdosta
Vidalia
Warner Robins

Hawaii
Hilo
Honolulu
Kahului
Kailua
Kaneohe
Lahaina
Waikiki Beach
Waipahu

Idaho
Boise
Coeur d'Alene
Ketchum
Lewiston
Moscow
Nampa
Pocatello

Illinois
Alsip
Carbondale
Champaign
Chicago
Decatur
De Kalb
Des Plaines
Elgin
Joliet
Kankakee
Moline
Peoria
Schaumburg
Skokie
Springfield
Urbana
Waukegan
Wilmette

Indiana
Elkhart
Indianapolis
Kokomo
Lafayette
Muncie
Rensselaer
South Bend
Terre Haute
Valparaiso
Vincennes

Iowa
Bettendorf
Davenport

Des Moines
Dubuque
Humboldt
Indianola
Ottumwa
Sioux City
Waterloo

Kansas
Emporia
Leavenworth
Manhattan
Osawatomie
Pittsburg
Topeka
Wichita

Kentucky
Bowling Green
Covington
Frankfort
Lexington
Louisville
Owensboro
Paducah

Louisiana
Baton Rouge
Bogalusa
Houma
Lafayette
Natchitoches
New Orleans
Shreveport
Thibodaux

Troublesome Place Names

Maine
Augusta
Bangor
Biddeford
Brunswick
Kennebunkport
Presque Isle

Maryland
Annapolis
Baltimore
Bethesda
Chevy Chase
Frederick
Gaithersburg
Hagerstown

Massachusetts
Amherst
Andover
Boston
Cambridge
Charlestown
Dartmouth
Framingham
Holyoke
Ipswich
Methuen
Nantucket
Northampton
Shrewsbury
Tewksbury
Waltham
Wellesley
Worcester

Michigan
Ann Arbor
Berkley
Cheboygan
Dearborn
Detroit
Escanaba
Grosse Pointe
Kalamazoo
Lansing
Mackinac
Marquette
Menominee
Muskegon
Saginaw
Wyandotte
Ypsilanti

Minnesota
Bemidji
Brainerd
Duluth
Edina
Fairbault
Mankato
Minneapolis
St. Paul
Winona

Mississippi
Biloxi
Hattiesburg
Jackson
Meridian
Natchez

Pascagoula
Picayune
Tupelo
Vicksburg
Yazoo City

Missouri
Affton
Cape Girardeau
Florissant
Hannibal
Jefferson City
Joplin
Sedalia
Tuscumbia

Montana
Billings
Bozeman
Butte
Havre
Helena
Kalispell
Lewistown
Missoula

Nebraska
Bellevue
Kearney
Lincoln
North Platte
Ogallala
Omaha
Papillion
Scottsbluff

Troublesome Place Names

Nevada
Carson City
Elko
Las Vegas
Reno
Winnemucca

New Hampshire
Concord
Laconia
Manchester
Nashua
Portsmouth

New Jersey
Bayonne
Camden
Englewood
Hackensack
Hoboken
Lyndhurst
Montclair
Paramus
Passaic
Paterson
Perth Amboy
Secaucus
Trenton
Wyckoff

New Mexico
Alamogordo
Albuquerque
Gallup
Las Cruces

Roswell
Santa Fe
Tucumcari
Zuni

New York
Albany
Batavia
Binghamton
Buffalo
Elmira
Ithaca
Massapequa
New Rochelle
Ossining
Patterson
Peekskill
Plattsburgh
Poughkeepsie
Rochester
Schenectady
Syracuse
Tonawanda
Utica
Yonkers

North Carolina
Asheville
Cary
Charlotte
Durham
Fayetteville
Fuquay-Varina
Greensboro
Raleigh

Roxboro
Winston-Salem

North Dakota
Bismarck
Fargo
Grand Forks
Minot
Williston

Ohio
Ashtabula
Bellefontaine
Berea
Chillicothe
Cincinnati
Columbus
Cuyahoga Falls
Dayton
Elyria
Lorain
Massillon
Piqua
Sandusky
Steubenville
Toledo
Van Wert
Wooster
Xenia

Oklahoma
Ardmore
Chickasha
Enid
McAlester

Muskogee
Oklahoma City
Ponca City
Stillwater
Tulsa

Oregon
Coos Bay
Corvallis
Eugene
Klamath Falls
Milwaukie
Portland
Salem
Tillamook

Pennsylvania
Aliquippa
Altoona
Carlisle
Edinboro
Harrisburg
McKeesport
Philadelphia
Pittsburgh
Punxsutawney
Reading
Scranton
Wilkes-Barre

Puerto Rico
Aguadilla
Arecibo
Bayamón
Caguas

Mayagüez
Ponce
San Juan
Trujillo Alto

Rhode Island
Coventry
Narragansett
Pawtucket
Providence
Warwick
Woonsocket

South Carolina
Beaufort
Charleston
Columbia
Greenville
Myrtle Beach
Spartanburg
Sumter

South Dakota
Aberdeen
Belle Fourche
De Smet
Pierre

Tennessee
Chattanooga
Gallatin
Knoxville
Memphis
Murfreesboro
Nashville

Sewanee
Tullahoma

Texas
Abilene
Amarillo
Austin
Corpus Christi
Dallas
Edinburg
El Paso
Galveston
Killeen
Laredo
Lubbock
Nacogdoches
Texarkana
Waco
Waxachachie

Utah
Ogden
Orem
Provo
Salt Lake City

Vermont
Brattleboro
Burlington
Montpelier
Winooski

Virginia
Alexandria
Charlottesville

Troublesome Place Names

Chesapeake
Fairfax
Lynchburg
Norfolk
Richmond
Roanoke
Suffolk

Washington

Bellevue
Edmonds
Kennewick
Olympia
Seattle
Spokane
Tacoma
Walla Walla
Yakima

West Virginia

Beckley
Charleston
Charles Town
Clarksburg
Follansbee
Huntington
McMechen
Weirton
Wheeling

Wisconsin

Beloit
Eau Claire
Fond du Lac
Green Bay

Kenosha
La Crosse
Madison
Manitowoc
Menomonie
Milwaukee
Neenah
Oshkosh
Racine
Sheboygan
Wausau
Wauwatosa

Wyoming

Casper
Cheyenne
Gillette
Laramie

Canada

Alberta

Calgary
Edmonton
Lethbridge
Medicine Hat
Red Deer

British Columbia

Chilliwhack
Kamloops
Matsqui
Penticton
Vancouver
Victoria

Manitoba

Dauphin
Portage la Prairie
Selkirk
Thompson
Winnipeg

New Brunswick

Campbellton
Chatham
Dieppe
Edmundston
Fredericton
Moncton

Newfoundland

Bonavista
Corner Brook
St. John's
Stephenville

Nova Scotia

Dartmouth
Glace Bay
Halifax
New Glasgow
Truro

Ontario

Ajax
Etobicoke
Guelph
Kitchener
Mississauga
Ottawa

Troublesome Place Names

Sault Ste. Marie
Sudbury
Toronto
Windsor

Prince Edward Island
Charlottetown
Montague
St. Eleanors

Quebec
Brossard
Charlesbourg
Châteauguay
Gaspé
Gatineau
Joliette
LaSalle
Longueuil
Montreal
Quebec
Trois-Rivières

Saskatchewan
Esterhazy
Humboldt
Lloydminster
Moose Jaw
Regina
Saskatoon

Mexico
Acapulco
Aguascalientes

Chihuahua
Ciudad Juárez
Cuernavaca
Ensenada
Guadalajara
Hermosillo
Mexico City
Monterrey
Oaxaca
Tampico
Taxco
Tijuana
Veracruz
Villahermosa
Zacatecas